America
and the
Automobile

A Historical Entertainment of the Mechanics, Moguls, and Moments that changed a Nation

William A. Cook

SUNBURY PRESS

Mechanicsburg, PA USA

Published by Sunbury Press, Inc.
Mechanicsburg, Pennsylvania

SUNBURY
PRESS
www.sunburypress.com

For information about special discounts for bulk purchases, please contact Sunbury Press Orders Dept. at (855) 338-8359 or orders@sunburypress.com.

To request one of our authors for speaking engagements or book signings, please contact Sunbury Press Publicity Dept. at publicity@sunburypress.com.

FIRST SUNBURY PRESS EDITION: July 2020

Set in Adobe Garamond | Interior design by Crystal Devine | Cover design by Lawrence Knorr | Edited by Lawrence Knorr.

Publisher's Cataloging-in-Publication Data
Names: Cook, William A., author.
Title: America and the automobile : a historical entertainment of mechanics, moguls, and moments that changed a nation / William A. Cook.
Description: First trade paperback edition. | Mechanicsburg, PA : Sunbury Press, 2020.
Identifiers: ISBN: 978-1-620064-14-6 (softcover).
Subjects: TRANSPORTATION / Automotive / History | HISTORY / United States / 20th Century | BUSINESS & ECONOMICS / Industries / Automobile Industry.

Product of the United States of America
0 1 1 2 3 5 8 13 21 34 55

Continue the Enlightenment!

For
Jonathan Pardini
A fantastic and talented great-nephew

Contents

Introduction

The automobile is synonymous with American culture. In 2015 there were over 253,000,000 registered cars and trucks with an average age of 11.4 years old on the nation's roads. To accommodate the swell of automobiles in the early twenty-first century there are four million miles of roads and streets in the United States and about half of them are paved, the rest are surfaced with gravel or stone. No other single entity tells the story of American history in the past 125 years better than the automobile.

What makes the story of the automobile and the persons who have advanced its technology appealing is that it is a story that is pure historical entertainment. This book makes no attempt to be an esoteric chronicle of the auto industry's history or be a ground-breaking biographical work on any of the characters included in the narrative. This work traces the history of the automobile in America through the development of its three most lasting and important manufacturers; The Ford Motor Company, General Motors and Chrysler, AKA, The Big Three. The work chronicles more than a century of technological development, triumphs and crises in the auto industry and it is my hope that I have created a work in which every page is enlightening, entertaining and sometimes controversial.

In addition, the book closely incorporates and examines the cultural changes that occur simultaneous in American society as the automobile becomes the primary source of transportation and recreation for the masses. The book examines how the automobile forced the need for modern highways onto the political agenda, it covers the rise of organized labor in the industry, the auto industry's supreme importance in building America's mighty arsenal in

World War Two and it even traces the automobile's effect on American popular culture in the rise of rock n' roll, growth of suburbs and as the primary mode of transportation for family vacations.

Despite the economic downturns and strong foreign competition that has occurred during the past forty years including, the Great Recession of the early of the twenty-first century, the US remains one of the largest automotive markets in the world. Automobile manufacturing remains one of the largest and most viable industries in the United States as well. In 2016 over 12 million cars and commercial vehicles were built in the US and over 17 million sold. Cars built in the US amount to 8.4% of all mechanical exports including such stalwarts as electronic equipment, aircraft, spacecraft, engines, pumps and medical/technical equipment. Currently there are over 950,000 people employed in auto manufacturing in the US with another 560,000 employed in the auto parts industry. Furthermore, since the early 1980s almost every European, Japanese and Korean auto manufacturer has wanted to build cars in the US.

On June 16, 1903 the Ford Motor Company was founded with a capital of only $27,000. The company was organized with John S. Gray as president and Henry Ford as Vice President. At that time the company consisted of only twelve Stockholders. Going forward from the humble beginning, on December 10, 1915 the one millionth Ford Model T would roll off the assembly line.

To enter the auto manufacturing business today on a fundamental basis would require an outlay of $250 million to build a modest plant and an additional $250 million for a basic tool and dye operation. So how did the American auto manufacturing industry evolve into such a giant while experiencing such an incredible economic roller coaster ride through-out its history?

The entire story of that industrial odyssey is told here. Every aspect is covered in the work from classic technological innovations of the Model T and the assembly line to the Thunderbird, Corvette, Mustang, K-Cars, SUVs and many others. There are also a few cars included that were either ahead of their time or simply an albatross such as the Edsel. Also included are the controversial and proven to be dangerous cars such as the Corvair, Pinto and others.

The work includes the beginnings of exports into the US market with Volkswagen in the early 1950s after Henry Ford II rejected an offer to take-over the company for free and continues with the surge of Japanese imports that begin to flood the American market in the early 1970s following the oil import crises that occurred after the Six Day War in the Middle East. Finally, Honda builds the first Japanese factory in the US in Marysville, Ohio in 1982 and the game changes forever.

Biographical information included through-out the work traces the lives of Henry Ford, Alfred P. Sloan, Walter Chrysler, Carl Fisher, Henry Ford II, Lee Iacocca and others. All are informative and show various dimensions of their personalities and talents. The Henry Ford bio material has a dark edge to it that shows a brilliant, but troubled man, held back by his strong penchant for anti-Semitism. Also, the Lee Iacocca bio material suggests that a dual personality drove the man that gave the world the Mustang and K-Car vacillating between being over-ambitions and having a true marketing brilliance.

All of the important characters relevant to the development of the industry during the period of 1890 to 2018 and their contributions are included, the moguls, mavericks, engineers, stylists, visionaries, union leaders, political leaders and critics who made it happen: Henry Ford, William Durant, Alfred P. Sloan, Walter Chrysler, William Knudsen, Edsel Ford, Henry Ford II, George Romney, Harlow Curtice, Virgil Exner, Louis Crusoe, Ed Cole, Robert McNamara, Charles Wilson, Carl Fisher, John DeLorean, Lee Iacocca, Hal Sperlich, Walter Ruether, Alan Mulally, Ralph Nader and many more.

The book takes the reader right up to 2018 as it chronicles how the current CEOs of the Big Three, Mary Barra, Mark Fields and the late Serigo Marchionne picked-up the pieces of an industry that nearly crashed and burned in America during the Great Recession and restored it to a position of distinction on the world economic stage. The work even examines the present-day futuristic technology with Tesla leading the way in the development of the electric car market and other manufacturers beginning to develop autonomous driver (self-driving) cars.

The work concludes with addressing the question of if the current president Donald J. Trump will be an advocate or adversary for the auto industry.

This story is an incredible ride through a wild and enormously entertaining 125 years in American History. It is suggested that you fasten your seatbelt before reading.

1.

Beginnings

In 47 B.C. Julius Caesar appointed dictator for ten years rode into Rome in a horse-drawn chariot. Then 1,960 years later in 1913 A. D., president-elect Woodrow Wilson rode to his inauguration in Washington, D. C. in a horse-drawn carriage. For most of human history, the horse that time-honored beast of burden, had been the source of power moving man and materials from place to place on land.

Railroads began to appear in America during the 1830s. By 1853 the Baltimore & Ohio railroad had been extended as far west as Wheeling. By 1860 there were 29,000 miles of railroad track in operation and the growth would continue for several decades.

As the bloody Civil War continued in the east and deep–south during the early 1860s Congress was looking ahead to western expansion awarding lands to homesteaders and to railroaders who were waiting to lay track for a trans-continental line. President Abraham Lincoln was looking forward to eventually taking the train from Washington, D.C. to California.

President Lincoln had been a railroad lawyer and recognized the strategic importance of moving troops, equipment and supplies by rail during the war. When a few railroad executives stalled at supporting the nation's war effort with using their line, Lincoln got a bill passed by Congress that authorized him to assume control of any line that did not fully support the war effort.

The Civil War also produced an unprecedented increase in railroad traffic in the south. Railroads in North Carolina provided a vital north-south link to the Confederacy moving men and materiel for General Robert E. Lee's Army of Northern Virginia and connecting the army with the vital port of Wilmington.

Following the Civil War construction of the transcontinental railroad began. The project had been government subsidized by a bill approved by President Lincoln.

The Central Pacific Railroad laid 690 miles of track eastward from Sacramento, California through a treacherous terrain including the Sierra Nevada Mountains, while the Union Pacific Railroad laid 1087 miles of track from Omaha, Nebraska while contending with a frozen Missouri River and the Rocky Mountains. The two lines met in 1869 at Promontory, Utah.

As western railroad expansion continued in the 1870s new railroad towns would be created such as Cheyenne, Denver, Topeka and so many more. In the northeast, railroads would expand to link existing towns and businesses from Boston to New York to Philadelphia and Washington. New lines would also be built along the Ohio River linking such cities as Cincinnati, Knoxville and Atlanta. Along the Mississippi River railroad lines would be rebuilt following the destruction from the Civil War and new tracks laid. Suddenly, the deep south would be connected with Chicago and Kansas City. By 1881 Los Angeles would be connected by rail with eastern-Texas.

The expansion of the railroads in the U.S. would continue through-out the remainder of the nineteenth century and by 1900 there were four transcontinental railroad lines and 225,000 miles of track The expansion of the railroads had occurred concurrently with the country's industrial revolution, opened the way for the development and settlement of the West and provided new individual economic opportunity and travel accessibility.

One of the most important aspects of the building of the railroad in America was that it eventually evolved into a network. The railroad had tied the nation together.

The railroad came before the automobile because the only engine and rail vehicle available to inventors of the era was the heavy steam engine using solid fuels such as wood and coal. Because of the large size and weight restrictions necessary for the use of steam engines those early inventors didn't see the difference between self-propelled road vehicles and steam engines.

So, the automobile would have to wait for three things to be available, the commercial availability of gasoline, the invention of the internal combustion engine and pneumatic tires.

Meanwhile the horse continued to do a large share of the heavy lifting. At the turn of the twentieth century there were three million horses in American cities. In New York there were 150,000 horses. In Rochester, New York there were 15,000 horses. In the early 1890s in Cincinnati you could still take a stage coach from Sixth and Main Streets to Hamilton, Ohio some 33 miles north of the city.

But the automobile was coming to America and its arrival would introduce a cultural phenomenon and personal freedom much larger than anyone could ever have imagined. And it would happen quickly.

In 1896 there were only four cars in all of the U.S.—a Duryea, a Ford, a Haynes and a Benz. By 1900 there would be 13,824 horseless carriages on the streets in America. By 1910 that number would rise to 459,000 being powered by a variety of sources—electric, steam and gasoline. The first drive-in gas station in the nation operated by Gulf Oil opened in Pittsburgh in 1913.

The question is often asked, who was the father of the automobile? The answer to who built the first automobile is the subject of great debate that is best generalized.

Almost all concerned agree that the first atmospheric pressure internal combustion engine had been invented in 1860 by a French engineer Jean Joseph Etienne Lenoir and soon after in 1866 a German inventor by the name of Nikolaus August Otto would develop a four-cylinder compression type engine. However, their use in the invention of the automobile would take several decades as technology to power automobiles would evolve through an evolution of fuel sources with the use of steam, electric and finally gasoline.

There is considerable historic support for Karl Benz an engineer and bicycle vendor from the southwestern province of Baden in Germany as being the first one to create a petroleum powered motor-vehicle. On January 29, 1886 Benz was granted a patent for what would become known as the Benz Motorwagen. The vehicle was equipped with three wire wheels that resembled those used on bicycles and was powered by a four stroke engine started by an electric coil ignition, and a transmission that was comprised of two-chains connecting the engine in the rear axle.

On August 5, 1888 Bertha Benz, wife and business partner of Karl, along with the couple's two sons made a 65-mile road trip form Mannheim to Pforzheim. The journey is often acknowledged as the first long-distance car trip. There were minor breakdowns along the way and Bertha purchased additional fuel at pharmacies she passed.

Consideration also has to be given to Charles E. Duryea who actually built a car in Massachusetts (the "buggyaut") in 1892 that ran and traveled on the road.

Pushing Henry Ford to the side of the road, the good citizens of Indiana will proudly tell you that it was Elwood Haynes of Kokomo, Indiana who built the first motor car in America sometime near the end of the nineteenth century. The fact is that Haynes built his car in 1894 a year after Ford built his. Nonetheless Hoosier's also claim that the first documented long-distance trip by an automobile in America was made by Haynes going from Kokomo to Indianapolis.

It should also be mentioned that in 1886 Ransom E. Olds shocked the populace of Lansing, Michigan when one morning at 3:00 a.m. he briefly drove some sort of a contraption on the streets of the capitol city that had lathe gears for the transmission and a main drive wheel improvised with spikes for sprockets. Whatever the thing was it had more capacity for noise than travel. But it ran.

While through-out the last two decades of the nineteenth century in both Europe and America while mechanics and engineers continued in their quests to produce a suitable automobile engine, the heart of the automobile, a lot of the basic essentials for an automobile already existed such as a differential, springs, steering mechanism, step-gear transmission and even brakes.

But something fundamental was lacking; an improvement to one of mankind's oldest inventions—the wheel. A fad taking place in the U.S. at that time would lead directly to the development of that critical part.

In the early 1890's a huge bicycle craze overtook America. Edouard Michelin had increased the craze with the introduction of detachable pneumatic bicycle tires in 1891.

Although a Scotsman, John Boyd Dunlop, had been granted a patent for a pneumatic tire in 1888, seven years later Michelin introduced a pneumatic tube sturdy enough to support an automobile. Prior to Michelin's invention the early automobiles had been running on iron tires and sometimes on solid rubber tires. When Michelin first approached the early automobile manufactures, he was both laughed at and scorned, most believing it was impossible to support the weight of an automobile on air.

So, Edouard Michelin built an automobile, equipped it with his pneumatic tires and entered it in the 1895 Paris to Bordeaux race. While the other cars with iron tires were bumping over the road, suffering breakdowns from excessive vibrations, the Michelin car raced along at speeds unheard of at the time.

Soon after, Michelin would introduce another innovation, the demountable rim, allowing a tire and rim to be removed at the same time. In 1907 Michelin purchased the A&V Rubber Company in Milltown, New Jersey and

Goodrich Silvertown Cord Tire, circa 1913. (Photo by Lawrence T. Hay)

began producing tires in America. Michelin continued to produce tires in New Jersey until 1930 when feeling the effects of the depression he closed the plant and moved back to France.

But it is somewhat ironic that Michelin, a Frenchman, lead the way in developing modern automobile tires while Europe's first mass-produced car, the Citroen Type A would not be launched until 1919 in France.

At first automobiles used a variety of power sources, electric, steam and gasoline and all were popular and had their advocates and fans. But the limitations of electric and steam cars quickly became apparent.

Steam powered cars were popular for a while. In fact, President William McKinley would be the first U.S. President to ride in an automobile when in 1899 Stanley Steamer inventor F. O. Stanley took him for a spin around Washington, D.C.

The steam car had serious limitations. It could not carry enough water except for short trips. During the winter one had to drain the boiler when parking or heat had to be maintained. Furthermore, control of the steam to meet variations in demand was complicated.

When Henry Ford introduced the assembly line the Model T became cheaper and more reliable than steam cars. Then with the advent of the electric starter and the advancement of the internal combustion engine, steam cars began to quickly fade into the background of popularity. Nonetheless the Stanley continued to be manufactured in limited quantities until 1924 and a few other models until 1930.

The electric car was equipped with heavy and expensive batteries with low power output. It was envisioned that an electric filling-station industry would evolve to service electric cars where occupants would pull-in and have lunch while the batteries in their cars were being charged.

On the other hand, the gasoline engine cars were lighter, more reliable and used a fuel which was widely available. The gasoline industry had been in existence since the 1860s. Gasoline was first marketed for the purpose of providing lamp oil. Then when Jean Joseph Etienne Lenoir (mentioned above) invented the first atmospheric pressure internal combustion engine that ran on illuminating gasoline, the focus for a new engine began in earnest.

While steamers would quickly be proven in-affective, the electric powered car just wouldn't yield to the internal combustion engine. In 1913 the *Indianapolis Star* reported that Mr. Nicolas Kilvert of Brooklands, Cheshire, England had owned a Waverly Electric for the past ten years and the car was still operative. The article stated that the car was, "used almost daily for ten years for station work and social purposes on country roads in Cheshire being driven almost exclusively by the owner's daughters."[1]

Electric cars would continue to have their devotees in the U.S. well into the first few decades of the twentieth century. The 1915 Detroit Electric Model 55 built by Andersen Electric Car Company of Detroit using an optional Edison Nickle Iron Battery would operate for 80 miles before requiring charging and had a top speed of 20 mph. The Detroit Electric was built between 1907 and 1939 and about 2000 cars a year were sold. In the early years of the car's production it was popular with women and physicians who wanted a dependable and quick start that didn't require the physical exertion of early internal combustion engine cars that had to be hand-cranked to start. (In 2008, the Detroit Electric brand was revived to produce modern all-electric cars by the Detroit Electric Holding Ltd. of the Netherlands.)

With the three critical factors in place, gasoline, pneumatic tires and the concept of the internal combustion engine, through-out the 1890s talented American mechanics for the most part continued to tinker in their garages to develop a saleable automobile. But European automobile manufacturers in

France such as Armand Peugeot, and in Germany the pair of Gottlieb Daimler and Karl Benz, were leading the way in developing automotive technology.

But the Americans would soon catch-up and take the lead. In 1901 the Oldsmobile became the first mass-produced gasoline-driven car being built at a rate of ten cars per week. That same year the Cadillac automobile company began producing cars in Detroit.

The Buick motor car had been the brainchild of David Dunbar Buick a Scottish immigrant. After spending a great deal of his first 47 years working as a plumber, Buick turned inventor. Fascinated by automotive technology, in 1899 Buick and his partner Walter Marr built the first Buick motor car.

But David Buick lacked knowledge of the fundamentals in business practices. To that end, in 1900 he sold Marr the rights to the Buick automobile name. Then in 1903 he sold 99% of the rights to the Buick Motor Car Company to brothers Frank and Benjamin Briscoe.

Nonetheless, both Buick and Marr continued to experiment with building a better car and in 1904 the pair came-up with a salable Buick—the Model B.

The Model B got the attention of William (Billy) Durant, a quintessential salesman and budding entrepreneur and he agreed to finance the company. In

1906 Durant built a new manufacturing plant for Buick in Flint, Michigan. While it was a start, Durant had much bigger ideas for Buick.

Sometime during the winter of 1907-1908 Durant began discussing a finance plan for expansion with the J.P. Morgan banking company. His plan called for a loan of a million dollars to be used to consolidate a group of fledging auto manufactures under the name of United Motors.

Although Morgan was skeptical of the auto industry, harboring a belief that it might be a passing fad, he agreed to the loan and Durant was off to the races in creating an automotive empire. When Durant learned that United Motors already existed in New Jersey he changed the name of the company to General Motors.

In 1908 General Motors (GM) was founded with the merger of the Oldsmobile and Buick companies and within two years was selling 50,000 cars a year.

Louis Chevrolet, the son of a watchmaker, was born on Christmas Day, 1878 in La Chaux-de Fonds, Switzerland. The community was the center of the French Dairy Industry. While Chevrolet had little desire to obtain a formal education, he demonstrated a keen interest and talent in mechanics. He started working on bicycles and racing them. In three years, Chevrolet won 26 competitive events

Around 1900 Louis Chevrolet immigrated to Montreal, Canada and was hired as a race car driver by Fiat. Soon after in 1901 Chevrolet moved to Brooklyn where he was hired by Billy Durant to race and test drive Buicks.

At Cape May, New Jersey in 1905 Louis Chevrolet made his American debut in auto racing with his brothers Gaston and Arthur acting as his pit crew.

Later Gaston Chevrolet would win the 1920 Indianapolis 500 driving a modified Monroe-Frontenac thereby breaking the early dominance of European cars in the race. That same year on November 25 Gaston Chevrolet would be killed in a race in California at the Beverly Hills Speedway board track when he attempted to pass another car and was struck by another racer on the outside.

In October 1909 the Motordrome opened in Atlanta, Georgia with Louis Chevrolet winning a 250-mile race in a Buick.

Louis Chevrolet wanted to build his own car. Billy Durant was impressed with Chevrolet's budding ingenuity and enthusiasm and backed him in the venture which by 1911 became the Chevrolet Motor Car Company. The company introduced the Chevrolet Classic 6 which became an instant hit with buyers allowing Durant to use the profits to buy-out stockholders who wanted more return on their investments.

In 1913 Louis Chevrolet returned to France for a visit and during his absence Billy Durant moved production of Chevrolets from Detroit to Flint, a move that would jeopardize the relationship between Durant and Chevrolet. When Chevrolet retuned his relationship with Durant deteriorated further over the design of the car. Chevrolet wanted to build huge, powerful cars, high performance models that would be bought almost exclusively by the rich. Durant, ever mindful of the success of Henry Ford with the Model T, wanted to build a Chevrolet that was simple in design, modest in price and that could be assembled rapidly to increase volume of sales.

It all came to a head in October 1915 when Chevrolet resigned from the company he had created and sold all of his shares of stock in GM to Durant.

By 1916 under the leadership of Billy Durant, GM had become one of the world's leading automobile companies. In 1917 Durant moved Chevrolet under the corporate umbrella of GM and it quickly became the largest division of the company.

Louis Chevrolet returned to his first love—racing. In 1915 he partnered with Howard E. Blood of Allegan, Michigan and the two proceeded to build the Cornelian race car.

The 1915 Indianapolis 500 was won by Ralph DePalma who racing historians acknowledge as the best driver to ever be entered in the race. Other entrants in the 1915 Indy included future World War One Air Ace Eddie Rickenbacker and Louis Chevrolet driving his Cornelian car to a 20th place finishing.

In 1919 Louis Chevrolet would finish 7th in the Indy.

With the on-set of the Great Depression Louis Chevrolet fell on hard times financially. GM took notice and in 1934 fearing consumer backlash from sympathetic consumers voted Chevrolet a modest pension. But it was hardly enough to provide more than the basic necessities. In 1941, Louis Chevrolet, a man whose name is one of the most iconic brands of the American automotive industry died nearly penniless and was buried in Indianapolis.

Still the man most responsible for taking the mass production of automobiles in the U.S. to the next level in the early twentieth century would be a Michigan farm boy by the name of Henry Ford.

2.

Henry Ford and the Model T

The horrific battle of Gettysburg had just been fought four weeks before when on July 30, 1863 Henry Ford was born in Dearbornville, Springfield Township, Wayne County, Michigan He was the eldest of six children.

Although Ford grew-up on a farm he never had much interest in agriculture. But all things mechanical fascinated him. By 1876 at the age of 13 Ford was making his own tools. When a farmhand brought a broken watch to Ford and explained the inner workings, he repaired it.

Ford's mother died in 1878. The following year at the age of 16 with only a sixth-grade education, Henry Ford left the family farm and went to the growing city of Detroit. He became an apprentice with the Drydock Engine Works. But within three years he had returned home and during the summer of 1882 ran a steam engine on a neighboring farm.

During the summers of 1883 and 1884 Ford worked for Westinghouse where he demonstrated and repaired steam engines. It was during 1884 that Ford received the only formal business education he would ever have when he took a few courses at Goldsmith, Bryant & Stratton Business University in Detroit.

Soon after, Ford went to work for the Detroit Edison Company where he was put in charge of a dynamo. During the time that Ford worked at the Detroit Edison Company in his spare time he began working on a gasoline engine. Ford's associates at Detroit Edison attempted to convince him it was a waste of time—that the future in power was electricity. He totally ignored their advice.

In 1887 there was an electrical convention held at Atlantic City, New Jersey, so Ford and his associates from Detroit Edison attended. Thomas Edison spoke at the convention and afterwards Henry Ford was able to speak with him for a moment.

Ford told Edison he was working on an internal combustion engine and wanted his opinion on whether it was a worthy endeavor. Edison told Ford, that he believed that there was a future for a light-weight self-contained engine with high horsepower as no one power source was ever going to do all the work of the country. The encouragement of Thomas Edison reinforced Henry Ford's strong belief in the future of the internal combustion engine and he became more determined than ever to produce one.

The following year in 1888 Ford married Clara Ala Bryant of Greenfield Township, Michigan and the couple set-up residency on an 80-acre farm in what today is Dearborn.

The couple's only son Edsel Bryant Ford was born on November 6, 1893. As the only heir to the Ford Motor Company, Edsel Ford would in his formative years work closely alongside his father devouring his automotive brilliance. But almost from the start Edsel Ford would have a desire to build very different cars than his father preferred.

In 1892 Henry Ford became employed as an engineer by the Edison Illuminating Company in Detroit. The following year Ford built a one-cylinder engine in two-story brick house that today sits in the heart of the Detroit business district.

When Ford was 32—years old and still working at Edison Illumination he built his first car in 1895—the Quadricycle. The vehicle was a lightweight runabout with a buggy chassis mounted on four bicycle tires. It only produced 29 horsepower from a massive two-cylinder air-cooled gasoline engine that was 540 cubic inches. But it was the forerunner of much bigger things to come. The vehicle steered with a boat-like tiller could go forward but not backwards. Ford ran the machine for about 1000 miles between 1895 and 1896 eventually driving it around the streets of Detroit and then sold it to Charles Ainsley of that city for $200.

However, Henry Ford was not the first person to drive a car on the streets of Detroit. That distinction went to Charles Brady King on March 6, 1896.

The Edison Illuminating Company offered Ford a promotion to general superintendent, on the condition that he give up his work on a gas engine and devote himself to something they considered more useful. Ford could see that his future with the company was taking a different course than that which he wanted to pursue. His heart was in the future of the automobile. So, on August

Henry Ford in first car built in 1896. (Courtesy of The Library of Congress)

15, 1899, after eight years employment with the company, Ford quit his job and went into the automobile business.

In 1900 Ransom Olds established the first automobile manufacturing plant. By now Henry Ford was a proven mechanic and began looking for ways to finance building his own cars and on October 10, 1901 he entered a 10-mile race at a one-mile race track in Grosse Point, Michigan just outside of Detroit. He had recently got his prototype car he called "Sweepstakes" up to 72 mph during a test a few months before. The speed record at the time was 65.79 mph held by a Belgian, Camille Jenatzy. The winner's purse was $1000 and with his mechanic Spider Huff riding along, Ford entered the race. It was supposed to be a three-car race but one car dropped out leaving Ford and Alexander Winton a Cleveland car builder and the favorite as the only entries. Ford took the lead on the 8th of 10 laps when Alexander's car began to sputter and crossed the finish line first having covered 10 miles in 13 minutes, 23.8 seconds for an average speed of 44.8 mph.

It would be Henry Ford's last race as a driver. He was jubilant in the fact that he had proven what he had set out to do. That he was capable of building a very fast and durable car. While Henry Ford would not race again, he realized the benefit of auto racing to marketing cars. Auto racing allowed a manufacturer to present his technology in front of very large crowds and Ford would be an enthusiastic backer of auto racing his entire life. As Ford was later to say, "Nobody sells horses anymore."[1]

Following his victory in the race at Grosse Point and with his name in newspaper, that same year Henry Ford was able to organize the Henry Ford Company with him acting as engineer. But the venture didn't last long as Ford became embroiled in a dispute with his bankers and fellow investors, mainly William H. Murphy a prominent businessman, over his desire to build a race car rather than a commercial car.

Murphy was even so bold to bring in a respected independent machinist Henry Leland to inspect the quality of Ford's work. At the time Leland along with his son was producing motors for the cars being manufactured by Ransom E. Olds. Leland's report on Ford's work was critical.

After three months of the company start-up on March 10, 1902, Ford resigned. On the way out the door Ford was given $900, the drawings, and the plans for the race car he had wanted to build and assurance by Murphy and the board that they would discontinue use of his name for the company.

Soon after Ford's departure the company reorganized as the Cadillac Motor Company and it began manufacturing high quality cars.

Walking out on William Murphy and his associates was a bold move by Henry Ford. Between 1900 and 1908, 503 companies would be formed for the purpose of building commercial automobiles. Within a few years 60% would fold and another 6% would cease auto manufacturing to concentrate on another product.

Undaunted, Henry Ford moved on. Later during 1902 in a little one-room brick shop at 81 Park Place, Ford began working on developing a four-cylinder motor. He built about 20 cars with the Detroit Automobile Company.

That same year, with help of friends, Ford also built the "999" race car. The famed race car driver Barney Oldfield would take the wheel of the "999" and win a 5-mile race at the Fair Grounds in Indianapolis that immediately attracted new investors allowing Ford to organize another automobile company.

On June 16, 1903 the Ford Motor Company was founded with a capital of only $27,000. The company was organized with John S. Gray as president and Henry Ford as Vice President. Stockholders included, Henry Ford, Alexander Malcomson, John W. Anderson, C.H. Bennett, James Couzens, Horace E.

Dodge, John F. Dodge, Vernon C. Fry, John S. Gray, Horace H. Rackman, Albert Strelow and Charles J. Woodfall.

A few of those stockholders would eventually standout out historically above the others. James Couzens would become the general manager of the Ford Motor Company from 1903 to 1915 running the business affairs of the company. After leaving Ford to enter politics, from 1919 to 1921 James Couzens would serve as the Commissioner of Police and then as Mayor of Detroit. Going forward Couzens would serve as a Republican U.S. Senator from Michigan from 1921 to 1936. James Couzens would become extremely wealthy from his association with Henry Ford. His initial investment in the Ford Motor Company in 1903 had been $2500. By 1921 Couzens was esti-mated to be holding $35 million in tax-exempt bonds. In 1923 he cashed-out his Ford investment taking away an additional $23 million

Two other stockholders, Horace Dodge and John Dodge, AKA the Dodge brothers, had been involved in the automobile business for several years making transmissions for both Ford and Oldsmobile. By 1913 the Dodge brothers de-cided that they had enough of Henry Ford and went out on their own making cars. In 1914 they would produce their first car the Dodge Model 30 which was acknowledged as a tougher version of the Ford Model T. Quality assurance in automotive engineering was key factor in the Dodge car. The Dodge brothers built a test track adjacent to their plant to test every car before shipment for engine and brakes performance. Nonetheless the brothers continued to hold on to their Ford stock

One curious fact about the early Dodges is that the brothers designed their logo for their early cars with the Star of David incorporated in it. Neither of the brothers was Jewish and no one really knows why it was included in the design.

In 1915 Henry Ford bought 2000 acres of land along the banks of the River Rouge west of Detroit. On the site Ford planned to build a massive auto-mobile manufacturing plant financed with company profits. The Dodge broth-ers strongly disagreed and argued that the Ford Motor Company profits should be diverted into dividends for stockholders.

Henry Ford fought the Dodge brothers in court and much to his chagrin was ordered to pay an extra-special dividend of $19 million to the stockholders. Ford challenged the court's ruling and a few years later the Michigan Supreme Court upheld it. The court's ruling so annoyed Ford that he became determined to buyout all the minority stockholders and convert the company into a family owned business.

Unfortunately, the automotive world would never know what heights the Dodge brothers could have taken their company to in the industry. During 1920 both Dodge brothers would meet their demise. John who had become one of the three most-wealthiest men in Michigan died from pneumonia then Horace died from cirrhosis. The Dodge brothers' car company would continue to operate without them until 1928 when it would be acquired by Chrysler.

The same month the Ford company was founded the first Ford Model A was on the market in Detroit. The first sale of a Model A occurred on July 15, purchased by Dr. E. Pfennig of Chicago for $850 paid in full. At the same time two additional buyers make deposits that provided the company with an important cash infusion. The company output in its first year was 1706 cars.

The first two Ford dealerships were also created in 1903. The first dealership was established in San Francisco with William "Billy" Hughson who had met Henry Ford at a bicycle show in Chicago in 1902. The second dealership was begun in St. Cloud, Minnesota, a farming community and a primary market that Henry Ford felt his cars fit perfectly. By 1923 there would be 9,000 Ford dealerships and 15,000 authorized Ford service stations thereby making 24,000 points of contract with the motoring public.

Production now began in earnest at the Ford Piquette Avenue facility in Detroit on the inexpensive lightweight Model N and in 1906 it would become the best-selling car in America.

It was in 1908 that Ford would begin manufacturing the Model T or "Tin Lizzy." Immediately the company began to establish new industry production standards. During the week of May 15, 1908, The Ford Motor Company assembled an amazing 311 cars in six working days. But that was just an opening act. In June Ford shocked the industry when it assembled 100 cars in one day!

The first Model T was introduced by Ford in October 1908. The car was a low-priced and efficient automobile, engineered and built for mass sale. You had to crank it up to get it going, but then it seemed to run for ever. The engine was capable of running on a mixture of kerosene and old candle ends. It was light, only 100 inches long and could turn within a twelve-foot circle. The Tin Lizzy was high enough off the ground to clear tree stumps and it had sufficient power in relation to its weight that it could pull itself out of loose sand and moderate muddy surfaces.

But the Model T was a bare bones car with no speedometer, windshield wipers or doors. Still the versatility of the Model T was significant. The chassis of the car accommodated a variety of body types—salon, buggy or pick-up

The 1910 Ford, Display Model of Ford Auto at the Automotive Industry Golden Jubilee in 1946. (Courtesy of The Library of Congress)

truck. The car was particularly popular with people living in rural communities of the mid-west.

The Model T was also easy to repair. About all the tools an owner required were a ball-peen hammer, a monkey wrench, a screwdriver and a paper clip. You could buy parts at a corner general store. A new fender cost $2.50 and a new muffler for $1.25. It was also possible to buy all the parts necessary to assemble a Model T. Many people did.

On January 1, 1910 Ford operations would be relocated to a factory in Highland Park, Michigan that occupied 300 acres with 123 under a roof. At the time Highland Park was the world's largest automobile manufacturing plant. By late 1913 at Highland Park, Ford would significantly improve the efficiency of automobile manufacturing through development of the movable assembly line. It was the beginning of mass production which changed industrial history.

The innovative mechanical skills and marketing success of Henry Ford did not go unnoticed by the other automobile manufactures and they quickly organized to put him out of business as early as 1903.

An association of automobile manufactures (Association of Licensed Automotive Manufacturers) filed suit against Ford in an attempt to force the company to follow a principle that there was only a limited market for automobiles and therefore a monopoly of the market was essential. The legal action was known as the Selden Patent Suit.

In 1879 George Baldwin Selden a Rochester, New York patent attorney, filed an application for what he described as the production of a safe, simple, and cheap road locomotive, that was light in weight, easy to control and possessed sufficient power to overcome an ordinary inclination. The patent application, Patent No. 549,160 that Selden filed was kept alive in the patient office until 1895 when the patent was finally granted.

When the patent had been filed in 1879 hardly anyone really could conceptualize just what an automobile was. But by 1895 a lot of people were familiar with the concept and actual existence of self-propelled vehicles. Henry Ford and a lot other men had been working on motor propulsion for over a decade and were surprised to learn that what they had been attempting to develop was covered by a patent application years before that had never been put into practice.

Henry Ford was not overly concerned with the suit because he believed that his engine had nothing in common with the one mentioned by Selden in his 1879 patent application.

George Selden had actually sold his patent to the Electric Vehicle Company of New York for $10,000 plus royalties. The Electric Vehicle Company manufactured electric taxis and street cars. The licenses for automobile manufacturing were sold by the company and the royalties divided up between themselves, George Selden and the association that was suing Ford.

The association had millions of dollars and it used the power of its purse to land a potential knock-out punch on Henry Ford when on September 15, 1909 a United States District Court issued an opinion against the Ford Motor Company.

The licensed association manufactures began an advertising campaign in an attempt to scare off potential buyers of Ford's cars by stating that they were illegal. The association was advancing an opinion that a buyer could be prosecuted. So, in affect you could buy a Ford and drive it to jail.

Henry Ford believing that further court action would exonerate his company counteracted the action of the association by taking out ads in major newspapers telling potential customers that at the request of anyone buying a Ford the company would issue a bond protecting them from prosecution. Only

50 customers asked for the bond and in 1910, customers remained extremely loyal and Ford sold more than 18,000 cars nearly doubling the output of the previous year.

Finally, in 1911 an appellate court ruled in Ford's favor. The court decision ruled out monopoly in the auto industry. It also led to the sharing of standardization of auto parts and processes. It was beginning of the modern automobile manufacturing industrial model.

The original price of the Model T had been $825. In 1912, Henry Ford attempted to make the car affordable to a vast number of working Americans by lowering the price to $575. Ford's marketing strategy was to build profit on volume. Immediately the Tin Lizzy's popularity with consumers increased three-fold and by 1913 there would be a Ford dealership in nearly every American town with a population of at least 2000. On December 10, 1915, the millionth Ford automobile would come off the assembly line. Ford continued to dominate the market until 1926 when Chevrolet outsold the Model T. Production on the Model T was stopped in 1927, but by that time there had been 15,007,033 sold.

With the popularity of Ford's Model T, the pressure on the U. S. Government to construct roads dramatically increased. The Great National Pike project began in 1806 and was completed in 1840. The road had extended 800 miles from Fort Cumberland, Maryland to Vandalia, Illinois. In 1913 there was a bill in Congress seeking to appropriate $20,500,000 to rebuild the old Great National Pike with extensions from Times Square in New York on the eastern end to Lincoln Park in San Francisco on the western end, thereby making it a transcontinental highway.

Meanwhile in Detroit on January 5, 1914, Henry Ford shocked the American industrial community when he and James Couzens held a news conference at Highland Park. It was announced that Henry Ford planned to share Ford Motor Company profits with workers. Effective January 12, Ford was cutting the daily workday from nine hours to eight and was immediately doubling the standard wage in his manufacturing plant to $5.00 for the eight-hour day. And there was one other thing; Ford was now going to begin three working shifts a day to enable the plant to build cars around the clock.

The "Five Dollar Day" and Henry Ford became synonymous. It was very big news. Politicians cautiously embraced it. Newspapers editorialized on it. Labor leaders endorsed it and the industrial moguls scolded it. At the time

Henry Ford appeared to be the workingman's best friend. Within 20 years he would be his worst enemy.

The announcement had opened up an estimated 4000 jobs at Ford and set-off a frenzy of hopeful job applicants rushing to Detroit to cash-in on the seemingly generosity of Henry Ford. There was a deluge of mail from job applicants pouring into the company daily. Steven Watts notes in his work on Ford *The People's Tycoon,* "Within one week of the announcement, nearly fourteen thousand such letters had arrived at the company's employment office; two months later, it was still receiving some five hundred letters a day."[2]

As the automobile manufacturing boom took center stage in Detroit people rushed to the city for economic opportunity. Between 1910 and 1920 the population of Detroit doubled from 465,766 to 993,768 making it the fourth largest city in the country.

Outside the Ford plant in the bitter January weather, stood other men, some looking extremely un-kept and in ragged clothes, building fires with scrap wood and cheering Henry Ford at every opportunity.

Many of those waiting and shivering in the cold outside the gate to the plant spoke in foreign languages. Some Ford managers were against hiring immigrants as they held the belief that they could not become effective workers much less loyal Americans unless they spoke English. It was in the opinion of a great number of Ford managers that the English language was the glue that kept the workforce productive and to emphasize safety. They considered it next to impossible to establish a constructive dialogue with foreign workers through the use of interpreters.

Henry Ford did not have a crystal ball; therefore he could have never predicted the mass migrations of Appalachian Whites and Blacks from the deep-south much less the large number of European immigrants that would arrive in Detroit in the years before World War One, during the Great Depression and the years after World War Two seeking jobs on his assembly lines.

At that time, Ford had big plans, he was getting ready to construct the River Rouge Plant and he was keenly aware that immigrant laborers were vital to further the expansion of the company. So, he became proactive.

Ford hired professor Peter Roberts in April 1914 to create an English language program for the company. Roberts was a YMCA teacher who had authored *English for Coming Americans* in 1911 published by New York Association Press. In addition, Roberts had experience working with immigrant laborers in the Pennsylvania coal fields. His book was more than a language instruction course it also concentrated heavily on socialization of immigrants in three areas of American culture, domestic life, financial dealings and the industrial environment.

The program Roberts developed for the company was called The Roberts Plan and it became the core curriculum for the Ford English School. In addition to English language instruction, the program emphasized safety in the workplace, thrift in personal finances, good manners, personal hygiene and citizenship.

When the school began in 1914 it had but a single instructor and 50 students, by 1917 the number of instructors had grown to 150 and the number of students to 2500. All of the instructors were Ford employees; foremen, machine operators, clerks and plain workers who volunteered their time.

As the second decade of the twentieth century reached the mid-point in 1915, the people of Detroit became benefactors of Henry Ford's philanthropy.

Henry Ford founded Ford Hospital in Detroit convincing a few physicians to come from Johns Hopkins Hospital in Baltimore and start the delivery of care. Originally the hospital was created to care for Ford's employees. But soon after opening the hospital began to accept patients who couldn't pay for their care.

Allowing the hospital to accept charity care cases is another example of how complicated Henry Ford's personality was as his general attitude toward charity was that it pauperized individuals, when they should be helped to help themselves.

Over the next one hundred years Ford Hospital continued to grow and is today the anchor of the Henry Ford Health Care System which handles approximately 3.2 million patient visits annually, has 23,000 employees and is the fifth largest employer in metropolitan Detroit.

Finally, in 1917 construction began on Fords new massive plant on 1200 acres along the banks of the River Rouge in Dearborn, Michigan. Initially Ford had intended to use the site only for making coke, smelting iron, and to build tractors. Ford had introduced its first tractor in 1907. However, over the next decade the company would turn the Rouge plant into the most fully integrated automobile manufacturing plant in the world. The plant had every component necessary to produce a car: blast furnaces, an open-hearth mill, a steel rolling mill, a glass plant, a huge power plant that even provided power to parts of surrounding communities and massive assembly lines. All were connected by 90 miles of railroad track and many miles of conveyor belts.

By 1927 Ford had shifted the final assembly line from Highland Park to the Rouge and the plant began mass production that was unparalleled by any manufacturing facility in the world.

In the late 1920s at the Rouge Ford was making between 3000 and 4000 complete units a day and also 6000 sets of parts. By comparison Chevrolet was making 1100 cars per day, Willys-Overland was producing 1800 during peak periods working five and a half days a week and Hudson-Essex was making 1350 cars per day.

In 1906 Percival Lea Dewhurst Perry was hired to be the managing director of Ford's British Agency in London. Although Ford demanded that his cars be paid in full in advance before leaving the docks in New York City, in 1911 Percival Perry sold 400 American built Model T's in England.

Perry saw a future for Ford in England. Time and again he would attempt to convince Henry Ford that the Model T needed to be adapted for use in Europe. Finally, Ford agreed to build standard American Model T's in England. So, Perry located an old carriage factory on the outskirts of Manchester and in October 1911 assembly of Model T's began at the Ford Trafford Park Assembly Plant.

When World War One broke-out in 1914, the Trafford Park facility was expected to build about 10,000 Model T's that year. Without blinking an eye or consulting Henry Ford who was a pacifist and who opposed the war, Percival Perry volunteered the Trafford Park facility to make munitions and military vehicles. The British government made Perry deputy controller of mechanical warfare at the Ministry of Munitions. Like it or not, the pacifist Ford was now indirectly involved in the war.

In recognition of his work toward victory for England in the war Percival Perry would receive knighthood. In 1919 Ford gave Perry his pink slip.

The World War had been raging across Europe for nearly two years in late 1915 when Henry Ford in his infinite wisdom came to the delusionary conclusion that he could bring about a cease fire among belligerent parties and get them to sit down and talk peace.

So, Ford charted an ocean liner the *Oscar II* and invited other known peaceniks of the time to join him on a cruise to Europe with the hopes of getting everyone out of the trenches for a while and into negotiations.

The liner commonly called the "Peace Ship" set sail from Hoboken, New Jersey on December 4, 1915. The ship reached Oslo on December 18 with a very ill Henry Ford suffering from the flu on board. At that point Ford was forced to abandon his mission and four days later return to the U.S.

The ship sailed on and reached Stockholm on January 16, 1916. A conference was held with representatives from Denmark, Holland, Norway Sweden and the United States, but without any representation from the waring nations it was an empty exercise at any attempt to discuss plans for ending the war.

Politically Henry Ford had always leaned toward the Republican Party. But in the 1916 presidential election Ford supported the re-election of Woodrow Wilson over Republican candidate Charles Evans Hughes. He not only liked Wilson's stance of keeping America out of the war, but also was pleased that Wilson supported eight-hour workday legislation.

After Wilson won re-election Ford continued to support him and continued that support even as the U.S. was about to enter the war in 1917. Ford declared, "I will stand with our President, and in the event of declaration of war will place our factory at the disposal of the United States government and will operate without one cent of profit."[3]

The actual contributions made to the war effort by the Ford Motor Company were marginal. The U.S, Navy had contracted with Ford to produce 100 Eagle-class patrol boats powered with Packard engines. But Ford delivered only a few and too late for any of them to see action. Nonetheless Ford produced thousands of ambulances and trucks for the Army, as well as a number of Liberty airplane engines.

As for Henry Ford's pre-war assertion that his factories would produce war materials without making a profit, that point has been the subject of great speculation and debate by historians over the years.

Following the war Ford continued to support Wilson. In 1918 President Wilson looking to fill a seat in a hardcore Republican state, asked Henry Ford to run for the U.S. Senate as a Democrat from Michigan against Republican Truman H. Newberry. Ford accepted the offer and then tried to play the game by his own rules.

Ford attempted to run in both the Republican and Democrat state primaries labeling himself as a citizen candidate. He campaigned on a platform of having a distaste for party politics and declared that if the people wanted him to run, so be it, but he would not lift one finger to help bring it about.

Ford's rhetoric resonated with workers and farmers in Michigan. While he lost the Republican primary to Senator Newberry, he won the Democrat nomination.

Truman Newberry had been the secretary of the Navy in the administration of President Theodore Roosevelt during 1908 and 1909. He attacked Ford as having helped his son Edsel to dodge the draft during the World War. Newbury was a veteran and so were his two sons.

Republican Ohio Congressman and former Speaker of the House Nicholas Longworth was to say in a speech before Congress in regard to the war, "There were seven, and only seven, persons in the whole world who were not injured by the fighting. These were the six sons of the Kaiser and Edsel Ford."[4]

There were plenty of issues on which to criticize Henry Ford. The press attempted to make him appear as a buffoon and made fun of his "Peace Ship" endeavor. One paper accused Ford of having taken a load of squirrel food to The Hague.

Ford's opposition to military preparedness also put-up a strong issue for many in the state of Michigan who felt that it was men like him who delayed the United States' inevitable entry into the war and that inaction had resulted in thousands of needless deaths.

Ford lost in the general election by only a few thousand votes to Newberry 220,054 to 212,487. He blamed the support of Wall Street for Newberry as the deciding factor in the election.

Senator Newberry would resign from the U.S. Senate on November 18, 1922 after being convicted of election irregularities under the Federal Corruption Practices Act. His conviction was later reversed by the U.S. Supreme Court.

On December 18, 1918 during a board meeting, Henry Ford still in a snit over the $19 million special dividend payment ordered by a Michigan court, resigned as president of the Ford Motor Company. Immediately, Ford began making threats to either buyout all the minority stockholders or resign from the company and start a new one.

The board elected Edsel Ford to succeed Henry Ford as president effective January 1, 1919.

In 1916 Edsel Ford had married Eleanor Clay and the couple would have four children: Henry Ford II, William Clay Ford, Josephine Ford and Benson Ford.

In contrast to the humble formal education his father had received, Edsel Ford had attended the Hotchkiss School in Lakeview, Connecticut and the Detroit University School. Later Henry Ford would donate generously to Hotchkiss and the school library would be named The Edsel Ford Memorial Library.

Edsel Bryant Ford. (Courtesy of The Library of Congress)

Edsel had served a long, arduous apprenticeship with his father's company. In 1912 he had went to work in the Highland Park plant as a laborer. He then progressed through the company as a designer and secretary.

While Edsel was now president of the company Henry remained in full control of the company's operations. But Edsel Ford's ascendency to the presidency of the company was hardly symbolic. Under Edsel's leadership a new era was about to begin at Ford that would within a few years see the company diversify.

In Dodge v. Ford Motor Company 170 NW 668 (Michigan 1919).in March 1919 the Michigan Supreme Court upheld the ruling of the trial court ordering Henry Ford to pay a $19 million special dividend to stockholders. The court ordered Ford "to operate the Ford Motor Company in the interests of its stockholders, rather than in a charitable manner for the benefit of his employees or customers."[5]

By 1920 Henry Ford had bought-out all minority stockholders for approximately $75,000,000 leaving him (58%), Clara (2%) and Edsel (40%) in complete control of the company. By 1923 Ford would be one of the largest industrial organizations in the world.

For years there had been a tale circulating that in 1905 Henry Ford had been so stretched financially that he was unable to secure a loan to buy a Thanksgiving turkey. While the turkey tale was no doubt folklore probably encouraged by none other than Ford himself, it was no myth that fifteen years later he had become enormously wealthy.

By 1920 Henry Ford had become the second richest man in America trailing only oil man John D. Rockefeller who was estimated to be worth a billion dollars. Ford's wealth was just ahead of Pittsburgh banker and soon to be U.S. Secretary of the Treasury, Andrew W. Mellon, whose vast $800 million in holdings included in part, the Pennsylvania Railroad, Gulf Oil Corporation, American Metal Company, The Aluminum Company of America and The American Locomotive Company.

The single factor which separated Ford's wealth from that of Rockefeller's and Mellon's was that his was tied to production and he had little opportunity to hide money behind loopholes in the tax code and in tax-exempt bonds. Although Ford had static investments in mines and forests which were the reservoirs of his raw materials, the vast majority of his money was used for production.

In 1921 it was estimated that Henry Ford paid the U.S. Government $76 million in taxes. However, a large share of that would have passed through his hands as the intermediary for the government collecting the 5% excise tax on cars and 3% on tractors was paid at the source by the buyer. So probably Ford's taxes were about $35 million.

Ford reportedly said that if he wished he could capitalize his company for a billion dollars and sell every share and he probably could have. At the time it seemed that Henry Ford could only get richer.

8.
Crazy Carl Fisher and the Indianapolis 500

In the early years of the twentieth century while Henry Ford, Billy Durant, Ransom Olds and others were rapidly making Detroit the auto manufacturing capital of America, 299.2 miles to the southwest in Indianapolis the automobile industry was also thriving.

Between 1898 and 1935 no less than fifty makes of automobiles would be built in Indianapolis by manufacturers that included American Motors, Cole Motor Company, Empire Motor Company, Ford, Marion Motors, Studebaker and several others.

The Duesenberg one of the most notable cars of the early twentieth century was built in Indianapolis between 1913 and 1937. The Duesenberg was a large sleek luxury car built exclusively for the rich and famous. Among the notables that owned the Duesenberg Model J were Washington socialite and owner of the Hope Diamond, Evalyn Walsh McLean, Chicago gang lord Al Capone, actors Clark Gable and Tyrone Power, actresses Mae West, Marion Davies and Great Garbo, tobacco heiress and socialite Doris Duke, industrialists Howard Hughes and Powell Crosley, Jr. (later owner of the Cincinnati Reds) and publisher William Randolph Hearst.

The 1935 Duesenberg SSJ was a powerful car equipped with an 8-cylinder, 448 cubic inch engine that produced 400 hp. The SSJ was capable of going from 0 to 110 mph in less than 20 seconds. Duesenberg also manufactured racing cars and three of their entries won the Indianapolis 500 races in the 1924, 1925 and 1927.

1929 Auburn 8-90. (Photo by Lawrence T. Hay)

Another classic car built in Indianapolis during its golden age of automobile manufacturing was the Stutz. The Stutz Motor Company owned by Bethlehem Steel tycoon Charles M. Schwab built high performance roadsters and luxury cars between 1915 and 1935. The most famous car produced by the company was the Stutz Bearcat. Also, the company produced the very popular Blackhawk line.

The Marmon, a popular luxury car, was also manufactured in Indianapolis by The Marmon Motor Car Company from 1902 to 1933. The company had been started as a flourmill machinery company before switching to automobiles at the turn of the century.

While Indianapolis held its own as an automobile manufacturing center during the early days, Detroit rapidly became the capital of such activity. Detroit had several advantages in taking the lead in auto production. First it is a port city. Furthermore, at the turn of the twentieth century Detroit had a solid reputation as being one of the largest marine gas engine manufacturing centers while Michigan was producing more carriages, buggies and wheels than any other place in America. In addition, there were many paint and metal processing plants in the state. All of these factors, including having a skilled, trained labor force at its disposal provided Michigan with an advantage over other states as being able to build auto bodies at a lower cost.

Eventually all the great Indianapolis auto manufacturers would be forced to close during the Great Depression. While automobile manufacturing would slowly fade away in Indianapolis after 1935, today the city's place in automotive history is stronger than ever due to a visionary Hoosier by the name of Carl G. Fisher.

Carl Graham Fisher was born in Greensburg, Indiana on January 12, 1874 the oldest of three sons born to Ida and Albert Fisher. While he would come to be referred to by many as "Crazy Carl," he was hardly what the moniker suggested. The fact is Carl Fisher was a brilliant serial entrepreneur and planner whose name historically belongs right up there alongside that of Henry Ford, Walter Chrysler, Ransom Olds and other auto pioneers.

Anyone who knew Carl Fisher growing up in Greensburg would have never believed that someday he would be worth $100 million. His peers considered him a showoff and a buffoon. One of his teachers considered him the stupidest boy in the school. Fisher was given the nickname "Crip" because he was constantly stumbling and bumping into things. In reality Fisher had a disability of a 50% vision loss.

Carl Fisher's parents separated when both he and his two brothers were still quite young. In order to provide a meager income for the family his mother, Ida Graham Fisher took the boys to Indianapolis and began to accept boarders into the home. The day-to-day struggle for family income and his inability to read textbooks with his sight disability forced Fisher to quit school at the age of 12 and seek employment.

For the next five years Fisher worked in a variety of jobs; he was a bookstore clerk, a bank messenger, and what was known as a "butcher boy," which was a newspaper, candy and sandwich vendor who boarded trains coming in and going out of Indianapolis.

Fisher was already known, despite his sight disability as a pretty fair bicycle racer. By the time Fisher reached the age of 17 he had been able to save $600 and invested it in starting-up a bicycle repair shop on Pennsylvania Street in downtown Indianapolis operated by himself and his two brothers that he had invited to join him

Fisher also spent some of his savings on two cheap paintings, one of Abraham Lincoln and the other of Napoleon. He hung the framed portraits over his bed, and they would remain there for the rest of his life.

It was during the period while Fisher was operating the bicycle shop that people started to refer to him as "Crazy Carl." Fisher had acquired a penchant

1903 Oldsmobile Curved Dash, the first mass-produced car between 1901 to 1907, 19,000 built. (Photo by Lawrence T. Hay)

for doing unusual and sometimes dangerous acts to promote his business. In one instance he took a bicycle to the top of an office building. Then as thousands watched below Fisher threw it over the side. He had promised a brand-new bicycle to the person who found the wrecked cycle and returned it to his shop.

On another occasion Fisher stretched a rope between two office buildings in downtown Indianapolis and despite the attempts by the police to prevent the stunt—Fisher rode the bicycle across the rope from one building to the other.

As Fisher's bicycle repair shop prospered and provided a modest but steady income for his family, he expanded the business into a dealership. Although still legally a minor and having no capital to invest, Carl Fisher had convinced an Ohio manufacturer to provide his store with $50,000 worth of inventory. It was a bold testimony to his budding salesmanship skills.

By the early 1900's Carl Fisher would evolve from bicycle mechanic to bicycle shop owner to Oldsmobile dealer.

Fisher owned one of the first horseless carriages in Indianapolis when prior to the turn of the century he imported a 2.5 hp de Dion motor tricycle. In 1900 he bought a mobile steam wagon. It wasn't long before he owned a Dayton-Stoddard. Fisher recognized the future in automobiles when he witnessed the large curiosity being expressed by people towards his car.

In 1903 Fisher bought two city blocks in what was then almost an exclusively residential area of Indianapolis on Capitol Avenue and Vermont Street and started the Fisher Automobile Company. His auto dealership is believed to have been the first in Indianapolis. At first people thought he really was crazy, but in a short time his block long dealership became known as Automobile Row and sales challenged those being made by dealers in Detroit and New York. While the primary car for sale behind the glass showroom windows was the curved-dash Olds, by 1911 Fisher's dealership was also selling Overland, Empire and Baker Electric cars.

In order to increase publicity for his auto agency Fisher continued his habit of performing daring stunts. One of the more memorable promotional tricks undertaken by Fisher occurred in 1908, when he suspended a Stoddard-Dayton automobile from a vermillion balloon and floated over a downtown street in Indianapolis.

Nonetheless, Carl Fisher believed that the best way to sell cars was by racing them. So, he joined forces with pioneering auto racing enthusiasts such as Barney Oldfield, Henry Ford, Tom Cooper and Alexander Winton and began to race cars on mile and half dirt horse racetracks in the Midwest.

Auto racing had been flourishing in Europe before 1900. The first major race covered internationally took place in 1894 when French auto maker Jules Albert de Dion won a race from Paris to Rouen in a steam car. Because of the huge crowds that swarmed upon the route, de Dion only averaged 11 miles per hour.

In 1899 international competition in auto racing began when Gordon Bennett millionaire owner of the New York Herald, offered the Automobile Club of France a trophy to be awarded to the winner of a race by entrants from automobile clubs of various countries. The Gordon Bennett Cup was awarded until 1905 after which the first Grand Prix racing event took place in Le Mans.

Auto racing was becoming a fad in the United States too and the whitewashed beaches of Daytona-Ormond in Florida had in 1902 become a mecca for speed. It was there that year Alexander Winton's racing car "Bullet" ran a match race against Ransom E. Olds "Pirate at 75 mph.

Of course, Carl Fisher had gotten into the act too. In 1904 Fisher had set a new world record for two miles on a dirt track driving a Premier Comet Racer at the Harlem Race Track in Chicago.

One day a local inventor by the name of P.C. Avery dropped in at Fisher's auto dealership and had a discussion with him in regard to a method he had

"Crazy" Carl Fisher driving a Stoddard-Dayton. (Author's private collection)

developed to provide lights for automobiles by compressing carbide gas into a cylinder.

At the time you couldn't drive an automobile at night because there were no lights on it. Some drivers attempted to use lanterns and the results were often tragic. But Avery's gas device had the potential for the use of illuminating automobile headlights.

In 1904 for $2,000, Fisher and a friend, Jim Allison became partners with Avery and began to produce the devices, under the name of the Prest-O-Light Storage Battery Company. Fisher would handle the sales/promotional end and Allison the business end of the company. They began production of the headlights in a shed on North Illinois Street in Indianapolis.

In a short time, Fisher and Allison expanded operations of Prest-O-Light with plants in Boston, Cleveland, Chicago, New York and Omaha. Despite several accidents at the Indianapolis plant where the devices were being manufactured when cylinders filled with carbide gas exploded, the venture became very profitable.

Eventually the Indianapolis City Council became concerned about explosions at the Pres-O-Light plant and ordered that it should be moved outside the city limits. The plant would be moved near the site of the present-day Indianapolis Speedway. Eventually Fisher became concerned that the employees of the racetrack and light plant should have their families close by, so he created the nearby factory town of Speedway, Indiana.

Over the course of the next decade Fisher and Allison bought-out Avery's interest in Prest-O-Light. Then in 1917 Fisher and Allison would sell the company to Union Carbide for $9 million.

Auto racing was already taking place in Indianapolis. In a 1903 race at the Fair Grounds, Barney Oldfield the most famous auto race driver in the country became the first driver to travel a-mile-a-minute.

There had been another race at the Fair Grounds in September 1908 that was promoted by the Indianapolis Automobile Trade Association in which the Mayor of the city, Charles Brookwater was the referee and Barney Oldfield participated. The Association had attempted to get Carl Fisher to drive his Stoddard-Dayton in the race, but he declined.

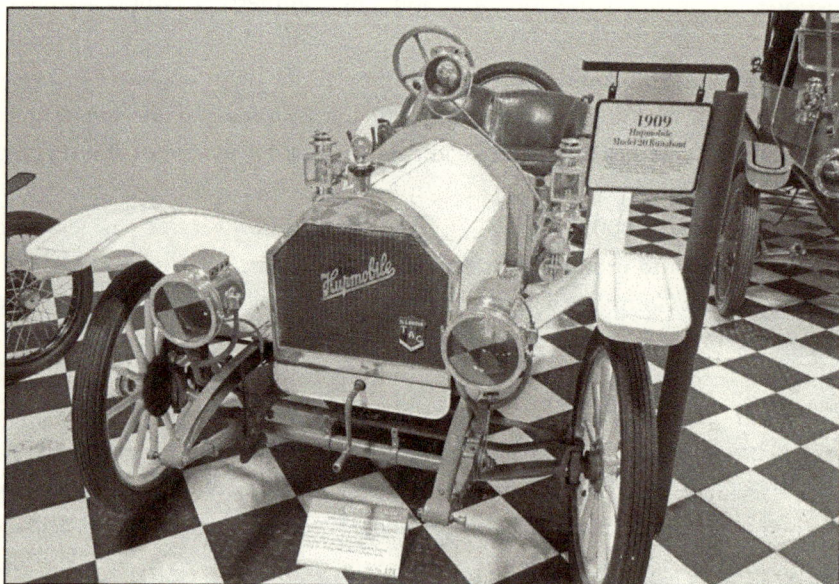

1909 Hupmobile Model 20 Runabout. Cost $750. Accessories included gas headlights and a Prest-O-Light tank. (Photo by Lawrence T. Hay)

As the second decade of the twentieth century neared American automakers had caught up with the Europeans in technology and styling. But there was no place for the American automakers to prove or test new technology such as four-wheel brakes, hydraulic shock absorbers, carburation suspensions or tires. Furthermore, there was no place where large numbers of people with a curiosity about these things could pay to see them tested or raced.

While Carl Fisher had moved on to manufacturing head lights, he was still interested in auto racing. In 1905 he had attended the Gordon Bennett Cup race in France and returned to the United States impressed with what he had seen in speedways and in public road construction. With the memory of his experience in France still fresh in his mind, Carl Fisher decided it was time to take auto racing in America to the next level.

In early winter 1908 Fisher invited his partner in Prest-O-Light, Jim Allison, and few Indianapolis businessmen, Arthur Newby, Frank Wheeler and Stoughton Fletcher to meet with him at Pop Haynes Restaurant located on North Pennsylvania. During the meeting Carl Fisher using a pencil would draw his conception of a proposed oval racetrack on the tablecloth. Fisher wanted the men to invest in building a large speedway and test track for the budding automobile industry in Indianapolis. It would require that all five of them put-up $50,000 each.

Initially all four men, Allison, Newby, Wheeler and Fletcher agreed. Then Fletcher backed out. His grandfather, also named Stoughton Fletcher, had been the founder of the Fletcher National Bank in Indianapolis and he quickly advised his grandson, as an officer of the bank, for him to indulge in such a risky venture as a racetrack was not in line with the best interest of the bank's conservative reputation. In short it was bad for business, so young Stoughton withdrew from the project.

The proposal was rescued when Carl Fisher and Jim Allison agreed to split Fletcher's pledge with both men putting-up an additional $25,000 each. On February 9, 1909 the Indianapolis Speedway was incorporated.

For $72,000 Fisher and his partners bought a group of farms totaling 400 acres just outside Indianapolis on the northwest fringe on Crawfordsville Pike where it intersected with Georgetown Road owned by Levi Munter and another family by the name of Presseley. Then with an early spring frost still clinging to the air, using hundreds of mules and a work force of 100 men paid $2 per day, they began to plow out the outlines of a 2 ½ mile track. Fisher and his associates had the intention of holding the first race sometime in late spring that year.

Not everyone in Indianapolis was impressed with Fisher's proposal. One of the city's newspapers ran an editorial that stated in part, "only a fool would build a racetrack five miles from downtown."[1]

Almost every day Carl Fisher would personally supervise the progress of the construction on the racetrack. Often, he would invite Jane Watts a 15-year old Indianapolis high school girl to ride along with him.

Fisher a quintessential publicity hound frequently featured in the Indianapolis newspapers was often the topic of dinnertime discussion in the Watts household. Jane Watts was 14-years old when she got her first glimpse of "Crazy Carl" as he pulled-off the stunt of sitting in an Olds suspended from a balloon several thousand feet above downtown Indianapolis.

In her book about her life with Fisher, *Fabulous Hoosier* that Jane wrote about ten years after his death, she describes her first glimpse of "Crazy Carl." She states that I was a 15-year-old schoolgirl walking along Meridian Street in Indianapolis when, "I noticed that all movement had stopped on that leisurely boulevard. I looked up. Against the clouds, thousands of feet above me I saw Carl Fisher for the first time. He was in a white automobile hung as the basket under a vermillion balloon."[2]

Jane's first close-up glimpse of Fisher took place at the Canoe Club. She even told a friend that day, "There goes the man I am going to marry!"[3] A few weeks later the home in which Jane Watts lived with her parents caught fire while they were away. Immediately, Jane called Fisher at his office and told him that she had seen him at the Canoe Club and her parent's home was on fire. Fisher told Jane he would be right over. It was the beginning of a romance.

Later that year as the speedway construction proceeded, Fisher would propose marriage to Jane. Fisher was a celebrity of considerable stature in Indianapolis and no doubt his proposal to make Jane Watts a child-bride was shocking to some. Nonetheless, the couple would marry in October that year.

The track was officially opened on June 5, 1909; but instead of an auto race—a balloon race took place. A crowd of 3500 paying customers came out to see what Fisher and his associates were building on the edge of town. An additional 40,000 people watched from outside the perimeter of the track. "Crazy Carl" Fisher was a participant in the balloon race but did not win. Fisher was no amateur balloonist; in fact, he was one of the first 25 licensed balloonists in the U.S.

The first auto race at the speedway was held later that summer on August 19. However, the track was made-up of crushed stone and a tar surface. It proved to be unsatisfactory for high speed auto racing and was the cause of a few fatalities. So, in 1910 the original surface of the track was replaced with 3,200,000, 10-pound bricks.

Fisher and his associates soon learned that crowd control would have to be improved at the track too. For the initial events confusion and mayhem had prevailed in the parking lots and streets outside the facility. Horses singly and hitched to carriages and wagons had broken loose and roamed in the adjacent fields dragging hitching blocks with them, knocking down fences, tearing-up shrubbery and some even wound up in the barns of property owners who refused to return them to their owners without paying a fee.

During 1910 a series of 42 separate races were held at the speedway and the new brick surface proved to be an excellent improvement for performance and safety. Although 40,000 spectators had come out for the series of races held in May and repeated on July 4th and Labor Day, Fisher and his associates came to the conclusion that it would be better to hold a limited number of races each year rather than a series. Holding only a few races they reasoned would attract the best drivers and racing teams. They eventually decided to hold one big 500 mile race each year in late May on Memorial Day.

Fisher and his partners hired T. E. "Pop" Myers and Eloise "Dolly" Dallenbach as his secretary and office manager with the responsibilities for coordinating the administrative functions of the yearly race. The pair would remain at their posts at the Speedway for 40 years.

On Memorial Day 1911 with Henry Ford in attendance and taking pictures, the first Indianapolis 500 race was held.

According to the *Indianapolis Star* all the cars entered into the 500 mile race were subjected to technical examinations and then received technical certificates from the American Automobile Association (AAA).[4] Two days before the race, Carl Fisher president of the Speedway, along with the race starter Fred Wagner and the race referees, held a school for the drivers to receive their final instructions. There were twelve cars lined up on the track with Carl Fisher as pacemaker along with the starter present to rehearse the start of the race while 4000 people watched. The intent of the exercise was to lessen the danger of accidents on the getaway.

Cars were limited to engine sizes of 600-cubic-inch displacement and had to reach 75 mph to qualify for the race. While 39 cars attainted the required speed, many did not. But Louis Chevrolet who had intended to be a relief driver qualified his model "100" Buick at 100 mph.

Where a car was placed in the lineup was determined by the date of its entry. Consequently, many of the faster cars that arrived at the track late were placed in rear starting positions. The prize was $35,000 for the winner.

A huge crowd was expected for the race and although tickets cost only one dollar, counterfeit tickets began to appear. To counter-act the bogus tickets Carl Fisher reminded race fans to buy tickets only at locations designated by the Speedway.

For the 1911 race Carl Fisher and his associates had really improved the facility by installing new fencing on the track, building new garages for the race cars and even installing drinking fountains. Fisher also paid $5,000 for a Stewart-Warner Electric Printer Timer to ensure accuracy in the race results. The device included a chronometer certified by the U.S. Naval Observatory along with a recording section that used a sprocket-wheel printer that printed the times of the race cars in one-one hundredth-second intervals on a continuous strip of paper.

Still a glaring dichotomy existed among the modern environment that Carl Fisher had created for the race; 3000 hitching posts were installed for the horses of spectators. Without them there would have been pandemonium from the frightened animals.

Memorial Day 1911 was a bright and sunny day and 75,000 crowded their way through the gates of the Speedway to witness the thrills, chills and tragedy of the initial Indy 500.

On the 12th lap Arthur Greiner who had started the race in 38th position, lost control of his car in the southwest corner and hit the wall. His ridding mechanic Sam Dickson became the first man to lose his life in the Indy 500. Greiner was lucky to be hospitalized with a broken shoulder.

Later in the race, Louis Disbrow driving a Pope-Hartford and Teddy Tetzlaff driving a Lozier collided on the front straight but neither driver was hurt.

Another dangerous incident occurred on the 87th lap when mechanic C. I. Anderson fell from the racer being driven by Joe Jagersberger as the two sped down the front straight. Harry Knight who was closely trailing Jagersberger swerved to avoid Anderson who was sprawled out on the track as the large crowd screamed in horror. While he managed to avoid hitting Anderson, Knight careened into the car of Herbert Lytle in the pits then flipped over on Caleb Bragg's machine. As a result of the impact, Knight sustained a mildly fractured skull and his riding mechanic, John Glover, a strained back.

Although Roy Harroun had been a late entry and started in 28th place he won the race. Harroun an automotive engineer for the Marmon Company had retired from racing the previous year but was persuaded by friends to enter the 500. He drove a six-cylinder, 447 cubic inch engine single seat racing car, painted black and yellow that he dubbed the "Marmon WASP," which covered the 500 miles in 6 hours 42 minutes at an average speed of 74.59 mph. The 1911 race would be the only victory in the 500 for a Marmon.

Harroun's car was the only single seater in the race. The purpose of having an extra man in the cockpit was to serve as an observer to watch the other cars and the pits, as well as to listen for sounds of trouble from the engine. To compensate for not having an observer Harroun mounted an eight-by-three-inch mirror on a tripod attached to the hood cowling, thereby putting into use the first rear-view mirror ever mounted on any car.

All during the early stages of the race Roy Harroun was challenged by David Bruce-Brown, but finally got by him in the later stages of the race.

"Smiling" Ralph Mulford finished second. However, Mulford would forever claim that a scoring error had occurred when four cars crashed on the starting line.

Future World War One fighter pilot Ace and future Indianapolis Speedway owner Eddie Rickenbacker was a relief driver for Lee Frayer in the 1911 Indy 500 and the pair finished 11th in an underpowered car. The following year Rickenbacker won a 300-mile race in Sioux City.

The following year one of the most dramatic moments in the history of the Speedway would be featured in the 1912 Indy. Ralph DePalma who many race experts list as one of the best drivers in Indy 500 history led the race for 196 of the 200 laps, then a connecting rod broke and stalled the car within sight of victory. DePalma and his mechanic Rupert Jenkins courageously attempted to push their heavy Mercedes the rest of the way while the crowd of 80,000 hysterically screamed and yelled their support for the two as Joe Dawson sped by them into victory lane. Dawson had led for only two laps in the race after DePalma was forced out.

In 1915 Ralph DePalma would win his only victory in the Indy 500 out of ten tries.

The Indianapolis 500 race really personified America's growing love affair with the car and it would not be long before automakers in Detroit would be producing them in the millions.

1919 Indianapolis 500 start. Race was won by Howdy Wilcox. (Author's private collection)

Soon racetracks were appearing all over the country. At Elgin, Illinois in the summer of 1919 a dirt speedway was made of a converted country road. Costing about $8,000 and using 25,000 gallons of oil, modern road making machinery and a lot of labor, a country road was converted to an 8 ¼ mile racecourse to hold a 36 lap 300-mile race.

Following the construction of the Indianapolis Speedway and organizing the Indianapolis 500 race, "Crazy Carl" Fisher continued to amaze everyone with his ingenuity.

With the popularity of the automobile growing Americans were quick to recognize that an inadequate road system existed. While there were streets in the cities they usually ended at the edge of town with no connecting roads. So, Carl Fisher got together with a group of people who wanted to see the construction of a national road that would connect America from east to west.

On July 1, 1913 Carl Fisher and a group of 70 businessmen and other interested persons, calling themselves "The Trailblazers," got in their automobiles and set out for San Francisco. A highway fund had been created for a transcontinental highway by Fisher and he and his party were hardily and generously greeted by all as they crossed the country. The trip heighted the awareness and support of Americans everywhere and began the campaign for the construction of a transcontinental highway. Soon after "The Trailblazers" auto trip Henry Joy, president of the Packard Motor Car Company became president of the campaign to build the road and it was incorporated as the Lincoln Highway Association.

When completed after World War One, The Lincoln Highway (Highway 40) would be America's first high-speed road connecting New York and San Francisco. The highway went through 14 states and 128 counties and all those along the route had Carl Fisher to thanks for his diligent advocacy.

As the construction of the Lincoln Highway was being planned, Carl Fisher undertook a second auto trip with another group going from Indianapolis to Miami. The sojourn would lead to the formation of The Dixie Highway Association and construction of the Dixie Highway that when completed in the 1920s would run from the upper peninsula of Michigan to Miami, Florida.

By now no one could predict what Carl Fisher would attempt to do next. In late November 1914 it was announced in *The Indianapolis Star* and *The New York Times* that Carl Fisher was about to introduce a gasoline substitute that he had acquired from John Andrus a chemist from McKeesport, Pennsylvania. The fuel which was a mixture of water and chemicals could be manufactured for 1 ½ cents per gallon. According to Fisher he was going to market it under the brand Zoline.

On November 21 and 22, 1914 Zoline was tested at Indianapolis Motor Speedway in a Marmon 41 stock car. The car ran on the fuel for 1030 miles over the course of two days and the only complication incurred was a frozen fuel line on the first day. The average temperature that day at the Speedway was 10 below zero.

While it is known that Carl Fisher was offered a $1 million for the formula, it is not known as to who made the offer. Soon after the substitute fuel's test at Indianapolis any mention of Zoline disappeared in the newspapers.

During the early part of the twentieth century there were several experiments with lighting for night sporting events. A Massachusetts inventor by the name of George Cahill had developed a system for field lighting that held promise.

In 1908 August "Garry" Herrmann president of the Cincinnati Reds organized a development company and raised $50,000 capital to install lights in The Palace of the Fans, the Reds ballpark, in order to play an experimental exhibition game at night. A year later on the evening of June 18, 1909 several towers outfitted with 14 flaming arch lamps were installed at The Palace of the Fans and an exhibition game between two teams from local Elks Lodges was played. The score of the game was 8-5 but there had been 18 errors committed. The results were judged inconclusive and it would be another 29 years until the first night game in major league baseball would be played at Crosley Field in Cincinnati.

In Indianapolis Carl Fisher decided to experiment with auto racing at night. Due to the massive size of the 2 ½ mile Speedway it was economically and technically impossible to illuminate the entire track for the experiment, so the one mile Fairgrounds track was used. For the experiment 180,000 candlepower was diffused over about 50 feet of the backstretch of the Fairgrounds track to provide a glimpse of what the course completely illuminated would look like. The rest of facility was illuminated with dull intermittent lighting.

The experiment took place on the evening of April 19, 1915. As Jane Fisher drove her limousine into the Fairgrounds she remarked to Carl. "I never saw so much light in my life."[5]

It was hoped that lighting would permit a car to attain the speed equal to what it got during the day. Eddie Rickenbacher representing the Maxwell Racing Team, now owned by Carl Fisher and Jim Allison, was the first driver to test the course under the lights and driving his Morcross Marmon roadster he did 65 mph. Then Carl Fisher tried the course.

Just as had been the case in the Cincinnati night baseball experiment in 1909, the results were judged inconclusive. To this day The Indianapolis Speedway remains dark at night.

It is estimated that it would cost $20 million to install lighting in the Speedway. Clint Beyer a NASCAR driver who has participated several times in the Brickyard 400 at Speedway says to light the track the electric bill would be considerable. "You're going to need a nuclear power plant to light this place. You're going to have to shut down downtown to have enough power to light the track. It's huge!"[6]

In late 1915 Maxwell had decided to get out of the racing business. So Carl Fisher and Jim Allison bought the remaining Maxwell inventory intending to use the cars for their Prest-O-Lite racing team thereby ensuring a competitive field for the 1916 Indy 500 as the war in Europe had caused all the European drivers to withdraw their entries. Fisher and Allison also decided to shorten the 1916 race to 300 miles.

Fisher and Allen made an agreement with Eddie Rickenbacker to be the Prest-O-Lite team manager and operate the cars in exchange for 75% of the gross prize money. While Italian born and British raised driver Dario Resta won

Eddie Rickenbacker. (Author's private collection)

the abbreviated race, Rickenbacker made around $60,000 as part of his deal with Fisher and Allen.

With the entry of the United States into the World War looking certain, Fisher and Allison cancelled the Indianapolis 500 race for the next two years.

Eddie Rickenbacker had been in England when the war finally drew the United States into the conflict. He quickly came home and joined the Army. Although Rickenbacker had learned to fly in California during 1916 he was assigned as the driver for General John "Black Jack" Pershing. But soon Rickenbacker was transferred to the Army Air Corps and went on to capture the imagination of all Americans shooting down 26 German planes.

The 1920's would usher in the first major changes in cars running in the Indy 500. During the first decade of the race it had been a contest each year between the Stutz, the Peugeot, Mercedes, Delage, Maxwell and Mercer cars. Then in 1920 the Speedway adopted the international formula for Grand Prix cars dropping the engine size to 183 cubic inches thereby making all the semi-stock cars that had run in the race obsolete.

On Memorial Day 1920 every car entered in the Indy 500 was built solely for racing, most in small shops around Indianapolis. Now it was a contest between Millers, Frontenacs and Duesenbergs. One historian was to remark, "Drivers had changed from the leather-helmeted, mustachioed daredevils handling huge, ungainly machines to young jousters in low-slung bombs."[7]

In the 1925 race Pete DePalo became the first driver to average 100 mph. In winning the race DePalo set a new track record with a speed of 101.13 mph driving a front wheel drive Duesenberg. At the 250 mile mark DePalo had let Norman Batten drive some laps while his blistered hands were bandaged. That stop and another dropped DePalo to 5th place, but he regained the lead when veteran driver Dave Lewis driving a front-drive Miller came in for relief from Benny Hill. Then DePalo drove the last few laps at reduced speed and won the race by a half lap over Hill.

The 1927 Indianapolis 500 was a very exciting event. The race was won by rookie driver George Souders who although a native of Lafayette Indiana, had worked his way up in the racing circuit through the rough and tumble dirt tracks of the southwest. Souders driving a two-year old Duesenberg built in Indianapolis took the lead on lap 149 and stayed there for the rest of the race. He had qualified at 115 mph.

There were some memorable and tense moments in the 1927 race. On the 120th lap 1926 winner Frank Lockhart broke a con rod and withdrew from the race. Two drivers; Henry Kohlert and Jules Ellingboe were seriously hurt when their cars hit a wall. Also when Norman Batten's car caught fire he drove the blazing racer down the front stretch and away from the other cars.

It should also be noted that in the 1927 Indy 500 Leon Duray ran his car on ethanol rather than gasoline. He was the first driver to do so. Today ethanol is the standard fuel for Indy cars.

The 1927 Indianapolis 500 would be the last in the Carl Fisher/Jim Allison era. Following the race Fisher and Allison sold the Indianapolis Speedway to Captain Eddie Rickenbacker for $700,000.

Following World War One Rickenbacker with backers from Detroit had got into the automobile manufacturing business and his 1922 Rickenbacker was a car with many fine innovations such as four wheel brakes. Eddie Rickenbacker had caught the automobile industry by surprise and their only recourse was to use adverse publicity to deem his car unsafe. Then the recession of 1925 dealt a fatal blow to Rickenbacker's company.

At first Eddie Rickenbacker brought new energy to running the Speedway and even added a golf course. But overtime he too lost interest as he became more involved with other ventures such as Eastern Airlines. During World War Two Rickenbacker was forced to close the speedway as the U.S. Government banned auto racing. So there was no Indy 500 during the period of 1942 to 1945.

However, Firestone gained permission from the government to use the track to test tires. Also Bob Hope and Bing Crosby used the facility for a War Bonds rally and a golf tournament. In November 1945 Rickenbacker sold the speedway to Tony Hulman.

Anton "Tony" Hulman, Jr. took the Indianapolis Speedway and the 500 race to unbelievable popularity. It was under Hulman's 32-year direction that the Indy 500 became popularly known as "The Greatest Spectacle in Racing." The Speedway was improved to include giant steel-and-concrete stands and a beautifully manicured-grounds.

There would be many changes in the Indianapolis 500 race over the years, but one moment in the history of the race stands out above the others when in 1977 the promoter announced to the drivers, "Janet and Gentlemen start your engines."

Janet Guthrie became the first women to qualify for the Indy 500 race on May 22, 1977. In the last day of qualifications for the race Guthrie achieved an average speed of 188.402 mph driving a Lighting Offenhauser.

At the time Janet Guthrie was a 39-year old physicist who had been driving race cars for 14 years. In the 1977 Indy 500 Guthrie would have to compete against such racing legends as A.J. Foyt, Johnny Rutherford and Gordon Johncock.

In 1976 for the first time since the bricks had been laid on the track in 1910, the entire Indianapolis Speedway had been repaved with asphalt in its entirety.

The 1977 Indy 500 witnessed by nearly 300,000 spectators was won by A. J. Foyt who edged out Tony Sneva to win for a record fourth time. Janet Guthrie finished 26th in the field of 33 entries. She had experienced engine trouble almost from the start of the race, then in her second pit stop, in the stifling heat a fuel mixture of alcohol and methanol expanded and spilled out to the bucket seat where she was. The pit crew had to pour water over her racing suit. Guthrie completed only 27 laps, but her presence in the race was a huge win for everybody.

The Indianapolis 500 race that Carl Fisher had been instrumental in forming is today the most attended sporting attraction in the United States. In 2015 for the 99th Indy 500, more than 220,000 fans attended and saw Juan Pablo Montoya win the race with an average speed of 161.341 mph. Montoya's speed was actually slightly slower than those of previous winners. Tony Kanaan won the 2013 Indy with an average speed of 187.433 mph.

Soon after Carl Fisher married Jane Watt in 1909, he had taken her on a yachting trip to Florida. During the trip Fisher met John Collins who at that time was attempting to build a bridge across Biscayne Bay.

John Collins was a 72-year old Quaker farmer originally from Moorestown, New Jersey who in 1891 had bought five miles of land (roughly 50 city blocks of present day Miami Beach) between the Atlantic Ocean and Biscayne Bay with the intent of growing coconuts, mangoes and avocados. By 1907 his land was clear and his groves successful, so Collins wanted to build a bridge to enable him to transport his produce across to Miami and points beyond. However his children, shrewder farmers than their father back in New Jersey, wanted the bridge to attract tourism on the land and enhance real estate value. So Collins agreed and the bridge construction began, but stopped when the money ran out in 1912.

Enter Carl Fisher, who offered $50,000 financial assistance to Collins in exchange for 200 acres of his land on the beach. The land was dense jungle filled with heavy growth of palmettos, vines and mangrove. It was only inhabited by alligators, rats, snakes and jungle flies.

The bridge was finished June 12, 1913. Then John Collins and a son-in-law built a hotel. By 1922 Collins had the largest avocado and mango groves in the world.

But Carl Fisher had a much larger vision for the land and almost immediately he began to develop what was then known as Alton Beach and buy as many additional acres as possible. Using men with machetes and mules who hacked their way through the jungle, the community would soon become Miami Beach. The name Miami Beach came from something Fisher had seen on a boxcar.

Following a difficult pregnancy on November 13, 1921 Jane had given birth to a baby boy the Fishers named Carl, Jr. Unfortunately the child lived for only 26 days. The death of his son broke Carl Fisher's heart. He told Jane there would be no more children; he could never again put her through such an ordeal.

By 1927 Carl Fisher was caught-up in the hard drinking, wild spending culture of the roaring twenties. He was spending most of his time becoming one of the pioneer developers of Miami Beach, Florida and bought a mansion on the edge of Biscayne Bay that he named Shawdows. He had for the most part lost interest in the Indy 500 race and the speedway was deteriorating. Furthermore the Indiana legislature was attempting to prevent Fisher from holding the Indy 500 race on Memorial Day.

The success of the Miami Beach project had raised Carl Fisher's estimated fortune to $100 million. With the success of Miami Beach, Fisher decided to attempt a similar project on the eastern tip of Long Island at Montauk Point. While Fisher was diverting his resources to the Long Island project a hurricane struck Miami Beach.

Fisher was on his way to Miami Beach aboard his yacht when he heard the news of the storm. At that point "Crazy Carl" Fisher made what was probably the only bad business decision in his life. He stopped work on the Montauk Point project and ordered his cash diverted to Miami Beach. The move rattled investors in Montauk and they withdrew their funds. While Miami Beach was saved, Fisher's fortune began to dwindle.

Montauk was never completed to the scale that Fisher had envisioned; but he had built a yacht club, golf course, bathing beach and the Montauk Manor. Unable to oversee the project Fisher made an agreement with Lindsey Hopkins of Atlanta to take over the project in exchange for income of $10,000 a year for life.

Not long after Fisher and Jane had an amicable divorce. Furthermore with Fisher's blessing, a few years later Jane remarried—this time to a much younger man. Now Fisher began to drink even heavier and his health gradually deteriorated.

As for Fisher's original partners in the Indianapolis Speedway, Jim Allison died in 1928 from complications associated with pneumonia. Allison had invested all of his money received from the sale of Prest-O-Lite into Allison Engineering which was eventually bought by General Motors following his death.

In 1921, Frank Wheeler committed suicide, despondent over his diabetes and the financial troubles he was experiencing.

Art Newby who had built the National motor car remained on the board as director of the Speedway until his death in 1933.

"Crazy Carl" Fisher's final project was to open the Caribbean Club in Key Largo, Florida in October 1938. It was billed as a sort of a poor man's fishing retreat that included a bar, kitchen and small hotel rooms. The bar was the oldest in the upper keys. Carl Fisher died on July 16, 1939.

Following Fisher's death, the Caribbean Club became a casino. In 1947 Warner Brothers used the location for inspiration and for exterior shots in the film *Key Largo* starring Humphrey Bogart and Lauren Bacall.

At the time of his death Carl Fisher was a hero in Miami Beach, residents knew what he meant to the community. The day he died at St. Francis Hospital in Miami Beach flags around town were hung at half-mast. Soon after at the corner of Alton Road & 55th Street a bronze bust of Fisher was dedicated. On it are the words chiseled in that read—"CARL GRAHAM FISHER—HE CARVED A GREAT CITY OUT OF A JUNGLE." [8]

In Indianapolis there is a school and street in Speedway, Indiana that carry his name.

When Captain Eddie Rickenbacker heard the news of Carl Fisher's demise, he remarked, "His vision made the world a more beautiful place in which to live." [9]

4.
Walter P. Chrysler's Rise to Power

As the roaring twenties began Henry Ford wasn't the only auto manufacturer making a lot of cars in America and getting very rich doing it, so was Walter P. Chrysler.

Walter Percy Chrysler was of American pioneer stock; his grandfather had driven a covered wagon across the plains and his father had been a drummer boy in the Union Army during the Civil War.

Born on April 2, 1875 in Wamego, Kansas, Walter Chrysler was the son of Henry (Hank) and Anna Marie (Breymann) Chrysler. The family soon moved to Ellis, Kansas where Walter grew up. His father was a railroad engineer on the Union Pacific Railroad on a wood-burning engine.

Walter's first job was during the summer school vacation delivering groceries. He went to school until he was 17 years old then he became a janitor at the Union Pacific shops earning five cents per hour. His father had instilled in him an appreciation for engines and Walter worked his way up to the position of mechanic's apprentice at the Union Pacific Roundhouse in Ellis.

In Ellis Walter enrolled in Miss Cartwright's music class where he learned to play the snare drum and later learned to play the B-flat clarinet and the tuba. Eventually Walter would play in the extremely popular Union Pacific Band. It was at Miss Cartwright's class that Walter would meet Della Forker who played the piano. Walter was instantly infatuated with Della.

Although Walter and Della became engaged in 1896 the couple was unable to marry because Walter was only making $1.50 a day. Eventually the two would be married on June 7, 1901 at the Methodist Church in Ellis.

Walter worked in the Union Pacific shops for four years then something happened that had a distinct effect on his career path. One day a locomotive pulled-in with a broken cylinder head. A mail train was scheduled to leave in two hours and there was not another locomotive available. The superintendent of Motor Power, John Hickey, needed to get the broken locomotive back on the track. Hickey told Chrysler that he didn't really believe that it was possible to repair the locomotive to leave on time with the mail cars, but if somehow he could do it, he would not forget what he had done. Walter assured Hickey that he could accomplish the task. Within two hours working feverishly with two assistants taking off nuts and crossheads with a wrench while Walter was machining parts, they had the locomotive ready to go.

John Hickey made good on his promise to not forget what Walter had accomplished for him. Three months later in early February 1902 on Hickey's recommendation, Walter Chrysler became General Foreman of the Colorado and Southern shops at Trinidad.

Walter was now in charge of ninety men He had a small office with a roll-top desk and a telephone. Because he had now become part of management the union required him to surrender his union card. Wisely, Walter requested a withdraw card just in case he ever became unemployed and needed work.

About a week after being promoted, on February 13, Walter and Della's first child was born, a daughter they named Thelma Irene.

Walter Chrysler continued to demonstrate a superior organizational skill set at Trinidad, but soon he moved on leaving the Union Pacific for the Atchison, Topeka and Santa Fe Railroad in Wellington, Kansas.

Nine years later Walter accepted the position as Superintendent of Motor Power of the Chicago and Great Western System. While he was making a decent salary in his new position, he came to the realization that he was now 33-years old and saw that it was dead-end career wise. "I realized that I had gone as far as I could in the line I was in," remarked Walter. "Mechanical men never got father than being the heads of their departments. Executive positions were not given to them. Tradition prevented any promotion."[1]

However, Walter Chrysler also came to the conclusion that being in a dead-end position, even in one that was perceived to be so, did not preclude him from taking another job. It became a personal edict with Walter Chrysler that would guide his career, you had to know when to move on, even if it meant entering an entirely new field and for less money.

Walter Chrysler. (Courtesy of The Library of Congress)

In this case, Walter went to work for the American Locomotive Company in the position of works manager for about half the salary he had been getting. He reasoned that there were possibilities for further advancement there.

He was right; his new job involved more than just the construction of locomotives. The element of competitive sales was inherent in the position and within two years he was general manager and the company was operating at a profit.

Walter Chrysler was a rising industrial star but he never forgot where he started. Years later when he had risen to the head of the company which would bear his name, at the entrance of the company's Detroit offices, there was a time card marked number one—it had Walter Chrysler's name on it. He used the timecard too. Every morning that he was in Detroit, he punched in at exactly eight o'clock.

During the first decade of the twentieth century when suddenly automobiles or horseless carriages began to appear everywhere, Walter Chrysler came to the conclusion that personal transportation was the future. In 1905 he attended the Chicago Automobile Show. It was there that he awestruck by a particular car. The price was $5000 and he only had $700. The reason he wanted the car was not to drive it—he wanted to perform reverse engineering on the car—to see how it was made.

He managed to borrow the additional $4,300 required to buy the car and had it shipped to his home. By the time he had taken the car apart and put it back together again, he had learned a lot about automotive engineering.

Chrysler began thinking about how he might get into the automobile business. Eventually he realized that he had to do exactly the same thing he had done to get out of the mechanical end of the locomotive business. So he quit his job with American Locomotive Company. Although he had been making $12,000 a year at that time, Walter took a job for $6,000 a year with General Motors. By 1912 he was the works manager for Buick in Flint.

By 1916 Walter had worked his way up to vice-president of Buick, helping the company to increase its production from 45 cars a day to 600. He was now making $10,000 a month with yearly a bonus of $500,000. Nonetheless all the time Walter Chrysler was working with GM he continued dreaming of the day that he would build a car of his own.

Following World War One in 1919, Walter Chrysler quit Buick and announced his retirement. He had been with GM and Buick since 1911. Chrysler left GM because he feared that Billy Durant was leading the company to certain disaster through constant over-expansion.

World War One was followed by a recession that hit the auto industry hard. Maxwell and Chalmers automobiles were being manufactured in the same plant, although there was no direct corporate connection between the two; movement was starting to take place to combine them.

As the recession deepened a group of bankers approached Walter Chrysler and enticed him to come out of retirement and take over the Willys-Overland Company based in Toledo, Ohio. At the time Willys-Overland was in debt $50 million and the banks that had put up the money were extremely worried. They had confidence in Chrysler's ability to turn the company around and offered him a 2-year contract with the title of executive vice-president. When Chrysler demanded a salary of $1 million a year in his contract, not one of the bankers blinked an eye.

Immediately Chrysler went to work on bringing Willys-Overland into solvency. He hired a trio of young engineers who had formerly been with Studebaker and had left to from their own automotive consulting company. Fred M. Zeder and Frank Breer were experts in designing and modifying engines and Owen Skelton was an expert in transmissions and axles.

They were sent by Chrysler to work in a new Willys-Overland factory in Elizabeth, New Jersey with a free-hand to build a totally new car that would bring the company out of its financial doldrums. But Chrysler's plan was second-guessed by the board who did not want to build a totally new car, but rather a redesigned version of its current car that would attract a larger market. While Chrysler would put the company back in the black, there would be no new Willys-Overland model.

While Walter Chrysler was turning Willy-Overland around, Maxwell's backers were in deep trouble too; the company was facing receivership and looking for someone to save the company.

Maxwell started to ramp-up production and manufactured 50,000 cars in 1919 which put it in 7th place for the year behind Ford, Chevrolet, Buick, Dodge, Willys-Overland and Oakland. But as Maxwell become more involved with Chalmers it found its profits being drained.

1915 Maxwell 25 Series Touring. (Photo by Lawrence T. Hay)

The move to combine Chalmers into the Maxwell operations was starting to have an adverse effect. Consequently, in 1920 only 34,168 Maxwells
were produced and the company fell to 11th place among auto manufacturers.
Furthermore the troubles were increased by the two company's accountants
who began to squabble as pressure was mounting to bring their respective books
into harmony. At mid-year in 1920 Maxwell had about 26,000 unsold cars and
was in debt $32 million.

The internal problems were extensive, Maxwell executives and Chalmers
executives were fighting with each other wanting to go their own ways. The
matter came to a head when Chalmers executives terminated the lease in their
Detroit facility where Maxwell was building its cars. As a result Maxwell ceased
production and relied on its unsold overstocked vehicle and parts inventory.

Ironically it was Chalmers that suffered the most from the squabbles.
Suddenly there were no Maxwell cars to build and no buyers for Chalmers
cars—so the company was forced into receivership. Maxwell made an attempt
to settle the matter and purchased the Chalmers Company for about $2 million.

But the acquisition of Chalmers did little to solve the over-all problems
confronting Maxwell as the company was deep in debt to the tune of about $30
million. While the 1921 Maxwell's were good cars they hadn't really changed
from those produced in 1919 or 1920 so sales sagged.

The Chalmers Motor Company, formerly known as the Chalmers Detroit
Motor Company that Maxwell had just acquired, had produced some notable
cars during the first decade of the twentieth century. The Chalmers Detroit
Model 30 manufactured in 1909 and 1910 won 69 major automobile competi-
tions establishing the car as strong running and dependable.

Most notable among those awards for the Chalmers was winning the
Glidden Tour in 1909 and 1910. The Glidden Tour had been sponsored by the
AAA and the trophy and name of the event came from the generosity of Charles
J. Glidden a financier and auto enthusiast.

The Chalmers Detroit Motor Company also had the historical distinction of being involved in a huge automobile controversy that occurred in the
National pastime in 1910 when Chalmers announced that they would give a
new car to the major league player that finished with highest batting average
for that season.

For a while Fred Snodgrass of the New York Giants in the National League
had been challenging American League players Ty Cobb of the Detroit Tigers
and Nap Lajoie of the Cleveland Indians; but he did a nose dive in late August

Ty Cobb and Nap Lajoie win Chalmers in 1910. (Author's private collection)

and began to fade from competition. So for most of the 1910 season the battle for the highest average in the major leagues was between Ty Cobb and Nap Lajoie. The final four weeks of the season found Cobb and Lajoie in a close contest and entering the final weekend of the season they were in a virtual dead heat for the highest batting average.

On the final day of the season Ty Cobb was in the lead. But suddenly the personalities of the two players came into play. Cobb was a feisty and fiery competitor and most opposing players intensely disliked him, so most of the players in the American League that were not Cobb's teammates preferred that Nap Lajoie win the batting title and the Chalmers car.

On the final day of season the Indians were in St. Louis to play a double-header with the Browns. Surprisingly, Nap Lajoie got eight hits in the twin bill to finish with a batting average of .384084. But it looked like Lajoie got a little help from the Browns. Six of his eight hits were bunt singles that the Browns fielders made a half-hearted attempt to field.

Ty Cobb finished the season with a batting average of .384044 and the decision of who was the official batting champion was one big mess. American League president Ban Johnson had the unsavory task of naming the champion and he named Ty Cobb the official batting leader.

Fans in Cleveland were outraged! The Chalmers Detroit Motor Company found itself in a pickle. Quickly Chalmers came to the conclusion that they sold automobiles in Cleveland as well as Detroit and to solve the dilemma they awarded a new Chalmers automobile to both Ty Cobb and Nap Lajoie.

Now in late 1921 Chalmers was facing extinction. In an attempt to bring peace to disgruntled factions at Maxwell-Chalmers, bankers approached Walter Chrysler who officially was still the executive vice-president of Willys-Overland. But some backroom wheeling and dealing by the bankers resulted in Chrysler being able to start work at Maxwell-Chalmers while still in a contract at Willys-Overland.

The offer was intriguing to Chrysler and rather than seek a $1 million a year contract as he had with Willys-Overland, he agreed to a salary of $100,000 a year with huge stock options. In a short time Walter P. Chrysler acquired controlling interest in the Maxwell Motor Company and became chairman of the board.

As soon as Chrysler came on board a Maxwell Reorganization Committee was formed and the company was forced to go up for auction. Chrysler was named head of the committee. The intent of forming the Reorganization Committee was to place it in a position to buy Maxwell. But to the surprise of all, there were some notable and unexpected bidders in the auction including Billy Durant, John N. Willys, The Studebaker Company and The White Motor Company of Cleveland. With Durant, Willys and others in the mix the price went well above what was expected. However in the end the Reorganization Committee bid $10.9 million and acquired the rights to Maxwell-Chalmers.

Immediately, the company was incorporated in the State of West Virginia as The Maxwell Motor Company. Walter P. Chrysler was named chairman and W. R. Wilson as president.

In 1922 driven by an improving economy and a redesigned car with a new look and lower price ranging from $110 on open cars to $210 on sedans, Maxwell-Chalmers doubled its previous year's production to 44,811 cars taking the company up to 9th place on the automobile production rank.

The reduced price on the cars ordered by Walter Chrysler surprised the bankers. Maxwell was only making an average of $5 profit per car. That was just the first shockwave as Chrysler then asked for another $15 million loan. In the end it would all work-out and Maxwell, despite absorbing a loss by the Chalmers division, made a profit for the year. Huge inventories of unsold cars were moved for a slight profit rather than a loss. Furthermore the additional capital provided the company with additional breathing room—perhaps as much as three years.

Meanwhile Willy-Overland was forced to put its production plant in Elizabeth, New Jersey up for sale. Included with the facility where the rights to the car that Chrysler had his trio of engineers, Breer, Skelton and Zeder, working on. The facilities were valued at $14 million. Chrysler authorized his agent to bid up to $5 million. The winner was Billy Durant who bid $5.25 million. A year later Durant started production of Chrysler's car calling it the Flint and it would become the cornerstone of his third automotive manufacturing company.

The Maxell Motor Company had also been attempting to merge with the Studebaker Corporation and when negotiations fell through in late 1923 Maxwell president Robert Wilson resigned. At this point Walter Chrysler began to take a much more active part in the management of the company.

By 1923 Walter P. Chrysler had become quite wealthy. His contract with Willys-Overland had ended and he was now turning his full-time attention to the future of Maxwell. Chrysler asked his bankers for another $15 million loan. Then together with Harry Booner, he began buying all the assets of The Maxwell Motor Company.

It would be a banner year for Maxwell as they produced 67,000 cars and held-down 9th place on the industry production list. However it would be the final year for Chalmers.

Walter Chrysler still holding his dream of building his own car authorized his private engineering team of Fred Zeder, Carl Breer and Owen Skelton, to design a new car at his own expense to replace the Maxwell. Zeder was the chief engineer on the project; he had just designed a new high compression engine. The three went to work on the project in a private garage and near the end of the year the car would be ready and it was planned to market it under the name of Chrysler.

Now all that Chrysler needed was an additional $5 million to begin production on the car, but bankers were hesitant to loan that much money on a new car, untested in the market.

Walter Chrysler decided to present the car at the highly popular New York Auto Show hoping that enough dealer interest would occur to stimulate orders. Then at the last minute Chrysler learned that he could not put the car in the show with his name on it because it was an experimental model, not a production model.

So Chrysler quickly introduced a back-up plan. The headquarters for the auto show was the Hotel Commodore. He rented the lobby of the hotel and put his new Chrysler on display there where every important person in the industry would be sure to see the car. The car was widely hailed and a huge volume of orders followed. So did the bankers with the production loan.

In 1924 Maxwell launched the mid-priced Chrysler Six The Six was a well-engineered car with a revolutionary six-cylinder high compression engine, 4-wheel hydraulic brakes, used a 112.75 inch wheelbase chassis and was fitted with the first replaceable cartridge air filter. The Six could accelerate from 5 to 25 mph in 7.5 seconds and had a top speed of 75 mph, had a price tag of around $1500 and it quickly helped the Chrysler brand to gain a reputation as reliable. In fact noted race driver Ralph DePalma used a Chrysler Six to win the Mt. Wilson Hill Climb in California that year.

The combined Maxwell and Chrysler production for 1924 was 79,144 of which more than 32,000 were Chryslers which were built on the former Chalmers assembly lines.

In 1925 Maxwell was renamed the Chrysler Corporation. On June 26, 1925 the company now in full control of Walter Chrysler and Harry Bonner would reorganize and be incorporated in the State of Delaware as the Chrysler Corporation.

That year a record 132,343 Maxwell and Chrysler cars now being equipped with Fisher bodies came off the assembly line and the company climbed to 8th place on the industry's production list. However it would be the end of the line for the Maxwell.

By 1925 Chrysler had developed a growing export market in Europe. In the fall of that year Walter Chrysler traveled to Germany, France and England to assess his market presence. Upon returning on the liner *Berengaria* on October 24, Chrysler announced that the company presently had 40 agencies in France, 312 in England and 3 in Germany, as well new startups in Spain, Italy, Switzerland and Belgium that had sold 10,000 cars during the year. Chrysler was predicting sales of 25,000 for 1926. His assessment of the European market would be correct as by 1927 foreign sales for Chrysler would increase by 30%.

By 1929 General Motors would have a presence in Germany after buying out Opel which controlled 45% of all auto production in that country. Ford had already established a European presence with manufacturing plants in both England and Germany.

Although both John and Horace Dodge had died during 1920, the existing management of the company they had founded continued to build cars. Then in 1928 Dodge was acquired by Chrysler. With acquisition of Dodge almost overnight Chrysler became the third-largest auto manufacturer in the U.S. That same year under Walter Chrysler's leadership the low-priced Plymouth line and the mid-priced DeSoto line were both launched.

There were some analyst and economists in the mid-1920s that began to express concern that saturation of the automobile market could begin due to over-production. But Walter Chrysler harbored no such fear believing that the automobile industry was going to continue to grow. Wages were growing and Chrysler believed that meant more sales and he maintained that families were now buying more than one car. If there was any concern in the automotive industry Chrysler saw it as a production arena for the survival of the fittest and he was predicting that by 1927 there would be 30 million cars on America's roads.

Walter Chrysler was building his market on trust. He was an auto executive who not only promised a fair deal to the consumer but he also delivered. In mid-year 1926 he announced that do to a tremendous increase in production he was immediately lowering the price of the six-cylinder "seventy" model by $50 to $200 with no changes to engineering or in equipment.

Chrysler was acutely aware of what producing low-cost cars for the masses meant to the over-all market. He saw the market in socio-economic terms rather than purely economic terms. He foresaw that an inevitable reaction from high quantity production and low price was quality. To that end Chrysler stated in 1928 that "When an article universally needed becomes cheap enough for practically every one to possess it the demand for high quality, better style and greater luxury naturally follows quickly."[2]

Using GM's multiple unit organization as a model, in 1928 after purchasing the Dodge Brothers Company; Walter Chrysler began to produce a low-priced Plymouth that would cut into Ford's profits. The Plymouth was a 4-cylinder car that replaced the Chrysler 52. At the same time Chrysler began to produce a low-priced 6-cylinder De Soto model sold through a separate division. Chrysler was now producing cars in every price class; on the low end with the Plymouth selling for $670 to the high end with the Imperial sedan selling for $3,495.

To compete with popularity of the Plymouth and retain his market share, Henry Ford cut his advertising budget to zero dollars. Eliminating advertising would allow Ford to keep the price of his cars down, so he told dealers to advertise independently.

No one could deny that during the boom years of the 1920s Walter Chrysler's ego had grown as large as one of his automobile manufacturing plants. To emblazon his status on the consciousness of America, Chrysler boldly announced in 1928 that he was determined to build a skyscraper in New York City of epic proportions that would represent the Chrysler automobile and the modern age.

In October 1928 Chrysler began negotiating for a lease held by former New York State Senator William H. Reynolds for a parcel of land on Lexington Avenue bound by East 42nd and East 43rd Streets.

Several years before Reynolds had obtained a long-term lease on the property from the trustees of Cooper Union. The land had been part of a massive tax free land holding in Manhattan that had been amassed by Peter Cooper who had started as an apprentice in an ironworks in the early 1800s and worked his way up to building locomotives for the Baltimore & Ohio Railroad and then entered the iron business in Trenton, New Jersey making iron structural beams and transatlantic telegraph cable. Later Peter Cooper was president of the North Atlantic Cable Company that controlled most of the cable lines throughout the United States.

In 1921 Senator Reynolds had intended to build a skyscraper and hotel on the land but failed to gain adequate financing.

Recently, S. W. Strauss & Company a large real estate mortgage company had offered Reynolds $7.5 million to construct a 68 story office tower on the site. Chrysler would take over the Strauss lease for a loan of $7.5 million that would take the form of a first mortgage 6% sinking fund gold bond issue.

Plans for the skyscraper announced on October 13, 1928 called for a building of 68 stories to be appraised at $14 million. When completed the building would be 16 feet higher than the Woolworth Building, the world's tallest office structure at 792 feet situated in lower Manhattan. Shops would occupy the ground floor then offices would rise to the 65th floor. The building would include a duplex three-story apartment on two of the upper floors. Above the 65th floor there would be a three-story observation dome constructed of bronze and glass culminating with a sphere. Thirty-three elevators would serve all floors running rapidly as 900 feet per minute. The first three floors would be faced in stone, with brick and terra cotta above that level.

But the finished building would be quite different from the one originally planned. Walter Chrysler took over the project and insisted that everything above the 61st floor be changed—the number of stories to 77 and that a

Chrysler Building. (Courtesy of The Library of Congress)

different look be designed for the tower. Considering plans for the building Chrysler said, "Thinking of Paris, I told the architect, "Make this building taller than the Eiffel Tower."[3]

The final version of the Chrysler Building designed by Craig Severance would feature gargoyles and eagles ornamenting the building. Corner ornaments were designed to look like the 1929 Plymouth radiator caps. The building was and still is the quintessential art deco building in the country.

The Chrysler Building topped out at 1050 feet with a 186-foot spire attached and would be the tallest building in the world and had its official opening on May 27, 1930.

There have been innuendos advanced over the years that the reason Walter Chrysler wanted an office and apartment built for him on the top floor of the building was so that he could install the highest toilet in the world and therefore he could defecate on Henry Ford and the rest of the world.

A spectacular feat of engineering and of beautiful design, the building's reign as the world's tallest building would last for just 11 months. Then the Empire State building located in mid-town Manhattan would top out at 1250 feet.

In January 1929 Walter Chrysler, soon to be literally sitting on top of the world in his magnificent skyscraper, was named *Time* magazine's Man of the Year. Then in mid-February customs officials seized 83 bottles of liquor from the Man of the Year's valet upon his arrival on the liner *Malolo* in Honolulu, Hawaii. Chrysler had sailed with his family to Hawaii for a two week vacation. Customs officials noted that a strong odor suggesting whisky was emanating from Chrysler's luggage as the bags were being unloaded from the ship. The matter was settled as Chrysler paid a fine of $5 a bottle.

Completely unlike his straight-lace automotive contemporaries Henry Ford and Alfred P. Sloan of GM, Walter Chrysler was by all accounts a free-spirit who engaged in wine, women and song of the Jazz Age. He was a man of the "roaring twenties." He loved music dating back to his time playing the tuba and clarinet in the Union Pacific Band.

When it came to prohibition, Walter Chrysler was a blatant hypocrite. Under the existing industrial standard guise of the time alcohol consumption compromised the workforce, particularly on Mondays. Chrysler publicly supported the Volstead Act. But privately he drank copious amount of liquor, sometimes all weekend long. There are some historians who look back at Walter Chrysler's life in retrospect and suggest that he was a functioning alcoholic.

Henry Ford's beliefs and personal habits in regard to liquor were diametrical opposite to those of Walter Chrysler. Ford was a flaming prohibitionist, privately and publicly. He held the mantra that business and booze were enemies. Ford was a bastion of advancing a dominant culture. He claimed that liquor never did anybody any good; it destroyed character and even the most casual use dulled initiative. Ford was also adamant that liquor divided families and heaped cruelty upon women and children.

So intense was Henry Ford's concern that imbibing alcohol would affect production in his company that after he created a sociological department at The Ford Motor Company to assist with the assimilation of immigrants, he hired detectives to spy on his workers at home to ensure they were not drinking. Of course it was an enormous invasion of privacy, but Henry Ford believed that he could control the habits of his workforce inside of his personal value set. Anything outside of his social beliefs left him uncomfortable and suspicious, even of his top executives.

On the other hand, while Alfred P. Sloan president of General Motors supported prohibition and never personally drank alcohol or smoked, he didn't exhibit the blatant paranoia of Henry Ford or the false pretense of support advanced by Walter Chrysler in regard to prohibition.

While the largest industry in Detroit during the 1920s and early 1930s was automobile manufacturing, the second largest enterprise was illegal bootlegging.

It is more than a bit ironic that Walter Chrysler, Henry Ford and Alfred Sloan were operating enormous automobile manufacturing enterprises in the City of Detroit which during the prohibition era of the 1920s and early 1930s was controlled by several Italian mobs and the infamous all-Jewish Purple Gang one of the most violent and largest bootlegging operations in the country.

The Purple Gang not only provided a flood of booze to Detroit's immigrant neighborhoods that the auto executives so abhorred, but also large shipments of Canadian whisky to the Chicago illegal market. The modus operandi of the Purple Gang was violence and they used it to the extreme to control territory, the gang was even suspected of being the assassins hired by Al Capone to carry-out the St. Valentine's Day massacre in Chicago in early 1929.

Even more remarkable is the fact that unwittingly the industry that Chrysler, Ford and Sloan had built was fundamental to the logistics of shipping illegal booze all across America and to some extent those vehicles became the war chariots in which the violent gang enforcement of territory was expedited.

Windsor, Ontario lies just across the Detroit River and Canadian officials turned a blind eye toward the illegal flow of whisky into the U.S. So traffic in illegal booze increased three-fold when the Windsor-Detroit tunnel opened in November 1930, prompting some casual observers to refer to the engineering marvel as "the funnel."

It was the absurdity of prohibition enforcement and violence of the illegal booze trade that in early 1932 brought Walter P. Chrysler to the reality that repeal of the Volstead Act was a necessity. He invited Pierre S. du Pont and several prominent businessmen to meet with him at the Cloud Club in the Chrysler Building to discuss the matter. At the gathering Walter Chrysler was named general chairman of a committee to raise $175,000 toward supporting a national fund for congressional candidates who were in favor of repeal of prohibition.

Other business tycoons such as S.S. Kresge and John D. Rockefeller soon got on board with Chrysler to lobby Congress for an amendment to the constitution to end prohibition. By December 5, 1933 the 18th amendment had been passed as Utah became the 36th state to ratify it and happy days were here again.

But happy days had never been apart from Walter Chrysler. In addition to booze and music, Chrysler also had an eye for pretty girls. In the late 1920s Walter Chrysler, although still married to Della, and ignoring the fact that the couple had four children, began dating flamboyant 'Gold digger' Peggy Hopkins Joyce.

Peggy Upton Archer Hopkins Joyce Mormer Easton Meyer, a barber's daughter, had been born in Norfolk, Virginia on May 26, 1893. At the age of 16, desiring a more glamorous and exciting life she ran away from home with a vaudeville cyclist. She went to New York where she became a Ziegfeld showgirl.

Peggy Hopkins Joyce was what today we would call a reality star. She had little real talent, yet had the keen sense of her personality that enabled her to market it as a brand. Nonetheless she did appear in a few movies.

Peggy was married six times, had several other highly publicized announced engagements and dated Charlie Chaplin. Her lavish shopping sprees spending rich husband's money were the stuff of tabloid headlines. In the early 1920s as a newlywed Peggy went on a whopping New York City shopping spree where it is alleged that she spent $1 million in a week buying such expensive goods as a Russian sable coat and a chinchilla. At one time she owned the Portuguese Diamond now in the Smithsonian.

Totally mesmerized by Peggy Hopkins Joyce, Walter Chrysler dated her openly in New York and showered her with expensive gifts. During their relationship Chrysler gave her $2 million in jewelry, including a 134-karat diamond strung on a necklace that was said to have cost $500,000. Walter even hired two secretaries to work for Peggy out of her townhouse and a body guard to look after her.

One morning in 1930 Walter went to Peggy's townhouse to awaken her. At Chrysler's direction she peered out of the bedroom window and saw two Isotta-Fraschinis parked at the curb. The cars were worth $45,000. One was a yellow roadster, the other a magnificent town car. Twenty years later one of these cars would be used by Gloria Swanson in the movie *Sunset Boulevard*. While Walter's automobile company made the luxurious Chrysler Imperial, he didn't believe the car was good enough for Peggy.

The blatant public affair carried-on between Walter and Peggy was terribly shameful to Della and the children. Rumors of a pending divorce circulated widely. There were those, including an executive in the Chrysler Corporation who tried to talk sense with Walter about the escapades. Just how the affair came to an end is not really known. But more than likely it was matter of Peggy just moving on to her next wealthy consort.

Peggy Hopkins Joyce died of throat cancer at the age of 64 on June 12, 1957 in New York City. She is said to have been the inspiration for 'Lorelie Lee" in *Gentlemen Prefer Blondes* portrayed by Marilyn Monroe in the 1953 film release.

Meanwhile the Chrysler Corporation continued to prosper. Between 1925 and 1940 the company would produce 8 million cars.

The only monetary loss for the company came in 1934 when the Airflow models designed by Carl Breer were introduced in the Imperial, Chrysler and DeSoto and they experienced production problems. According to auto critic and *Los Angeles Times* columnist Dan Neil, the 1934 Chrysler/DeSoto Airflow's "worst"-ness derives from its spectacularly bad timing. Twenty years later, the car's many design and engineering innovations—the aerodynamic singlet-style fuselage, steel-spaceframe construction, near 50-50 front-rear weight distribution and light weight—would have been celebrated."[4]

The bodies in the Airflows were extremely strong. As a publicity stunt not seen since days of " Crazy Carl" Fisher, an Airflow was driven off a 100 foot cliff

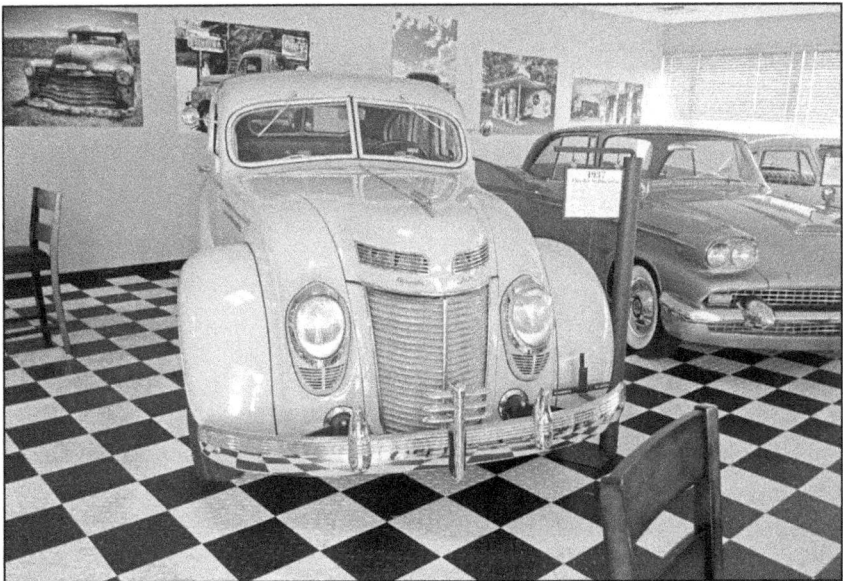

1937 Chrysler Airflow Sedan. (Photo by Lawrence T. Hay)

and proceeded to bounce down the cliff face, landed on all four wheels, and was promptly driven off under its own power.[5]

But this was 1934 the depression era, many buyers had temporarily returned to the Model T mentality and the car's dramatic streamliner styling antagonized Americans, some on a very personal level.

Production in Canada on the Airflow model was halted after the completion of 40 cars. The problems with the car were compounded due to a few early Airflows having had major, engine-falling-out-type problems that stemmed from the radical construction techniques required. Chrysler and Desoto made an attempt to re-engineer the Airflow stylistically to give it a more conventional grill and raising the trunk into a kind of bustle, but the damage had been done. It was simply a case of American car buyers of the era looking at the future and saying, "no thanks." It was a harbinger of the Edsel to come.

5.
Alfred P. Sloan and General Motors

Henry Ford had grown-up on a farm in Michigan and Walter Chrysler grew-up in a frontier rail head in Kansas, both had limited formal educations, but Alfred P. Sloan, Jr. unlike his contemporaries was a city boy and college educated.

Alfred Sloan was born in New Haven, Connecticut on May 23, 1875. He was the eldest of five children. His father Alfred Sr. was a well-to-do coffee and tea importer in New Haven and a wholesale grocer.

In 1885 Alfred Sr. would move the family to Brooklyn and they would take-up residency at 240 Garfield Place situated in Park Slope. Alfred Jr. attended public school in Brooklyn until he was 11-years old, then entered Brooklyn Polytechnic Institute where he established a stellar reputation in mechanics and engineering. At the age of 17 Alfred enrolled in the Massachusetts Institute of Technology (M.I. T.) in Cambridge, Massachusetts where he continued to excel in his studies graduating in three years in 1895 at the age of 20.

Following graduation from M.I.T. Sloan through a connection of his father's was employed as a draftsman by John F. Searles in one of his many companies the Hyatt Roller Bearing Company in Harrison, New Jersey. The company's founder John Wesley Hyatt had invented the roller bearing. But Hyatt is better known for his ingenuity when during a shortage of elephant tusks in 1869 used to make billiard balls he invented a synthetic billiard ball by combining pyroxylin and camphor.

In 1897 Alfred Sloan left Hyatt Company and took a job with the Hygienic Refrigeration Company a start-up venture that was manufacturing a new concept called electric refrigeration.

On September 28, 1898 Sloan would marry Irene Jackson. Soon after Sloan's marriage the Hygienic Company dissolved.

About the same time John F. Searles went broke. So Alfred Sloan, Sr. and an associate bought Searles out for $5,000. Now the elder Sloan owned the Hyatt Roller Bearing Company and he put his 23-year old son Alfred, Jr. in charge of the company. It turned-out to be a great move for Alfred, Jr. as the company would turn a profit of $12,000 over the first six months and over time he would build-up considerable equity in the company.

One of the key factors in turning the Hyatt Company around was the vision of Alfred, Jr. that it should be directing its products toward the fledgling and dis-joined automobile industry.

Alfred P. Sloan worked closely with an associate at Hyatt by the name of Peter Steenstrup. At that time automakers had been using heavily greased wagon axles. In 1899 the two determined that automobiles required bearings to make wheels turn efficiently on their axels.

Steenstrup suggested that they approach Elwood Haynes, an automobile maker from Kokomo, Indiana who had building cars for about six years.

Elwood Haynes was not your typical heartland Hoosier who stereotypically would be seen as someone at the rear of a plow working the back forty. Haynes was an eastern college educated engineer and had even learned to read and speak German so he could closely follow the workings of Teutonic automobile pioneers such as Karl Benz and Gottfried Daimler. But Alfred Sloan nixed the idea of contacting Haynes, he had no faith in such rural engineering ventures and paid little attention to what Haynes was doing. Sloan could not conceive as to how an automaker in Kokomo, Indiana was going to be beneficial to the Hyatt Company. So Haynes was never contacted. It was a mistake, but Sloan was young and learning how to manage a company.

One of the first significant customers of the Hyatt Company was Cadillac being managed by Henry Leland and one that would immediately raise the consciousness of Sloan. In 1901 Cadillac began building cars in Detroit. After a shipment of Hyatt bearings were rejected by Leland, Sloan jumped on a train and headed for Detroit as fast as possible. Although Sloan got an ear-full from Leland about quality, the lesson would be ever-lasting in his thought process as he created an automobile manufacturing empire.

In 1901 the Oldsmobile became the first mass-produced gasoline-driven car being built at a rate of ten cars per week. Alfred Sloan persuaded the Olds Motors Company to try his bearings. By 1905 the Hyatt Company was supplying Henry Ford's company and within a decade Hyatt would become one of the leading auto parts manufactures in America turning a very high profit.

In 1904 William "Billy" Durant the grandson of a former governor of Michigan had entered the automobile business as the managing director of Buick. Then in 1908 General Motors was founded by Durant with the merger of the Oldsmobile and Buick companies. But Durant didn't stop there. Using speculative stock sales and profits from Buick, Durant began buying-up any automotive associated business that was for sale. He purchased A-C spark plugs, a truck manufacturer, an axel manufacturer and even Cadillac from Henry Leland.

By 1916 General Motors had become one of the world's leading automobile companies and Alfred P. Sloan, now 41-years old, was not only supplying parts for GM but also the Ford Motor Company which used Hyatt bearings in the Model T.

At that time Billy Durant had come up with a plan to integrate General Motors directly with manufactures of parts and accessories. One of the latest companies on Durant's corporate shopping list was Alfred Sloan's Hyatt Company.

By 1916 Alfred Sloan had made a considerable amount of money through purchasing stock in the Nash Motor Company. At that same time General Motors had replaced Ford as Sloan's best customer and the Hyatt Company was doing a gross business of $10-million a year and making profits as high as $4-million. Of equal importance, Sloan had made a name for himself in Detroit as a knowledgeable and reliable businessman with keen insights into the auto industry.

Billy Durant was seeking to implement what we call today vertical integration into GM. Simply defined vertical integration is a merger of companies at different stages of production and/or distribution in the same industry. So Durant invited Sloan to a meeting in New York in his mid-town Manhattan office where he popped the question. Would Sloan like to sell the Hyatt Company and for how much? In order to reinforce his point Durant also casually added that GM was considering making its own bearings.

After Sloan informed the Hyatt board and some simple negotiations, Durant's accountants did their due diligence and a purchase price of $13.5 million was agreed upon.

Of course Alfred Jr. split his share of $10,125,000 with his father Alfred Sr. who nearly two decades before had provided his industrial "grub-stake" with a few thousand dollars in the Hyatt Company. So Alfred P. Sloan, Jr. had made his first $5 million. It was the tip of the fortune iceberg that Alfred Sloan would amass during his lifetime topping out at about $250 million.

Alfred Sloan however just didn't walk away from the automotive business a wealthy man. Billy Durant merged Hyatt with some other of his parts and accessory companies into the United Motors Corporation and installed Sloan as president

The next step up on the corporate ladder for Alfred P. Sloan occurred in 1918 when as a result of an initiative by John J. Raskob, GM took over United Motors and designated it as its own parts division. As part of the deal, Alfred Sloan came along as the division's executive head and was named as a member of the GM board of directors and a vice-president.

All this was happening at the same time that Pierre S. du Pont and those supporting him had acquired controlling interest in GM through stock purchases thereby sweeping Billy Durant, Sloan's mentor, from the company. In fact, two and a half million shares had passed to the du Pont interests in a single day.

While Billy Durant had been quite capable of building the company, he lacked a plan to market all the brands that he had acquired independently. Suddenly, GM was competing against itself as much as Ford.

Pierre Samuel du Pont was a member of the famous Delaware family that built a fortune in the dynamite and gunpowder business during the Civil War and in the last half of the nineteenth century. Pierre had run the company from 1915 to 1919 and handled lucrative government contracts during the World War.

When du Pont became president of GM, Alfred Sloan became vice president of operations in 1920. However after serving for three productive years du Pont stepped-down. GM was losing money and by du Pont's own admission, he didn't know much about the automobile industry.

Alfred P. Sloan was named to succeed du Pont as president. At the time, GM's net sales were $698 million; six years later after Alfred Sloan took over they would grow to $1.5 billion and the company would surpass Ford as the sales leader in the low-priced car market.

Alfred P. Sloan was an imposing figure; a string-bean of a man he stood six feet tall and weighed 130 pounds. He was always impeccably dressed in what was then the height of fashion-a dark, double- breasted suit, a high starch collar, conservative tie fixed with a pearl stickpin, a handkerchief cascading out of his breast pocket and spats.

Alfred P. Sloan, 1937. (Wikipedia Commons)

He was a predictable person too. Sloan always arrived at his office in the General Motors Building located at 1775 Broadway (at 57th Street) by 9:30 AM. In winter he drove from his 14-room apartment on Fifth Avenue. But in the summer he commuted to Pennsylvania Station from his 25 acre estate in Great Neck, L.I., and rode the subway to the West 59th Street station.

Sloan always knew the agenda for the day and would with metronomic precision tick off the day's conferences. Some associates said he was a bit restless, squirming in his chair, gesturing, putting his small, well-polished spats-covered shoes on the table. When Sloan spoke, it was in a quiet voice that curled out of the side of his mouth in which just a trace of a Brooklyn accent could be detected. When he listened the speaker had his full undivided attention. Nonetheless at 5:30 PM each day Sloan was ready to go home. So he stuck his briefcase under his arm and with quickness of dispatch departed his corporate lair.

At home he had dinner with Irene then usually worked for a few hours before climbing into bed at 10 PM. The couple seldom entertained quests.

Two weeks each month Sloan spent in Detroit. However as he never drank or smoked, didn't care for sports, he often said that sports were a waste of a man's time, he would rarely stray out of the GM building, not even to a hotel.

Under Sloan's leadership during the 1920's the price of GM stock rose 480 per cent. Alfred Sloan personally monitored that growth by visiting as many of the GM dealerships as possible in as many cities as possible in the U.S., Canada and Mexico. While he was cautious to never let friendships influence his decisions, on these trips he would meet with five to ten dealers a day and solicit suggestions from them and listen to their complaints in regard to their corporate relationships with GM.

Sloan ran GM on the staff principle, with himself as the chief executive. He knew who he was. Despite the loftiness of his position he did not function as an autocrat, he didn't rant and rave and refrained from ordering subordinates about. He was known throughout the company as "Silent Sloan." But his presence was felt. His success as president of the company was realized through his management principles. He centralized administration and decentralized operations, grouping together those with a functional relationship. He also initiated realignment of the company's products so that the different brands of automobiles did not conflict with another. Each product within GM—cars, electric iceboxes, etc.—was manufactured in its own division.

Just as Walter Chrysler did, Alfred Sloan also saw the automobile market as a socio-economic model. It fact, Sloan's market was stratified. He believed that his Chevrolets were cars for people of modest but steady income, blue collar workers, newlyweds, etc. Pontiacs were a step-up on the economic ladder designed for people who were somewhat upwardly mobile and wanted a sporty car to demonstrate the fact. Buicks and Olds were for young lawyers and managers, perhaps doctors. But the Cadillac was for top executives or the guy that owned the factory. The Caddy was the car you bought when you had made it. Alfred Sloan would continue to have this marketing mindset through-out his career at GM.

When Sloan had ascended to the presidency of GM he had taken over a company that was losing money. At that time there were 8.1 million cars on the nation's roads and he considered the possibility that the automobile market was saturated. In order to move GM forward Sloan determined that the company was going to have to find ways to open new markets.

During the early 1920s cities across the nation were starting in earnest to build and improve infrastructure; new streets, highways and parkways were

General Motors Building. (Wikipedia Commons)

being planned and under construction. So that fact did increase the possibility more cars could be sold, especially low priced cars that had been the domain of Ford.

Sloan began to look at urban mass-transit systems and reached the conclusion that the electric mass-transit systems, i.e. streetcars and inter-urbans, being used in America's cities since the 1880s might be on the way out.

In Cincinnati a pre-World War subway system that had been under construction was abandoned by city officials as too expensive to complete in favor of more buses and improved city streets. As more cars continued to be sold streetcar ridership in the country had peaked in 1920 at 13.8 billion. It would decline to 11.8 billion by 1929.

It occurred to Sloan that urban populations might prefer to start traveling by gasoline driven buses and GM could sell a lot of units.

So Sloan arranged a merger with a bus manufacturing company—The Yellow Cab Company of Chicago which built Hertz Yellow Coach Buses. The company had been started by John D. Hertz of rent-a-car fame and in 1925 was merged into GM with its motor trucks company as a subsidiary.

But what followed in retrospect was that Alfred P. Sloan would be wrongly accused of attempting to destroy the nation's streetcar system and create an addiction in the nation to oil. Of course "the streetcar conspiracy." is an urban myth. But there have been those during the years that have pressed the theory to the outer-limits of suspicion.

One such conspiracy theorist is Bradford Snell who as a young government attorney in 1974 alleged that General Motors killed the streetcar and without the company's influence that mode of public transportation would be alive and serving America's cities today.

Snell suggested that in 1922 Alfred P. Sloan established a special unit within GM charged with formulating a plan to get rid of electric railways and replace them with cars, trucks and buses. At the time there were approximately 1200 separate electric-street and interurban railways with 44,000 miles of track operating in the country.

The alleged strategy that GM came up with was to combat the electric street railway systems was freight leverage. By that point in time GM had become the largest shipper of goods on America's railroads. Therefore the conspiracy theory holds that GM quietly began to persuade rail lines to abandon various electric rail subsidiaries. As a result, suddenly through pressure applied on company management by ruthless gangsters, the street railway system in Minneapolis-St. Paul was scrapped. The New York Central Railroad shut-down 600 miles of street railways and portions of the Southern Pacific which owned the Los Angeles Pacific Electric interurban were shut-down and replaced by buses.

Snell's conspiracy theory has had a long shelf-life. In August 1996 PBS aired the documentary *Taken for a Ride* which was funded by the National Endowment of the Arts. The film was an expose that intended to expose GM's role in dismantling streetcar systems in the 1930s in an attempt to move automobiles to the center of the national culture.

The narration in the film alleges, "They had to get rid of the streetcars. They wanted the space that the streetcars used for automobiles. They had to find something they could put in place of the streetcar. (Alfred) Sloan had the idea that he wanted to somehow motorize all the major cities in the country. That meant replacing all the street railways with buses ultimately thinking that no one would want to ride the buses and therefore they would buy General Motors automobiles. Sloan wanted to get in very big in this field. What he bought was phenomenal: the largest bus-operating company in the country and the largest bus-production company. And using that as a foothold, GM moved into Manhattan. They acquired interests in the New York railways and between 1926 and '36 they methodically destroyed the rails."[1]

Of course the rise in the popularity of the automobile caused the demise of the streetcars in cities across the nation, but it was hardly a conspiracy. It was simply a matter of supply and demand. When the Ford Model T had first come on the market in 1908 the price was $850. The price continued to go down and by 1923 the price to buy a Model T was just $269, even though most roads in the nation were sub-standard.

Meanwhile Chevrolet kept coming and by 1927 surpassed Ford in sales. By 1929 there were 23.1 million cars in use—a rise of 65% in less than a decade. That year the Chevrolet division of GM was producing 6000 cars a day and the automotive world was rocked when the Chevrolet AC Coup was released. It featured a six-cylinder engine which was standard across the board and was promoted as six for the price of a four.

Because of the high utility of buses being able to travel wherever transportation was needed and being a self-contained unit that required neither electric lines nor tracks, they permitted easy route changes and they were in part responsible for the suburban booms of the late 1920s and in the 1950s.

Over the decades following the 1920s GM was at the forefront of improving bus style and technology. In 1931 GM introduced monocoque body construction. In 1936 the first diesel engine and automatic transmission for buses was introduced.

The famous Greyhound "silversides" bus was built by Yellow Coach and first displayed at the New York's World Fair of 1939–1940.

Between 1940 and 1942 GM built 500 transit buses a year. Then in 1943 GM took control of Yellow Coach and formed the GMC Truck & Coach Division.

Following World War Two GM continued to improve its transit bus technology. In 1948 GM introduced the first 50+ passenger bus and the first buses with air-suspension in 1953.

It stands to reason that the GM was chosen to replace more streetcars than any other manufacturer because they were in the forefront of bus technology, not because of a conspiracy to eliminate streetcars launched by Alfred P. Sloan.

If there had been a formal plan developed by Sloan to eliminate streetcars in the nation it is doubtful it will ever be revealed. Upon Sloan' death in 1966 GM destroyed his corporate papers and since that day no one has been talking.

Although by 1930 there were still fifteen automobile companies, the automotive manufacturing triumvirate of Ford, General Motors and Chrysler (the Big Three) had been forged and they dominated the industry. Ford set the pace in pricing and the others competed with style changes, advertising campaigns and various methods of organizational efficiency.

Alfred Sloan had been responsible for creating demand among automobile consumers for yearly model changes. It was profitable for GM and car buyers anticipated the new models with excitement. In forcing yearly model changes on the market GM forced the industry to abandon "Fordism."

As the nation entered into the dark days of the Great Depression GM was the leading industrial Company in the United States and it was clear to Alfred Sloan that the company was going to have to play a major role in finding a path to recovery. To keep up consumer interest in automobiles in tough times, Sloan began to implement yearly model changes. The plan enabled GM to make a modest profit in 1932. While Sloan knew he was a national public figure he shunned the lime light, but nonetheless began to take a public position on various issues. A life-long teetotaler he joined Walter Chrysler in calling for the end to prohibition as a means of stimulating the economy and advocated cuts in federal spending as a way to balance the budget.

In early 1933 prior to the presidential inauguration of Franklin D. Roosevelt banks were crashing all over the nation. Henry Ford showed little concern and adopted a laissez-faire attitude stressing that he felt young enough to start all over again.

Two of Detroit largest banks failed; the First National Bank and the Union Guardian Trust Company prompting the governor of Michigan to declare a "bank holiday." But unlike Henry Ford, Alfred Sloan took action. He sent some of his accountants to work on the Detroit bank problems and put-up $12.5 million which would be matched by the federal Reconstruction Finance Corporation that President Hoover had started and was continued by President Roosevelt. The result of Sloan's efforts to save the Detroit banks resulted in the formation of the National Bank of Detroit.

Although Alfred Sloan had supported President Hoover in the 1932 presidential election, when Franklin D. Roosevelt took office in 1933 at first he cooperated with the new administration. He even became a member of the Industrial Advisory Board of the National Recovery Administration. But when the dollar was devalued Sloan turned his back on the Roosevelt Administration and became a persistent critic.

6.
Henry Ford, Presidential Ambitions and Bigotry

In 1918 Henry Ford purchased the *Dearborn Independent* a small weekly community newspaper. Then Ford hired Edwin G. Pipp away from the *Detroit Press* to be his editor and launched a business plan to increase circulation by selling subscriptions door-to-door and by pressuring his dealers across the country to buy subscriptions and provide copies to customers for free.

Henry Ford had through-out his life harbored a deep hatred of the Jews. His prejudice was troublesome to many in the Ford Motor Company including his son Edsel Ford who felt that the company was becoming systematically linked to anti-Semitism.

There were reports that the foul feelings of Ford toward the Jews had permeated the operations of the company. There was a policy that Jewish boys could not work in the shop. On one occasion a new employee was told by a veteran employee, "Don't ever let Mr. Ford see you using brass. It's Jew metal."[1]

Many have alleged that Henry Ford even blamed the Jews for the assassination of President Abraham Lincoln. Peter Collier and David Horowitz state in their chronicle of the Ford family *The Fords—An American Epic,* that Henry Ford believed in a conspiracy theory whereby supposedly Jewish bankers had hired John Wilkes Booth to assassinate President Lincoln and then spirited him off to the West Coast and given him a new identity. When a body embalmed in the late 1800s was discovered in California and alleged to supposedly be that of Booth and linked to the conspiracy theory, Henry Ford wanted to buy the mummified body and bring it to Detroit and have it studied.

Henry Ford. (Author's private collection)

In May 1920 the *Dearborn Independent* would become Ford's first amendment platform to expose his deep-seeded feelings of bigotry and anti-Semitism. Henry Ford, in his infinite wisdom believed that he was going to use the newspaper to promote his belief for the necessity of a dominant culture and provide readers with a more narrow based analysis of issues facing the nation and world. He felt in effect that he was going to educate Americans about forces detrimental to the establishment of a hard-working, productive society. But what Henry Ford was about to undertake was a massive campaign of Jew-baiting.

Seeing where the paper was heading and wanting no part of it, Edwin G. Pipp resigned in April 1920.

In the May 22, 1920 edition of the *Dearborn Independent* Henry Ford began his attack on Jews with a front page article titled "The International

Jew: The World's Problem." Then for the next two years these deplorable texts would appear in the paper as Henry Ford attempted to convince his readers that there was a Jewish conspiracy in place to capture wide social, cultural and economic power and thereby achieve world domination.

The anti-Semitic diatribe advanced by Henry Ford was in part borrowed from the standard European style rhetoric of the times that railed against Jazz, short-skirts, money lending and Bolshevism. Ford was able to advance his hatred on a very personal level in every edition in a spot reserved for him titled "Mr. Ford's Own Page." Although these hateful editorials were written by William J. Cameron, the views expressed in them were a result of daily conversations with Ford and the notes taken by the ghostwriter.

Jew-baiting was a common practice in1920s America and extreme views towards Jews were often expressed by highly educated Ivy League men and women, even by a few Catholic and Protestant clergymen. It was a ready-made explanation for unwanted cultural changes taking place in the nation.

The *Dearborn Independent* became popular in various rural sections of the Southern and Midwestern U.S. where racial and religious tolerance were low and the Ku Klux Klan fed the population a continuous diet of hate. Still it is inconceivable by today's standards that at that point-in-time, any potential car buyer in the early 1920s that wandered into a Ford dealership anywhere in the nation would have access—gratis—to a tabloid of hate authored by the car's manufacturer.

The paper did include articles other than those promoting prejudice. There were articles promoting the League of Nations, supporting the 1919 Southern Race Congress, urging the government take-over of telephone companies and others. Also some noted writers also had articles published in the paper including, Robert Frost and Hugh Walpole.

As Ford still believed that the 1918 Senate election had been stolen from him, he would also use the paper to take political revenge upon Senator Truman H. Newberry who had defeated him.

By 1924 the circulation of *Dearborn Independent* would rise to 650,000 and in 1926 peak at 900,000.

The International Jew would eventually become a compilation of 91 articles in a four volume set of booklets published in the *Dearborn Independent.* The articles would cover a wide-range of suspicion and hatred advanced by Henry Ford that included such articles as "Does Jewish Power Control the World Press," "Jewish Copper Kings Reap Rich War Profits," "Jewish Idea Molded Federal Reserve System" and "Jewish Hot Beds of Bolshevism in the U.S."

Ford would even link the Jews in a disparaging way with the national game. In his essay "Jewish Degradation of American Baseball" Ford remarked in part.

"Every non-Jewish baseball manager in the United States lives between two fears, and they are both describable in the Biblical term "the fear of the Jews." The first fear concerns what the Jews are doing to baseball; the second fear concerns what the Jew would do to the manager if he complained about it. Hence, in spite of the fact that the rowdyism that has afflicted baseball, especially in the East, is all of Jewish origin—the razzing of umpires, hurling of bottles, ceaseless shouting of profane insults; in spite of the fact that the loyalty of players had to be constantly guarded because of the tendency of individual Jewish gamblers to snuggle up to individual players; in spite of the evidence that even the gate receipts have been tampered with—the managers and secretaries of baseball clubs have been obliged to keep their mouths closed. Through fear they have not dared say what they know. As one manager said, "Good God, man, they'd boycott my park if I told you!" This is in free America, and in the "cleanest game"! It is time for baseball to begin to look round."[2]

It has been said that Adolph Hitler admired Henry Ford and was a loyal reader of translated articles in the *Dearborn Independent*. It's just possible that Ford could have fed Hitler's enormous hatred of the Jews with articles such as his "Germany's Reaction Against the Jew" which stated in part.

"The Jew in Germany is regarded as only a guest of the people; he has offended by trying to turn himself into the host. There are no stronger contrasts in the world than the pure Germanic and pure Semitic races; therefore, there has been no harmony between the two in Germany; the German has regarded the Jew strictly as a guest, while the Jew, indignant at not being given the privileges of the nation-family, has cherished animosity against his host. In other countries the Jew is permitted to mix more readily with the people, he can amass his control unchallenged; but in Germany the case was different. Therefore, the Jew hated the German people; therefore, the countries of the world which were most dominated by the Jews showed the greatest hatred of Germany during the recent regrettable war. Jewish hands were in almost exclusive control of the engines of publicity by which public opinion concerning the German people was molded. The sole winners of the war were Jews"[3]

The blatant bigotry of Henry Ford did not go unchallenged. In October 1922 a reporter for *The New York Times* caught up with Ford in Boston and asked him to explain his venomous articles that appeared in his paper.

Ford began to back-peddle but fell head over heels as he denied hating Jews. He said they were victims of a money system that is all wrong and that he had no hatred in his heart for Jews. "In fact, I do not blame the Jew money-lender for bunking humanity just as long as humanity lets him get away with it. However that does not wipe out the fact that the Jew, who is a victim of a false money system, is the very foundation of the world's greatest curse today—war. He is the cause of the abnormality in our daily life because he is the money maniac"[4]

The solution to the Jewish problem Ford believed was to abolish all interest—the whole world would benefit. He then added that the only reason that the Jew money-lender didn't take the pocketbook of everyman was because they wouldn't let him.

Henry Ford concluded his remarks by coming as close as possible to blaming the Jews for the World War. "Through education the everyman will one day refuse to let the Jew bunk him with this institution called war, because it is these same money-lenders who create war today. War is purely a financial institution."[5]

The remarks of Henry Ford inflamed the sensitivities of many Jews in America. They called Ford's remarks an attack that was unwarranted and based upon forgery and bigotry of the lowest order, by a millionaire in ignorance of basic truth and swollen in egotism.

The American Jewish community took particular exception to Ford's war-monger accusations among its people. It was pointed-out by many that when America became involved in the World War, Jews rushed to volunteer for military service. The facts are that at the time of the World War the Jewish population of America formed approximately 8 percent of the population, who furnished over 200,000 soldiers to the army, one-third more than their quota, 40,000 of whom volunteered their services.

In a letter to the editor of *The New York Times,* F. P. Merritt of New York City stated, "While the Fords were making millions in safety of person and pocketbook, the Jewish element of our A.E.F. (American Expeditionary Force) earned nearly 5 percent the United States military awards for valor in battle. Three men of the seventy-eight selected by the Commander-in-Chief for the highest award of the nation, the Congressional Medal of Honor were Jews, and it so happens they represent the first, second and third generations of their families in our country. The love of home and country, even adopted country, of the Jewish citizen, reverence for freedom, sacrifice of life and fortune for those principles are characteristics of Jews in America. Can that be said of Fords?"[6]

From time-to-time the Jewish community fought back against Ford's prejudice. The American Jewish Committee led by attorney Louis Marshall led a boycott of Ford Motor Company advertising in Jewish newspapers. There were also boycotts of Ford automobiles in urban areas. In addition, thousands of telegrams and letters of protest periodically streamed into the offices of the *Dearborn Independent*.

There were also many non-Jews who objected to the vicious and vile journalistic mission of the *Dearborn Independent*. The Federal Council of Churches adopted a resolution in December 1920 condemning the "International Jew" series. Also the paper was branded as vicious propaganda against Jews by former presidents Woodrow Wilson and William Howard Taft. Cardinal William O'Connell signed a petition condemning the paper.

The Ford "International Jew" essays continued for two years in the *Dearborn Independent* concluding in January 1922. The final installment of the venomous articles was an eye-popping essay entitled "An Address to Gentiles on the Jewish Problem," in which it warned people to limit Jewish influence in the country. The thesis urged citizens to be vigilant about the Jewish subversion and peacefully bring it to an end.

Meanwhile it was business as usual at the Ford Motor Company and business was very good. In 1921 Ford had dominated automobile production with 55% of the industry's total output.

On February 4, 1922 it was announced that Henry and Edsel Ford had purchased the Lincoln Motor Company for $8 million at a receiver's sale in Detroit.

Then a year later Henry Ford shocked the automotive manufacturer's world when he voluntarily agreed to pay to the Lincoln Motor Car Company creditors $4,000,000 in unsecured debt they had accumulated with 900 firms. Under the terms of the purchase Henry Ford was under no obligation to pay the Lincoln creditors and his action set a precedent in the business world.

When Ford announced plans to take on the embattled auto manufacture they also announced that the company would continue to be managed by its founders Henry M. and Wilfred C. Leland, but production for Lincolns would now begin on an enlarged scale and prices for the cars would drop from $800 to $1200, depending on the body type. Although Lincoln had been going through hard times the car was considered one of the finest constructed in the world.

Now with Ford's limitless resources the future seemed very bright for Lincoln. About the only major policy of the Lincoln Company that was agreed to be left intact was the practice of not having yearly models. The Lelands as had Henry Ford always believed that yearly models led to unjust deprecation in cars and lower resale values.

The next action for the Ford Motor Company came in late March of that year. Back in 1914 Henry Ford had shocked the American industrial establishment when he introduced the $5 work day. Now he was about to introduce the five-day work week to the automotive industry.

While historically Henry Ford, due to his high industrial profile has been given credit for innovating the five-day work week, the facts are that Ford was actually following a precedent set three months earlier by Arthur Nash, president of the Nash Clothing Company of Cincinnati when in early January 1922 he placed his 2000 employees on a basis of a forty hours a week, eight hours a day, five days a week.

Nonetheless Edsel Ford president of the company made the official announcement of the new work week policy stating that the intent of the five day work week was to provide more work for idle workers and extend through an additional day of rest to employees an opportunity for self-development.

1931 Lincoln Limousine Model K. (Photo by Lawrence T. Hay)

Labor leaders across the county rallied behind the new Ford work week policy. Samuel Gompers, president of the American Federation of Labor stated, "Mr. Ford will find the introduction of his new plan—the five day work week— as beneficial per man and in the aggregate as he found in the introduction of the eight-hour day both as to the quantity of output and as to quality."[7]

While Henry Ford was ambitious and hard-working, he began to find time for recreation. In 1913 Ford had made the acquaintance of naturalist John Burroughs. The two instantly bonded through a common love for nature and birds.

Henry Ford and Harvey Firestone. (Courtesy of The Library of Congress)

Beginning in 1914 as a way to get away from the pressures of the business environment in Detroit, Henry Ford began making annual summer camping treks into the woods to refresh him mentally. Soon Ford was making these annual trips accompanied by a trio of high profile Americans and their families that included, Thomas Edison, Harvey Firestone and Burroughs. They called themselves the "Four Vagabonds" and their annual get-a-ways into the back-water areas of America attracted a large following through the newspapers that began to tag along.

While the intent of these camping trips by Edison, Firestone and Burroughs was without a doubt a respite from the rigors of their respective fields of endeavor, it would be disingenuous to suggest that was the only intent of Henry Ford.

While the others found the constant presence of the press uncomfortable during their outings, Ford liked publicity. He was well aware that these trips highlighted a growing habit of many Americans in seeking recreation and a great many were now doing so in automobiles. So in regard to Henry Ford it is fair to say these annual trips were part vacation and in part just taking care of business.

The usual destinations for the Four Vagabonds were in rural areas of the upper Midwest, New England, upstate New York and Pennsylvania.

Where ever they traveled locals in the small towns and villages their caravan passed through would expect speeches and turn-out in mass to honor Ford, Edison, Firestone and Burroughs. After a few years as movie cameras began to record their every step and the number of reporters began to resemble an army, the trips became so widely publicized that Harvey Firestone began to refer to the annual jaunts as a traveling circus.

A great deal of Americans were in a romantic state of mind in regard to the wilderness frolicking of the Four Vagabonds imagining them in a bucolic setting almost in the spirit of a Currier and Ives print as the four geniuses sat around a campfire at peace with world.

But it would be a misnomer to suggest that the Four Vagabonds roughed it on these forays. The truth is that Ford, Edison, Firestone and Burroughs enjoyed the most modern of conveniences in outdoor equipment.

During the 1918 trip the Vagabonds traveled to their destinations in six motor vehicles that included two Packards, two Ford Model Ts and two Ford trucks. They were accompanied by a staff of seven drivers and helpers. The group was also accompanied by a Japanese cook who prepared their meals and the group ate well, being served huge breakfasts consisting of eggs, bacon, biscuits and pancakes. Dinners included steaks and chicken and various fresh provisions picked-up along the way, including deserts of pies and cookies.

In 1919 Ford retrofitted two vehicles to support the trip. One automobile was turned into a kitchen equipped with an ice box and gas stove. Ford also retrofitted an automobile with a truck chassis that included many special compartments for the transportation of tents, beds and other camping equipment. In addition Ford had built a portable generator so that electric lights could be strung in the tents used for sleeping and dinning.

Each tent was equipped with a fold-out cot, mattress, blankets, sheets and pillowcases. All this prompted one attendant to remark that it was just like staying in a hotel.

During the 1921 summer outing the Four Vagabonds would be joined by President Warren G. Harding and his wife.

Although Harding had been in the White House only a brief time since being inaugurated on March 4 he had quickly grown restless with the routine of being president. He had always been one of the guys. Harding liked to play poker, go to burlesque shows, play golf and had an eye for pretty girls. The White House with all the servants, staff and business being conducted each day was too much of a close quarters and he was too close to the demanding personality of his wife Florence, aka the Duchess.

The 1921 outdoors adventure for the Four Vagabonds was to be held at the Maryland property of Harvey Firestone near the Licking Creek. This year the Vagabonds would be joined in the woods by Edsel Ford and his wife and the younger Firestones.

On July 24 the group would be joined by President Harding and Florence accompanied by a secret service detail that was not exactly happy about it all. For the next three days Harding would act like a pioneer chopping wood, sleeping on canvas cots and taking walks with Henry Ford and Thomas Edison in the woods. Harding had even brought along a Methodist Bishop William Anderson from Cincinnati, so on Sunday a pine-grove service was held.

Many believe that the presence of President Harding with the Four Vagabonds was just another of Henry Ford's publicity stunts.

In 1918 at the urging of President Woodrow Wilson, Ford had run and lost a race for the U.S. Senate in Michigan against Republican Thomas H. Newberry.

In the 1920 presidential race Henry Ford had supported James Cox a Democrat over Warren Harding a Republican.

According to early Henry Ford biographer Allan L. Benson, former president Theodore Roosevelt had once predicted that Ford would be a candidate for president in 1924.

In late May 1922, less than a year after Henry Ford had camped and chopped wood with President Warren G. Harding in Maryland, in Dearborn, Michigan a grass-roots campaign led by William T. Kronberg, editor of a Dearborn newspaper, along with 140 others, many who were neighbors of Henry Ford, had been formed to urge Ford to run for president against Harding in 1924. In fact, they had already organized a "Henry Ford for President Club."

The Dearborn group immediately began to print large quantities of hat bands with the lettering on them stating *We Want Henry* and from a small office they sent 45,000 letters to friends all over the U.S. urging the formation of Ford for president clubs. In order to finance their efforts they sold the hat bands for one dollar each. The ultimate goal of the Dearborn Ford club was to solicit enough signatures on petitions in every state in the union through Ford clubs to place Henry Ford's name on the ballot in each district.

When William Kronberg and a delegation from the Dearborn Ford for President Club called on Henry Ford he informed them, that if the people of the country wanted him to run for president then he would do so, but he would not put forth one dime of his own money to bring it about.

It was a fact that despite his extreme and biased views on the Jewish community, Henry Ford was one of the most popular men in America.

But there was the huge question looming over the possibility of a Ford candidacy of whether he was a Republican or a Democrat. While most of those near Ford believed the past few years he had moved closer to the GOP, he still maintained close ties with William F. Connelly, a member of the Democratic National Committee for Michigan. So many believed that if Ford did indeed run for president he would run as an independent.

Charles W. Wood of *Colliers* magazine interviewed Henry Ford in August and was left with the following impression. "Henry Ford," according to Wood, "cannot well be a member of a political party today. To him the parties are exactly what the politicians call them. They are organizations and they exist to serve the organization instead of existing to serve. Whether he could accept a nomination from one these parties—well, it is conceivable, but it is hard to visualize."[8]

The fact was that at that moment Henry Ford's head was not in the White House, it was in his River Rouge plant. He was making cars, not presidential plans. He was concerned about getting other manufactures to accept higher wages and getting workers to accept maximum production. Ford believed these two factors would permit dealers to lower prices substantially resulting in the government not needing to do anything. With nothing to do all government officials could take a vacation.

Ford was convinced that full-employment would end war. Busy people he reasoned do not stop work to make war. Ford felt that "When the time comes that every one, everywhere, has a job, and lasting prosperity has been created as a result, the people of any nation will be too busy and too happy to even think about war."[9] While no endorsement had been made by Henry Ford or any member of his family by early 1923 the Henry Ford for president movement was gaining popularity and Ford for president clubs were springing up everywhere. In Chicago a headquarters had been opened on Michigan Avenue and 50,000 circulars were circulated to 'feel out" the sentiment of potential voters.

While there was a Ford for president club in New York located on Broadway in the Wilson Building, the club president George H. Proctor was complaining that not one cent had been received from Ford. Meanwhile in Detroit large portraits of Henry Ford were being sent-out to every auto agency with his biography soon to follow. Ford liked the idea. He was strong with the farmers' votes; not only had he made life easier on the farm with the Fordson tractor introduced in 1917, but he had also attempted to make fertilizer cheaper by gaining control of a Muscle Shoals nitrate plant.

At that time a debate was taking place both locally in Alabama and in the U.S. Congress in regards to what the government should do with the facilities that included, land, a dam and powerhouse that it had used to produce nitrogen for explosives during the World War at Muscle Shoals on the Tennessee River.

The Federal Government was willing to sell the facilities at Muscle Shoals to a private company that would produce fertilizer. So in 1921 Henry Ford made a proposal to buy the unfinished Wilson Dam and two nitrate plants. The Ford proposal was cause for much local enthusiasm as a lot of locals felt that Ford could do for Muscle Shoals what he did for Detroit. The Ford plan called for building a city at Muscle Shoals that would encompass 75 miles of north Alabama and possibly employ one million people. But when various members of Congress opposed the sale of the facilities to Ford he withdrew his offer in 1924.

Eventually in May 1933 Congress would create a government corporation out of the facilities called the Tennessee Valley Authority (TVA) to provide flood control, agriculture and industrial development and improvements to navigation on the Tennessee River.

There still remained the question of what party's nomination the Ford clubs were aiming at for their candidate and that was a big question with labor. Labor was split over Ford and set to endorse a Democrat over Republican incumbent president Warren Harding. In February the Michigan Democrats failed to endorse Henry Ford for president at their state convention. To that end the Detroit Ford club was floating the possibility that if neither of the major parties nominated Henry Ford they would attempt to run him as an independent.

There were a considerable number of voters, particularly on the east coast that felt that Henry Ford's extraordinary attitude of credulity toward the Jews demonstrated a limited mentality.

By early 1923 reports began to appear in newspapers such as the *Chicago Tribune* and *New York Times* that a young Bavarian monarchist revolutionary in Munich by the name of Adolf Hitler was receiving financial support from Henry Ford. According to the vice-president of the Bavarian Diet, Herr Auer, Herr Hitler had as part of his program extermination of the Jews in Germany. Hitler was openly boasting of the support he was receiving from Henry Ford and hung a photograph of him on the wall of his quarters on Cornelius Street which was the center of the monarchist movement.

At the same time allegations were being made by Sydney S. Cohen, President of the Motion Pictures Theatres Owners Association that emissaries of Henry Ford were attempting to gain control of the moving picture theatres throughout the country looking to control the screen for a future presidential run.

All through the spring of 1923 Henry Ford kept denying that he had any presidential aspirations. In fact, Ford's wife was telling people that if her husband ever went to Washington to live in the White House he would have to live there without her.

But there were a lot of people that wanted Ford to run. It was being predicted that he could win every state Democrat primary election in the south but in Alabama where he had attempted to gain control of Muscle Shoals.

Then in May 1923 *Colliers* canvassed its readers for their preference for president. In the poll 19,744 readers cast their votes and Henry Ford came in first with 5,547 votes. President Harding was second with 4,460, while William G. McAdoo, Secretary of the Treasury under Woodrow Wilson came in third with 1,693, followed by Senator Hiram W. Johnson of California with 1,409 votes. James M. Cox, former Governor of Ohio who had been the Democrat nominee for president in 1920 finished fifth in the poll with 1,335 votes.

In the poll Henry Ford had virtually smoked such notable political figures as Al Smith, Governor of New York 908 votes, progressive Senator Robert M. LaFollette of Wisconsin 778 and Herbert Hoover, Secretary of Commerce 754 votes.

Following the poll, newspaper baron William Randolph Hearst publicly came out in favor of Henry Ford for president. But there was a caveat to Hearst's endorsement, that being Ford had to run as an Independent. Hearst was of the opinion that Ford's radical ideas would prevent him from winning in the Democratic convention and that his strength lie with the common people.

The *Colliers* poll and the Hearst endorsement of Ford caused growing concern among the Republican and Democrat ranks. Was there a third party movement taking place? To that end, the Executive Committee of the Democratic National Committee met in Washington to discuss the fact that Ford's boom was a serious enough to consider if he should be taken seriously as the party's nominee. While there was hardly any enthusiasm for Ford among those who would have to run his presidential campaign there were questions that needed to be answered. Could Ford sweep the party's primaries? If so, the Democrats needed to find a way to stop him.

By the time the meeting adjourned the Executive Committee had reached the conclusion that Hearst's endorsement had hurt Ford more than it had helped him. It was believed that Henry Ford would not allow himself to be used as a third party candidate where in the end it would only be a boost for one or the other of the major party candidates and weaken his own prestige.

Soon after Democrats across the country began lining-up against Henry Ford. Senator Edward I. Edwards of New Jersey was blunt when asked about the so-called Ford boom. Edwards exclaimed, "Why he's no Democrat. We don't want him and we won't have him. Does anyone know if he is a Democrat or a Republican? Let him run on a third ticket, if he wants to. I guess that's where he belongs."[10]

The Jewish community was now organizing and going on record to voice their disapproval of Henry Ford. Around Memorial Day at their national meeting in Atlantic City the Grand Lodge Order of B'rith Abraham an organization with a membership of 35,000 passed a resolution condemning Ford for his antagonistic attitude and charged him with being a financial backer of the Ku Klux Klan. The resolution stated in part,

"Be it resolved that the order of B'rith Abraham now in session, go on record as follows:

"The delegates assembled condemn the attitude of Henry Ford for his attitude against the Jews as un-American and that his candidacy for President is an insult to the fundamentals which this country is based."[11]

The Order of B'rith Abraham was not the only Jewish organization expressing dissatisfaction with the thought of Henry Ford running for president. The Federation of Hungarian Jews in America an organization with a membership of 200,000 also passed a resolution condemning Ford as a candidate while calling him a menace to peace and prosperity of the inhabitants of the land.

In a second poll conducted by *Colliers* 53,703 readers responded and this time President Harding finished first with 13, 080 votes to 12, 379 for Henry Ford.

In Dearborn officials in the Ford for president club were beginning to realize that neither the Democrats nor Republicans were likely to nominate Henry Ford. Furthermore up to this point no authoritative group had signified that they wanted him to be a candidate. Therefore Ford's backers began to advance the idea that he should run as an independent candidate.

To many observers it seemed that Henry Ford's presidential backers were for all intents and purposes jumping into an empty pool. Henry Ford had still not expressed any interest in seeking the presidency and had not contributed one dime to those working on his behalf and furthermore, had not indicated that he would accept a presidential nomination if tendered. On the other hand, Ford did nothing to discourage his backers from promoting him as a presidential candidate.

Just when it seemed like Ford's candidacy might be fading in early June, *Colliers* canvased its readers for the third time and this time a whopping 83,883 readers responded. Henry Ford came out on top beating President Harding by a margin of 21,374 votes to 20,170. In this poll it was New Jersey that put Ford over the top.

In summing up the results *Colliers* stated, "The Ford sentiment disclosed in our first two weeks count has already become a political sensation, but the more some politicians think about Ford the more they fail to hit upon any solution. They simply say he can't be nominated, at least in any way that they can think of now."[12]

Henry Ford was receiving over 200 letters a day at his office urging him to run for president and recently a petition had been signed by 50,000 people in

Kansas supporting his candidacy. Suddenly the Ford for president campaign became a coast-to-coast affair as a Ford club opened in Fresno, California. Polls were being taken by the Golden State group and if they proved favorable for Ford then additional offices would be opened in Los Angeles and San Francisco. At the same time a Ford club opened its doors in Waco, Texas.

Two weeks later in a fourth *Colliers* poll Henry Ford began to pull away from President Harding beating him by 11, 297 votes 38,467 to 27,170. The closest competitor to Ford and Harding was Secretary of the Treasury William G. McAdoo with 10,526 votes.

While Henry Ford remained aloof with his supporters about his true intentions of running for president, he realized that all the publicity surrounding him provided a huge platform to express his personal values.

He lost no time in seizing the opportunity to promote his support of the Volstead Act. Ford was quick to tell any captive audience that booze did nobody any good and he was convinced that production in his auto plants had risen since the prohibition law was passed. "Booze had to go out when modern industry and the motor car came in," said Ford. "Upon only one condition can the nation safely let it come back. That is if we are willing to abolish modern industry and the motor car."[13]

Living in Detroit across from Canada presented a significant challenge for prohibition agents from keeping illegal booze from crossing the border in the U.S. So Henry Ford proposed that the Army and Navy be put in charge of enforcing the Volstead Act. "Turn the Volstead Act enforcement over to the army and navy," declared Ford. "They haven't anything to do in peace time anyhow, but to go through a few drills and idle their time away cruising or maintaining the social relations at some isolated post. Why not give them something to do for the money we give them? They would surely put the rum runners on the blink."[14]

On June 16, 1923 the country took notice through a press release that it was the twentieth anniversary of the Ford Motor Company. The company reminded all that the production had been increased in 1903 from 1,790 cars to an expected 1,500,000 cars in 1923.

The Ford Motor Company which had been started with $27,000 had grown in two decades to become one of the largest industrial organizations in the world. At that time Ford was employing 100,000 men in Michigan alone.

There were now 9,000 Ford dealerships in the country and 15,000 authorized Ford service stations therefore offering 24,000 points of contact with the company. In addition to having manufacturing plants at the River Rouge in Detroit, Hamilton, Ohio, Troy, New York and several other Michigan locations, the company had its own glass plants at Glassmere, Pennsylvania and Highland Park, Michigan. Ford also had its own coal mines in Kentucky and West Virginia and had its own railroad, The Detroit, Toledo and Ironton which connected with most of the trunk lines east of the Mississippi.

During the summer of 1923 President Warren Harding, although he had been ill for several weeks, had been on campaign trip in the western United States to judge the strength of his support for re-election and support for a World Court when on August 2, he died at the Palace Hotel in San Francisco. A few hours later vice-president Calvin Coolidge was sworn-in as the 30th president of the United States. Harding's presidency had been riddled with personal philandering and political scandals, most notably Teapot Dome which involved oil drilling by private individuals on tracts of land the government had acquired through the exercise of public domain and turned over to the U.S. Navy for future use.

President Harding's remains were transported by train back to Washington, D.C.'s Union Station and taken off as a band played the mournful strains of "Nearer to Thee My God" in the concourse. His remains were then taken to the White House and placed in East Room until the following morning. Then they were taken on a caisson followed by a large cortege to the Capitol building and placed on a black catafalque directly under the core of the central dome. President Coolidge entered and placed a large wreath on the catafalque. A brief service ended at three minutes before noon. Then at the noon hour a moment of silence was observed all across the country as a bugler sounded taps on the Capital steps. For the next four hours Harding's body lie in full view as tens of thousands of mourners passed by. The coffin was then closed and taken to Union Station for transport to the final funeral to be held at Marion, Ohio

At Marion Cemetery a huge service was held. Flanking the coffin were six admirals and a Marine general, Mrs. Harding, President Coolidge, Chief Justice William Howard Taft and various relatives, while standing in an enclosed space just beside the vault were President Harding's friends including, Henry Ford, Thomas Edison and Harvey Firestone.

The fact was that President Harding had indeed been very friendly to Ford and Firestone in a business sense. His administration had created 10,000 miles of new roads in the U.S.

In would have seemed that with the death of Warren Harding a path may have been cleared for the nomination of Henry Ford for president with the

Republicans. But at that moment Henry Ford showed no interest in pursuing the presidency. Instead of leaving Marion to begin campaigning, Ford went camping.

Once again Henry Ford, Harvey Firestone and Thomas Edison set-out on their summer sojourn in quest of recreation. This year's journey would first take the Vagabonds to Milan, Ohio to visit the birthplace of Edison where they were greeted by a crowd of 5,000. Then the trio traveled to Ford's country home near Detroit and finally without any definite itinerary they wandered aimlessly through Northern Michigan and Wisconsin.

On Halloween, October 31, 1923 any hidden presidential aspiration of Henry Ford took a huge hit when Senator James Couzens ridiculed his potential candidacy in a speech delivered to the Republican Club during a dinner at the Hotel Statler in Detroit.

James Couzens had been one of the original stockholders in the Ford Motor Company and general manager of the company from 1903 to 1915. He became a U.S. Senator from Michigan in 1921 after serving as a popular mayor of Detroit.

Couzens clearly loved Henry Ford and stated that he had never thought so much of any other man. But he was also less than candid in proclaiming any Ford presidential campaign would be as big a fiasco as his peace ship. Couzens told the members of the Republican Club that night, "Ford for President. It is ridiculous. How can a man over 60 years old who has done nothing except make motors, who has no training, no experience, aspire to such an office. I want to save Ford the greatest humiliation of his career and save the United States Government the humiliation of having him as President."[15]

Couzens concluded his remarks by asserting that many of those advocating Ford's candidacy were sincere, but there were also many supporters who were dishonest citizens surrounding him with hopes of getting personal advantage or gain.

While both the leadership of the Dearborn Ford-for-President Club and Henry Ford had no response to the attacks made by Senator Couzens, it was clear that the possibility of any possible presidential run by the auto tycoon was waning.

The Democrats began to way in too expressing the view that Henry Ford was an undesirable candidate for several reasons; first it was unclear if he were a Democrat or a Republican. Then there were his extreme views of prohibition pointing-out that the Democratic organization in Michigan was pro-wet. So how was he going to win that state's primary? Finally there was the matter of Ford's antagonistic and alienating views on the Jews which categorically made him unfit for the presidency.

The knockout blow to any presidential aspirations that Henry Ford may have had took place in late November in South Dakota. In the Democratic county proposal meetings 80% of the delegates for the State convention chosen supported William G. McAdoo over Ford.

In the Republican meetings in South Dakota the votes for delegates was split between President Coolidge and Senator Hiram Johnson.

Consequently, Henry Ford was now faced with the fact that if he truly wanted the presidential nomination, be it Democrat or Republican, he was going to have fight for it and he just didn't have the fire in his belly for the challenge.

On December 20, Henry Ford announced he would not run as a candidate for president on any ticket and endorsed the re-election of Calvin Coolidge. In a statement released to the press Ford stated, "I believe it is the wise and natural finding for the people to agree on the nomination and election of Mr. Coolidge. I am satisfied that 90 per cent of the people feel perfectly safe with Coolidge, and I feel too, that the country is perfectly safe with him. And if this is the feeling of the country, why change?"[16]

On November 4, 1924 Republican incumbent President Calvin Coolidge won election to a full term by a landslide over Democrat candidate, former West Virginia Congressman, John W. Davis by a margin of 15,714,068 votes to 8,384,341. In the Electoral College Coolidge won 382 to 136. Also in the race was third party candidate Democrat Senator Robert M. LaFollette of Wisconsin who finished with 4,833,821 popular votes and 13 Electoral College votes.

In 1925 Aaron Sapiro a Jewish-American launched a legal battle against the *Dearborn Independent*. In 1919 Sapiro began organizing farmers' groups into the Farmers' Cooperative Marketing Association. The organization would ultimately represent about one million farmers in the U.S. and Canada. One of the tactics used by the organization was to withhold crops from the market to push up prices. In 1924 Sapiro would be forced to step-down as head of the organization as a result of discontent with his leadership.

Nonetheless, while acting as the head of the farmer's organization Aaron Sapiro had grown tired of the attacks on his character made by Henry Ford. In January 1925 Sapiro sent a letter to Henry Ford demanding an apology. None would be forthcoming. About six weeks later on February 20, Aaron

Sapiro filed a one million dollar libel suit against Henry Ford and the *Dearborn Independent* over a series of articles published in the paper that characterized his attempts to organize farm collectives as a plot by Jewish international financiers to control the American economy.

Astonishingly, Henry Ford was eager to meet Aaron Sapiro in court. Ford had never understood the hurt and division that his articles had caused in many communities. He was hallucinatory in his belief that he was only taking on bad Jews and that the good Jews would follow his crusade.

In March 1926 depositions in the case were taken and a trial date set for March 15, 1927 in U. S. District Court in Detroit.

The trial would be a bizarre legal battle with Sapiro's attorneys charging that Ford's attacks on their client were not only personal slander but a slanderous attack on Jews as a whole.

Ford attorneys that included U.S. Senator James A. Reed of Missouri countered the charges against their client by charging that Sapiro was a fraud, grater and cheat. Furthermore they claimed that under the law you could not libel a race and that it had be proven that Ford either wrote the articles or directed that they be published.

All during the trial Henry Ford hid behind the testimony of William J. Cameron as the author of the hateful articles as he attempted to avoid being subpoenaed and having to appear on the witness stand.

Ford even had a mysterious auto accident between his office and his home as process servers chased to serve him with a subpoena.

While Sapiro's attorneys sought to have Ford examined by an independent doctor to determine if he was capable of testifying it was alleged that a juror had been offered a bribe by a Jew to convict Ford. While the juror Ms. Cora Hamilton denied the charges in a statement to the press, the trail judge Fred S. Raymond had no choice but to grant a motion by the defense for a mistrial.

While a new trial was scheduled to begin in September, Henry Ford decided that it was in his best interests to bring the matter to a close. First, he ordered that the *Dearborn Independent* cease publishing and on September 30, 1927 the paper was dissolved.

Second, he arranged for an out-of-court cash settlement with Aaron Sapiro.

Regarding the issue of healing the wounds he had inflicted upon the American Jewish community at large, Ford enlisted two men, Earl J. Davies of Detroit and Joseph A. Palma of New York to negotiate for him with Louis Marshall of the American Jewish Committee.

A meeting was arranged at Marshall's New York office where the two Ford representatives were introduced to him by former Congressman Nathan D. Perlman.

Davis and Palma told Marshall that Henry Ford felt that he had been taken advantage of by those he had put in charge of the *Dearborn Independent* by publishing the series of articles attacking the Jews. They stated that Ford had taken umbrage and that he was convinced that all of the charges made against Jews, individually and collectively were without foundation and unjust. To that end, he wanted to know what could be done to put an end to the strained relations on the part of the Jews toward him.

Louis Marshall told Davis and Palma that it was necessary for Henry Ford to make a complete retraction of all the false charges that had been made against the Jews, a full apology and a request for forgiveness, as well as, a discontinuance of the attacks and a withdraw of the pamphlets consisting of "The International Jew" and a pledge they would never again be made.

On July 8, 1927 in a formal press release Henry Ford pledged to make amends to the Jewish people by asking for their forgiveness for the harm he had unintentionally committed upon them. Ford promised the Jewish community that such articles reflecting upon them would never again appear in his newspaper.

Ford's mea culpa was accepted by Marshall representing the American Jewish Committee and stated in part the following,

> Those who know me can bear witness that it is not in my nature to inflict insult upon and to occasion pain to anybody, and that it has been my effort to free myself from prejudice. Because of that I frankly confess that I have been greatly shocked as a result of my study and examination of the files of The Dearborn Independent and of the pamphlets entitled "The International Jew." I deem it to be my duty as an honorable man to make amends for the wrong done to the Jews as fellow-men and brothers, by asking their forgiveness for the harm that I have unintentionally committed, by retracting so far as lies within my power the offensive charges laid at their door by these publications, and by giving them the unqualified assurance that henceforth they may look to me for friendship and good will.

It is needless to add that the pamphlets which have been distributed throughout the country and in foreign lands will be withdrawn from circulation, that in every way possible I will make it known that they have my unqualified disapproval, and that henceforth The Dearborn Independent will be conducted under such auspices that articles reflecting upon the Jews will never again appear in its columns.[17]

It seemed as if Henry Ford had suddenly reconsidered his views on the Jewish community. Humorist Will Rodgers may have captured the reasoning of Ford correctly when he stated, "He (Henry Ford) used to have it in for the Jewish people until he saw them in Chevrolets, and then said, "Boys, I am all wrong."[18]

7.

The 1930s and the Rise of Organized Labor

By 1927 the number of registered cars in the nation for private and public use had swelled to 17,481,001. In Detroit auto manufacturing was in high gear during the roaring twenties and by1929 there would be 292,228 men employed in the industry.

The annual National Automobile Show held in New York had become an enormously popular event with tens of thousands flocking to the Grand Central Palace to view the new models from GM, Chrysler, Franklin, Hudson and Packard and meet sports celebrities such as Babe Ruth. Although Ford didn't offer much in the way of new models, the company still put on a service show at the Ford Building located at Broadway & 54th Streets.

During the 1920s automotive technology had advanced rapidly. Cars were now available with shatter-proof glass, powerful brakes, varied sizes of wheel-bases and increased horsepower.

Then in the early 1930s the first commercial radios were made available for cars. Suddenly a whole new cultural experience began to descend on the use of the automobile. Drivers and passengers were now entertained electronically as they were transported. A complete evolution in the car radio would take place over the following eighty years as new products became available; radios with an FM band, eight track tape players, stereo sound, cassette tape players, CD players and today satellite reception.

On March 11, 1929 a new land speed record of 223.2 miles per hour was set by Henry Seagrave at Daytona Beach, Florida driving in his streamlined car

"Golden Arrow." Seagrave's record would be short-lived though as on February 24, 1932 at Daytona, British racing driver Sir Malcomb Campbell would surpass him setting the new land speed record at 253.968 miles per hour.

The prohibition era would create the need for speed by both a sub-culture of entrepreneurs known as bootleggers and some infamous outlaws.

On April 13, 1934 the Ford Motor Company would receive a letter from Clyde Barrow who along with his partner Bonnie Parker and his gang would rob numerous banks and store owners between 1930 and 1934 while also committing several murders of law enforcement officials.

The letter written on paper, dated April 10, 1934 and addressed to Mr. Henry Ford, Detroit, Michigan, stated the following: "Dear Sir, While I have still have got breath in my lungs I will tell you what a dandy car you make. I have drove Fords exclusively when I could get away with one. For sustained speed and freedom from trouble the Ford has got ever other car skinned and even if my business hasn't been strictly legal it don't hurt anything to tell you what a fine car you got in the V8. Yours truly Clyde Champion Barrow"[1]

Six weeks after the letter was received at Ford "Bonnie and Clyde" were shot dead in an ambush by Texas Rangers ending their four-year crime spree.

While handwriting analysts have questioned the authenticity of the letter, it certainly is something that the publicity seeking Clyde Barrow would have been likely to do.

Bootleggers of the 1920s and 1930s needed to have automobiles to haul their illegal moonshine and whisky at speeds that permitted them to outrun revenue agents and law enforcement officers. So very skillful mechanics souped-up various cars and Appalachian area bootleggers from West Virginia, Kentucky, Tennessee, North Carolina and Georgia began transporting their illegal cargo over mountain and back roads while outrunning the law. With the repeal of prohibition, the moonshine trade continued. The favorite car of the bootleggers was a souped-up Ford V-8 coup that Clyde Barrow championed.

With the repeal of prohibition, a lot of former bootleggers began to race each other and it would become the genesis of another popular form of racing in America—stock car racing. Following World War Two as the sport became more popular tracks were built and in 1947 at Daytona Beach, Florida, NASCAR (National Association for Stock Car Racing), was founded.

The 2016 Daytona 500 attracted 101,000 spectators as Denny Hamlin driving a souped-up Toyota edged out Martin Truex, Jr. also driving a Toyota, by an incredible 1/100 of a second.

Bonnie Parker and Clyde Barrow, sometime between 1932 and 1934.
(Wikimedia Commons)

The Federal Highway Act of 1921 signed into law by President Warren Harding was instrumental in creating an organized system of roads. Under the Act, north to south roads were assigned odd numbers. East to west roads assigned even numbers.

One of the most lasting undertakings created by the Act would be the creation of Route 66. In its beginning in 1926 Route 66 would be a hodge-podge of connections of existing roads, but within a decade would become an organized system with many new roads. Eventually Route 66 would become the most iconic highway in the United States.

1930 Ford Model A Rumble Seat Coupe. (Photo by Lawrence T. Hay)

Covering 2446 miles between Chicago and Los Angeles Route 66 would become the escape route for tens of thousands of people fleeing the despair of the Great Depression created by the collapse of Wall Street in 1929 and perils of the Dust Bowl that wreaked drought and crop failures in Kansas, Oklahoma and Texas in the early 1930s. Route 66 would be forever immortalized in American popular culture as "The Mother Road" in John Steinbeck's epic novel of the Great Depression *The Grapes of Wrath*.

Other famous highways were also coming into their own such as U.S. 101 that runs from San Diego to the Oregon border, while in the east with the construction of U.S. 9, popular vacation destinations in New Jersey such Cape May and Atlantic City were now only a few hours away from New York City.

The automobile was stimulating tourism and creating a growing demand for even more roads. By 1922 there were nineteen National Parks under the jurisdiction of the Department of the Interior, covering 10,000 square miles and attracting a million visitors a year. The automobile had made Yellowstone Park the most popular destination in the park system.

The first white man to have entered the Yellowstone was trapper, hunter and soldier, John Colter in 1807 who had intended to open up trade negotiations with Chief Blackfoot only to be chased and injured by hostile Crow Indians before making a harrowing escape on the Missouri River.

Yellowstone National Park was created by Congress in late 1872 and signed into law by President U.S. Grant on March 2, 1873. But Americans were slow to embrace Yellowstone Park as their own. In 1910 Yellowstone Park attracted just 20,000 visitors of whom most all of them came by train. But with the growing popularity of the auto by 1922 Yellowstone was attracting over 100,000 visitors annually.

Nearly a century later in 2015 Yellowstone was the fourth most visited National Park in the U.S. with 3,447,729 visitors trailing Great Smoky Mountains National Park 9,685,829 visitors, Grand Canyon National Park 4,421,352 and Yosemite National Park 3,853,404 visitors. And nearly all came by car or bus.

In South Dakota in 1924 the concept for of a huge man-made national memorial had begun. In the Black Hills it was planned to carve the faces of four American presidents, George Washington, Thomas Jefferson, Abraham Lincoln and Theodore Roosevelt on the side of Mt. Rushmore a thousand feet above the chasm below. In the sculpture Lincoln's nose would be larger than the Sphinx in Egypt and Washington's head would be sixty feet from the hair line to his chin. The memorial would be visible sixty miles away.

Work officially began on the sculpture in 1927 after being dedicated as a national memorial by President Calvin Coolidge. By 1936 President Franklin D. Roosevelt would unveil the head of Jefferson.

But the memorial was located many miles away from the nearest roads. So, between 1927 and 1941 when the memorial was 99% complete, the State of South Dakota spent over $500,000 to construct scenic modern highways and byways to and around the memorial. In 1941 the memorial attracted 393,000 visitors.

America's first super-highway was also in the making. Dubbed as the highway of tomorrow the 160-mile Pennsylvania Turnpike was opened in 1940. One year after its opening two and a half million automobiles and trucks were operated over the highway. The state-run highway which initially had no posted speed limit had eleven points of entrance staffed night and day by officers available to provide direction to motorist. Also, along the expanse of the highway there were eleven restaurants and service stations. By the early 1950s the Pennsylvania Turnpike was carrying ten million vehicles a year.

The on-set of The Great Depression in 1929 had a devastating effect on the auto industry and Detroit—when 60,000 workers were laid off the welfare roll expenses in the city increased by $1 million. Ford laid-off workers and cut wages for thousands who had been working 14-hour days for 10 cents an hour.

On March 7, 1932 a Hunger March was organized and protestors selected the Ford Rouge plant as a symbolic target and approached the gates of the facility to petition for relief. But things turned ugly as protestors threw rocks and police responded by firing weapons into the crowd wounding fifty and killing four, another protestor died from injuries.

A year later in September 1933, Henry Ford announced that he would hire 5000 local war veterans for $3 a day. The next morning 10,000 men showed-up to apply for work.

During Franklin D. Roosevelt's first term as president, Alfred P. Sloan had been appalled by the New Deal tactics to stimulate the economy through new tax plans and federal deficit spending. But the larger part of Sloan's discontent with Roosevelt's New Deal was aimed at his dislike of the pro-labor legislation that Congress had passed and the president signed into law. This included the National Industrial Relations Act of 1933 (NIRA), which authorized the president to regulate industry in an attempt to raise prices after sever deflation in order to stimulate recovery.

The second legislation that that left a bad taste in Sloan's mouth was the Wagner Act passed by Congress and signed into law by President Roosevelt on July 5, 1935. The Wagner Act (Section 7A) guaranteed basic rights of private sector workers to organize into trade unions and engage in collective bargaining for better terms and conditions in the workplace.

This was a very troubling event for the automobile industry. Almost since the founding of the industry the manufactures had tightly controlled the workplace. Henry Ford was anti-union to the core proclaiming that labor unions are "a great scheme for interrupting work and speeding up loafing."[2]

Although GM made a substantial profit in 1936 after its sales of vehicles world-wide topped two million, three times what sales had been in 1932, Sloan backed Republican candidate Alf Landon in the presidential election. Of course Roosevelt won in a landslide winning every state in the union.

Through-out its existence GM had experienced labor peace. That changed in late December 1936 and suddenly Alfred. Sloan would encounter one of the most frustrating crises of his business career. In Flint, Michigan newly organized

Franklin D. Roosevelt. (Author's private collection)

workers in the General Motors plant staged a 44-day sit-down strike to obtain union recognition.

Alfred Sloan, still holding fast to the belief that automobile industry was better served by the workers not being organized and under the thumb of management decrees was of the opinion that all the trouble was caused by Franklin Roosevelt and the NRA.

To counter-act union organizing GM used a strategy of putting in place a network of anti-union activities in every one of its plants across the nation, including the use of industrial spies. The company even went so far as to hire private detectives to spy on the spies hired by division and plant managers. While these tactics were never the direct result of an order by Alfred Sloan, he knew about the anti-union operations and signed-off on them.

While the strike at the Flint plant was caused by production increases, while the work force and wages were cut, Alfred Sloan was stead-fast in refusing to deal with the strikers contending that they were holding GM plants unlawfully. He joined the growing forces assailing John L. Lewis, head of the Committee for Industrial Organization (CIO), as seeking to dominate the auto manufacturing industry. In fact, Lewis was attempting to cash-in his political collateral by calling for Roosevelt to settle the strike in favor of the UAW.

At first President Roosevelt criticized Alfred Sloan; then as public opinion ran against him; he beat a hasty retreat. It would ultimately be newly elected Michigan Governor Frank Murphy that brought labor and management together in the first attempt at a resolution.

Governor Murphy was a former Mayor of Detroit and had been appointed governor-general of the Philippines in President Roosevelt's first administration. Governor Murphy also owned a large bloc of GM stock that he would sell during the strike to avoid a conflict of interest allegation and to ensure his profits.

As the strike in Flint continued into January 1937 it started to spread to other GM plants around the country including a walkout at the Cadillac plant led by Walter Reuther and the UAW. Workers at a Chrysler plant also staged a sit-in.

As GM was contending that the strikers were occupying their property illegally, Governor Murphy was confronted with the possibility of using the National Guard and Police to remove them from the Flint Plant.

On January 11, 1937 the strike turned violent. A rumor had spread that GM security guards were being held hostage in the Flint Fisher Body Plant. About thirty Flint police offices reinforced by other departments attacked the strikers with tear gas canisters being shot into the plant. Outside labor organizer Walter Reuther shouted through a bull horn for the strikers to fight back. Suddenly, they turned fire hoses on the police and hurled bottles and door hinges at them. With a large number of picketers outside the plant becoming disgruntled the police retreated

Then the police regrouped and using pistols and riot guns opened fire on the plant, strikers and picketers. While thirteen people were wounded, miraculously none was killed. Nine police officers were wounded during the riot.

The violence continued through-out the night with the police hurling more tear gas canisters into the plant and the strikers answering back with more debris. Finally, in the morning Governor Murphy called in the National Guard and peace was restored. Still about 800 strikers remained barricaded in the plant refusing to back down.

The week after the riot Governor Murphy brought the parties together for negotiations at the state capital in Lansing. Homer Martin represented the UAW. Alfred Sloan chose not to carry on the negotiations personally and instead remained in New York. He delegated the job to William S. Knudsen, vice president of operations. But negotiations broke down when Knudsen, with Sloan's full support, refused to recognize the UAW as the sole barging agent for the GM workers.

By February 1 with John L. Lewis boldly proclaiming that he and the strikers would not back down, the strike had spread further as a group of workers seized the Chevrolet plant in Flint. Once again Governor Murphy was considering removing the strikers by force.

Alfred Sloan fought back by getting an injunction against the striking workers from a Michigan judge, but Governor Murphy refused to enforce it.

Finally, the Roosevelt administration got involved in the troubles at Flint. The same day that the injunction order had been obtained by Sloan, William Knudsen was informed by Francis Perkins, Secretary of Labor, that President Roosevelt requested that he sit-down with John L. Lewis and seek a resolution to the strike. It was an opportunity for both Sloan and Knudsen to save face and Knudsen announced that he had agreed to the meeting because the president had requested it. In New York Alfred Sloan was conspicuous in his silence.

On February 4, 1937 Knudsen met with Lewis and the two worked-out an agreement for GM to end the sit-down strikes. The terms of the agreement were simple and straight forward, UAW was granted exclusive bargaining rights until October of that year. The strike at Flint against GM had resulted in the first-ever contract between the UAW and an automobile manufacturer. Going forward the UAW would be a permanent part of the industry. By 1940 GM would agree to the first paid vacations for workers in the auto industry.

The UAW victory at GM was followed by a massive rally at Cadillac Square in Detroit where the union's national president Homer Martin addressed 150,000 sympathizers. Now there was a surge in the union's spirit, and they turned their attention to Ford which was the only remaining major auto manufacturer that had not negotiated with the UAW.

Henry Ford who only a decade before had been billed as the auto workers' best friend now became their worst enemy and fought legally, illegally and violently to keep the union out of his plants. Ford had recently distributed cards to their employees that stated, "We have never had to bargain against our men, and we don't expect to begin now." UAW leaders termed the rhetoric "Fordism."

The UAW attempt to organize Ford employees in the spring of 1937 would be led by Richard Frankensteen and Walter Reuther.

Richard T. Frankensteen was a native of Detroit, born March 6, 1907. He attended Central High School, where he played football and was named to the All-City and All-State teams. A big man, Frankensteen stood 6' 2" and weighed 250 pounds. He was awarded a scholarship to The University of Dayton where he was named an All-American on the gridiron. After graduating from Dayton in 1932 Frankensteen had intended to teach school, but the depression had made opportunities scarce. So, he came back to Detroit and went to work for Chrysler. By 1935 he was involved with organizing workers for the AIWA which was merged into the UAW in 1936.

Walter P. Reuther was born the second of four sons of German immigrants Valentine and Anna (Stocker) on September 1, 1907 in Wheeling, West Virginia. Reuther's father Valentine who was employed as a steel and brewery worker was a socialist and he trained his sons in trade unionism and public debate. In 1922 Reuther left high school after completing two years and began an apprenticeship as a tool and die maker. He would be fired for attempting to organize workers against working on Sundays and holidays.

Reuther moved to Detroit and began working in the Briggs plant while he finished his high school education at night. He then attended classes at Wayne State University for three years where he was a campus activist organizing a social study club and organized debates. During the time Walter was attending Wayne State his brother Victor who was studying economics and sociology at the college was his roommate.

Hired at Ford as a die maker for the Model A, Walter Reuther rose to the job of foreman at the Rouge plant before being fired in 1932 for again attempting to organize workers.

During the 1932 presidential election Walter Reuther campaigned for Socialist Party candidate Norman Thomas.

In 1933 Walter along with younger brother Victor left Detroit and began bicycling through Europe attempting to study labor conditions. The brothers went inside Nazi Germany, where they learned the cruel lesson that labor unions had become extinct under a dictatorship. They also went to France, then Walter worked for a time as a tool and die maker in Russia's famed Gorky automobile plant. Before returning to the U.S. the brothers made stops in India, China and Japan.

Upon his return to the U.S. Victor Reuther went to work on the assembly line at the Kelsey Hayes Wheel Company where in 1936 he helped organize West Detroit UAW Local 174 of the new automobile workers' union.

The year before Victor Reuther had become the leader of a sit-down strike using a tactic he and his brother Walter had observed in France and making Kelsey-Hayes one of the first plants to be struck in Detroit. The strike was successful and won union recognition and a wage increase at Kelsey-Hayes.

Meanwhile in 1935 Walther Reuther had met May Wolf a physical education teacher, modern dance enthusiast and a Socialist party activist. The two would be married in March 1936 and raise two daughters.

Reuther had joined Local 86 representing employees at GM's Terristadt plant. Soon he was elected to the UAW's National Executive Board and became a paid union representative. Then it wasn't long before he became president of UAW Local 174 which represented 30,000 workers and 76 shops. In late 1936 and early 1937 Reuther had played a key role in the sit-down strike at the GM plant in Flint, Michigan.

Ford Motor Company River Rouge Plant, Dearborn, Michigan. (Photo by Detroit Publishing Co., 1927)

Now Reuther was ready for the challenge of attempting to organize the Ford plant at the River Rouge. A Dearborn municipal ordinance mandated that the city clerk had to issue a permit for the distribution of literature or leaflets. So, the UAW applied for and was granted permission. The UAW intended to distribute leaflets that were entitled "Unionism not Fordism" to the 90,000 workers at the Ford River Rouge plant seeking to change the current 8-hour work day and $6.00 minimum wage to a 6 hour work day with a $8.00 minimum wage.

On May 26, 1937 UAW union leaders, organizers and several women arrived by streetcar at the Rouge plant. Walter Reuther, who was then president of the UAW West Side Local and union organizer Richard Frankensteen along with two other men, J. Kennedy and Robert Cantor, climbed up on an overpass near Gate 4 of the massive River Rouge plant to pass out leaflets as shifts changed. Dozens of women joined them and dozens of news reporters and photographers too.

At that time about fifty men, many in work clothes were loitering on the overpass which was located above a streetcar line. Henry Bennett, Ford's chief of security, sent his goons out on the overpass and ordered the UAW activists and their supporters to leave. Reuther refused yelling that he saw no reason why he and his party should get off the overpass. At that moment, all hell broke loose and eighteen minutes of hand-to-hand fighting ensued as Bennett's men with swinging fists assaulted Reuther and knocked Frankensteen to the ground and rushed the UAW party down the stairs to the streetcar tracks while kicking them and beating them to a bloody pulp.

On the street level several of the women who had accompanied Reuther and Frankensteen to the Rouge plant were also beaten while a Dearborn police officer watched. In all sixteen union members, including seven women were injured in the attack. In addition, near the plant eight additional UAW members were beaten by men wielding blackjacks.

Richard Frankensteen said later, "They bounced us down those concrete steps. They would knock us down, stand us up and knock us down again. It was worst licking I've ever taken."[3]

The incident was explicitly photographed by newsmen and the brutality of Ford's union-busting tactics shocked a depression-weary nation and brought national attention to Walter Reuther. "The Battle of the Overpass" as the incident became known was featured on the cover of *Time* magazine and led to charges against Ford by the National Labor Relations Board. Ford would eventually lose a challenge after an appeal to the U.S. Supreme Court.

Ford blamed the incident on the news media. An official statement issued by Ford stated "The demonstration on Wednesday against the Ford workmen on Ford property was staged by newspapers which, for the last six months, have demanded the production of a Ford strike story,' and by the UAW, which required some dramatic occurrence to cover its conspicuous failure to influence Ford employees."[4]

Walter Reuther who like Richard Frankensteen suffered severe bruises and cuts on his face alleged that the attack on them had been carried-out by thugs and mobsters employed by Harry Bennett's Ford service department to halt union organizing efforts.

Harry Bennett was an ex-boxer and sailor in the U.S. Navy who at the age of 24 in 1916 was employed by Ford. He took over operations of the service department at the Rouge plant in 1921 and remained in charge until 1945. It was Bennett's job to keep peace in the massive plant and to do it he hired associates with questionable backgrounds, even mob affiliations.

Henry Ford knowingly had connections to Detroit underworld figures. As Ford's fortune and public stature grew over the years, he became somewhat paranoid about needing protection for himself and his family to avoid being physically harmed or even kidnapped. To provide the perceived needed protection Ford developed ties with Detroit mafia figures such as Peter (Horseface Pete) Licavoli, Cesare (Big Chef) LaMare, Joseph (Joe the Baron) Tocco, Anthony (Tony Cars) D'Anna, Giuseppe (Joe Uno) Zerilli and Joe (Legs) Larnan.

Licavoli, head of the River Gang, LaMare, leader of the Westside Gang and Tocco the boss of the Downriver Gang operating out of Wyandotte, Michigan and Zerilli head of the Eastside Gang, were notorious Detroit bootlegging kingpins during prohibition. Cesare LaMare, a non-Italian was a specialist in kidnapping. During the 1920s Henry Ford occasionally socialized with LeMare.

Also, Detroit mafia don Salvatore (Singing Sam) Catalanotte had concessions contracts with The Ford Motor Company to provide food trucks at its auto plants.

The most notorious of the Detroit gangs the ultra-violent Purple Gang made up of Jewish mobsters was out of business by the end of prohibition through attrition as their members had all either been sent to jail or killed. Regardless, due to the gang's religious heritage Henry Ford would have never associated with them.

In 1930 Salvatore Catalanotte died from pneumonia. His death set off a mob war for control of the rackets in Detroit. During the struggle LeMare was killed by his own men inside his mansion. Zerilli and Tocco were ultimately the victors in the war and they proceeded to organize the modern-day Detroit mafia uniting all the city's gangs into a regional crime syndicate.

Joe Tocco had been a confidant of Henry Bennett and no doubt supplied some of the muscle for Ford Motor Company anti-union activities. In 1938 Joe Tocco was gunned down in front of his home. It was said that Tocco had been feuding with Tony D'Anna over Ford stock options. While D'Anna was suspected of ordering the hit on Tocco, he was never charged. Following the murder of Tocco, D'Anna became capo of Detroit's Downriver mob.

In April 1938 two masked gunmen invaded the home of local UAW head Walter Reuther in an attempt to abduct him. The kidnapping was foiled when one of Reuther's dinner guests escaped from the house and called the police for help. The attempted assailants were arrested. A trial followed with an acquittal for both men. One of the would-be kidnappers had provided security for the Ford Motor Company. While the prosecution believed the motive for the botched kidnapping had been retribution for Reuther's union activities at the Ford Motor Company, the jury had been packed with Ford supporters and the attorney for the defense charged that Walter Reuther had staged the event.

The botched kidnapping of Walter Reuther would not be the last attempt on his life. Ten years later in April 1948, would-be assassins fired shotgun blasts into his home at 20101 Annoline Avenue located in a quaint Detroit neighborhood as he went to the refrigerator to get a bowl of fruit salad. At the time his wife May was only a couple of steps ahead of him when the blast came roaring in shattering both the regular kitchen window and the storm window with an impact so strong it knocked Reuther down on the floor where he continued to lay until being taken to the hospital.

A neighbor, Helen O'Keefe, told police that she had seen a red Ford stop in front of the Reuther home and two men get out. A moment later she heard a shot and saw the two men run back to the car and drive away.

Reuther suffered chest and arm wounds and he never recovered the full use of his right arm and hand. No one was ever convicted of the crime.

A little over a year later on May 24, 1949 Victor Reuther who had gone on to play a central role in unionization of Ford was shot in the face by a shotgun blast while sitting in his living room. The attack caused him to lose sight in his right eye. As was the case with the attack on his brother Walter, no one was ever convicted of assault.

That same year there was an attempt to bomb the UAW headquarters in Detroit. Neither the Detroit Police Department nor the FBI under the direction of J. Edgar Hoover attempted to discover who the perpetrators were.

It would take four more years after The Battle of Overpass before the UAW was recognized at the Ford Motor Company. It would all begin with the firing of eight workers at the River Rouge plant on April 1, 1941. Suddenly rolling mill workers stopped production and then as word of the labor action spread through-out the Rouge other workers joined in. Outraged, nearly 50,000 workers at the plant joined a wildcat strike.

Meanwhile Ford security and about 1000 workers who were either long-time employees or loyal to Henry Ford stayed in the plant. Many of the workers were black men. Nonetheless in a show of solidarity outside the plant picket lines were formed that included both black and white workers.

The following day on April 2 a large group of black workers charged out of the plant and attacked the mostly white picket lines. Henry Ford claimed that the strike was basically a racial conflict as he attempted to mobilize the black community against the UAW.

Before 1935 only about 4% of the labor force in the automobile industry in Detroit was black. Most of those were hired by Ford in foundry and janitorial positions. Both Chrysler and GM did not hire black workers.

Henry Ford had a self-contradictory relationship with Detroit's black community going back many years. He used black churches in Detroit to assist him in recruiting black workers. Ford would make monetary contributions to various black churches on the condition that they promised not to allow their facilities to be used for union activities, such as representation rallies. If ministers supported Ford, he promised to hire parishioners for $5 per day—which at that time was a tidy sum considering what most black workers were being paid in other jobs. For ministers who refused to work with Ford they faced the possibility of losing their congregation to other churches that did.

The UAW had not always been a model of fairness in regard to black workers. In 1937 the UAW accepted the idea of a separate seniority list. But in the spring of 1941 Black ministers decided to support the UAW and went to the Rouge and made an appeal to the black workers still inside to leave. The NAACP joined in distributing 10,000 pro-union leaflets.

Then the NLRB ruled that there had to be a collective bargaining election at Ford within 45 days which surprised many, the usual timeline issued for an election by the NLRB was 60 days. But the Roosevelt administration was adamant in expressing its belief that Ford had violated the Wagner Act.

As the strike at the Rouge entered its second week, Henry Ford at the urging of both his son Edsel and wife Clara, capitulated and agreed to a union vote. The results were a resounding victory for the UAW as 97% of the workers voted for union representation. Henry Ford would not take part in the contract negotiations but stated that there would be no reprisals on strikers. On June 21, 1941 Harry Bennett signed the first contract for Ford with the UAW.

In 1935 Walter Chrysler retired as president of his namesake company but remained as chairman and CEO. He was succeeded as president by K. T. Keller who had first met Walter Chrysler in 1915 when he was working as a master mechanic at Buick. At the personal invitation of Chrysler, Keller had joined the company in 1926 as vice-president of manufacturing. Keller would remain president of Chrysler until 1950.

During 1937 The Chrysler Corporation which had experienced a sit-in strike would also be organized. At that time Chrysler workers were making 49 cents per hour. Two years later there would be another strike at Chrysler and when black workers attempted to cross a picket line fist fights broke out.

On May 26, 1938 the dynamic life of Walter Chrysler came to an abrupt halt when he had a stroke. Then on August 8 while he continued convalescing on Long Island, his beloved wife Della suffered a cerebral hemorrhage. She died a few hours later. Her passing left Walter over-whelmed with grief and he never recovered. Suddenly he was confined to a wheelchair. The tragic end for Walter came a little over two years later on August 18, 1940 when he had another stroke and died at the age of 65.

Franklin D. Roosevelt might have appeared outwardly as a jovial soul with his belly-whopping laughs and his family hour fireside chats to the American public on radio, but he was also a tough politician, one who rewarded his political friends and went after his political enemies' hell-bent on revenge.

To that end, in June, 1937, Alfred Sloan was in the headlines again when Treasury Department agents reported to a Congressional committee that he and his wife had avoided payment of $1,921,587 in income taxes over a three-year period between 1934 and 1936 through personal holding companies. Sloan was accused of moral fraud.

In the early 1930s a friend told Sloan that a man of his position ought to own a yacht. After some hesitation, he agreed and bought an elaborate 236-footer for $1 million. Sloan incorporated it and christened it *Rene*. Then he hired a crew of 43 at an annual cost of $119,609 and embarked on a few cruises But Alfred Sloan was hardly a sea-fairing man and he quickly became bored with cruising. Consequently, the yacht was virtually dry-docked until 1941 when Sloan sold it to the Maritime Commission for $175,000.

But by that point in time the Treasury Department was alleging that the Rene Corporation, a holding company that Sloan had set-up to buy and maintain the yacht was in fact a tax loop-hole scam.

President Roosevelt even sent a message to Congress and although he was not named, Alfred P. Sloan was clearly targeted. "All are alike in that failure to pay resulting in shifting the tax load to the shoulders of others less able to pay and in mulcting the Treasure of the Government's just due."[5]

While there was no Government charge that such a means of tax avoidance was illegal, Sloan was furious that his reputation had been challenged. He issued a statement categorically denying that he had ever sought to evade paying a just share of the tax burden. Sloan said that he and his wife had received income totaling $2,876,310 in 1936. Their Federal and state income taxes paid were $1,725,790, and the remainder-$1,150,520—was divided evenly between charity and themselves.

While no charges were ever filed by the government, the damage had been done as it gave the public a perception of Alfred Sloan being a money-grubbing automobile baron and an economic glutton in the middle of the Great Depression.

To counter-act the negativity caused by the Treasury Department allegations Sloan donated $10 million and created the Alfred P. Sloan Foundation with the intention of making it a research-based organization.

The first half of 1937 had been a wild ride for Alfred Sloan and a few months later, now 62-years old, he turned-over the company presidency of General Motors to William Knudsen, then became chairman of the board as Lamont du Pont stepped down.

During his tenure as president of GM (1923-1937) Alfred P. Sloan had built the company into one of the world's largest and well-known manufacturing enterprises. Under Sloan's leadership GM evolved from a group of loosely coordinated companies into a highly efficient centralized corporation. Even during seasonal lulls GM assembly plants continued manufacturing at a rapid pace producing 100,000 Chevrolets in the third quarter of 1928.

Alfred Sloan's modus operandi was simple; "I never give orders," he once said. "I sell my ideas to my associates if I can. I accept their judgment if they convince me, as they frequently do, that I am wrong. I prefer to appeal to the intelligence of a man rather than attempt to exercise authority over him."[6]

Sloan's formula for success was simple, "Get the facts. Recognize the equities of all concerned. Realize the necessity of doing a better job every day. Keep an open mind and work hard. The last is most important of all. There is no short cut."[7]

The market share of GM by the late 1930s had grown to 50%. Although there was a new administrative structure at GM with Alfred Sloan in the lead that was attempting to keep GM's market share at about 45% to avoid federal anti-trust action, the Roosevelt Administration continued to challenge the company's business practices.

In 1919 GM had created General Motors Acceptance Corporation (GMAC) a wholly owned subsidiary as a way to assist dealers in providing financing for car buyers.

On May 28, 1938 in South Bend, Indiana, the Justice Department successful sought and was granted a criminal indictment against not only GM, but Ford and Chrysler as well, charging each with illegally restraining trade by requiring their dealers to only provide financing through each of the manufacturer's controlled finance companies.

By November 7, 1938 Ford and Chrysler reached agreements with the Justice Department through consent decrees.

In regard to Ford and Chrysler a document from the *Congressional Quarterly (CQ)* archives states, "Both the Ford and Chrysler decrees forbid the manufacturers to advertise a particular finance company exclusively and limit their right to advertise any named finance company at all. The Chrysler decree requires the company, if it advertises any named finance agency, to advertise by name all finance companies which will furnish services which conform to the plan of financing considered most efficient in distributing the maximum number of automobiles. The Ford decree prohibits that company from advertising or endorsing any particular finance company by name. Its advertising is to be restricted to the recommendation of a plan of financing, leaving it to the finance companies themselves to compete in selling their own services on the basis of their individual merits."[8]

But William Knudsen and Alfred Sloan of General Motors and its subsidiary GMAC decided to fight on. On November 17, 1939 both were convicted of violating the Sherman anti-trust laws and fined $5,000.

At the end of World War Two Walter Reuther achieved equal media status with the big three auto barons Henry Ford, Alfred P. Sloan and the late Walter Chrysler when on December 3, 1945 he appeared on the cover of *Time* magazine.

In 1946 Walter Reuther would be elected national president of the UAW and serve until 1970. His younger brother Victor would be elected educational director and be the union's envoy on the international stage. The eldest of the Reuther brothers Roy would also be instrumental in the union's rise serving as the political representative and legislative director. During the span while the UAW was under Walter Reuther's leadership the union grew to 1.5 million members and became a force world-wide and in the Democrat party.

The attempt on Walter Reuther's life in 1948 would have far-reaching psychological effects. Marvin Miller who would become president of the Major League Baseball Players Association in the mid-1960s stated that several years before becoming the leader of the players association he had asked his wife what she thought about the possibility of him running for president of the United Steelworkers union. According to Miller, "She hated the idea. Or to be more accurate, she was scared to death, thinking, no doubt, about the attempted assassination in 1948 of Walter Reuther. She thought the potential for violence was greater than I admitted. And, she might have been right."[9]

In October 1968 Walter and Victor Reuther narrowly missed being killed in an airplane crash. The small private plane that they were flying into Washington, D.C. was making its approach at Dulles International Airport. The skies were clear, and the pilots realized that the plane was too low and the altimeter was malfunctioning. While they were forced to make a crash landing all on board were not injured. Victor Reuther would remain convinced until the day he died on June 4, 2004 at the age of 92 that the crash was not an accident.

On May 9, 1970 Walther Reuther and his wife May did die in a plane crash in northern Michigan. The Reuthers along with four others were about to land in their chartered Learjet in the fog and rain at Emmett County Airport near Peliston, Michigan. The plane was cleared for landing and broke through the scattered clouds at about 400 feet. But it was short of the runway and clipped treetops. The plane came down burning, crashing a mile and half southwest of the airport. The Reuthers were flying to a union recreation and educational center at Black Lake about 25 miles from Peliston.

8.

World War Two and the Auto Industry

In the late 1930s Alfred P. Sloan saw the second-world war on the horizon and began to ruminate on what it meant for General Motors. Sloan came to the conclusion that the entry of the U.S. into the conflict would mean uncertainty for GM, so he decided to stay on as CEO & Chairman of the Board longer than he had intended.

Sloan was cognizant of the fact of what was happening to the Jews under the leadership of Adolph Hitler and that his company had assisted re-arming Nazi Germany. In 1939 as Germany occupied Austria and Czechoslovakia GM was coming increasingly under attack from stockholders and non-stockholders alike. Most took a dim view of the Nazi's anti-Semitic doctrines.

By 1940 the GM Opel plant in Germany was being run under the direction of the economics ministry headed-up by Herman Goering and the Nazis made it nearly impossible to take profits out of the company's operations.

But prior to 1940 the Wehrmacht, the German military, had been GM's best customer in the country. Sales of trucks to the military yielded a greater per-truck profit than civilian sales—about 40% more. Therefore, GM highly preferred selling trucks to the military which seemed to be in constant need of more equipment as the Nazis prepared for war in Europe.

In 1935 in agreement with the German military GM agreed to construct a new truck factory in Bradenburg where it would be strategically less vulnerable to possible aerial bombardment by those countries Germany was secretly mobilizing against such as Great Britain, France and the Soviet Union.

According to a report by the Jewish Telegraph Agency (JTA), GM's sales figure to the Wehrmacht was increased to 29% in 1938—totaling 6,000 Blitz trucks. "Expanding the German workforce from 17,000 in 1934 to 27,000 in 1938 also made GM one of Germany's leading employers. Unquestionably, GM's Opel had become an integral part of Hitler's Reich."[1]

Meanwhile Adolph Berle, Assistant Secretary of State in the Roosevelt administration, was starting to pressure Alfred Sloan and GM to focus on a pro-American agenda. Berle wanted Sloan to sever relationships with various Latin American auto dealers that were reported to be Nazi sympathizers. This caused Sloan to go ballistic! He openly professed that it was not the responsibility of GM to police the political feelings of people in various countries.

Still some friends attempted to warn Sloan that if he did not capitulate with the wishes of the State Department, he and GM might be branded Nazi sympathizers.

Adolph Berle was smitten by what he perceived as arrogance by Alfred Sloan and his response was to have the FBI investigate various GM executives including James D. Mooney, Graeme K. Howard and Alfred Sloan.

Several of Sloan's colleagues were interviewed during the investigation and all categorically stated that the GM boss was indeed patriotic and that was the bottom line in the final FBI report issued to J. Edgar Hoover on September 5, 1941.

As for Mooney and Howard, while James Mooney was running the GM Opel operations in Germany he had been advised by Alfred Sloan to be cordial with the host country. Some government officials in the United States believed that Mooney had been more than courteous, even chummy with the Nazis. From time-to-time on visits back to the States, Mooney had given briefings to President Roosevelt. But Harry Hopkins, one of Roosevelt's closest advisers, believed that Mooney was a Nazi appeaser and cut-off his contact with the White House.

Then there was the incident of James Mooney having received the Merit Cross of the German Eagle, First Class on August 10, 1938 for his work that the Nazis appreciated in his running of the operations at GM's Opel plant

The medal that Mooney had received was the same Nazi medal that had been bestowed on aviator Charles Lindbergh and Henry Ford that would continue to cast a shadow on their legacies as American patriots.

In fact, prior to World War Two the CIO had threatened a campaign against Henry Ford due to the fact that he had received the Merit Cross of the

German Eagle from Hitler complaining to the U.S. Government that Ford had $55 million in defense contracts. To defuse the tension, the government in a token gesture took away one contract from Ford.

The day after Adolf Hitler occupied the Sudetenland by way of the Munich Agreement, Charles Lindbergh began an eighteen day visit to Germany. (October 11—29, 1938). During this visit Lindbergh would be subjected to one of most controversial political events involving a private citizen in American history.

On the evening of October 18, 1938, at the invitation of Ambassador Hugh Wilson, Lindbergh attended a Stag dinner held at the American Embassy in Berlin. Guests included, German Air Marshall and Nazi party leader, Hermann Goering, German Field Marshall, Ehard Milch, both who would later be tried for war crimes by the U. S. Military Tribunal at Nuremberg, General Ernst Udet, who had been the 2nd highest German flying Ace in World War One, the Italian Ambassador, the Belgian Ambassador, and several American military officers, including Colonel Truman Smith. Also in attendance were noted German aeronautical pioneers, Dr. Ernst Heinkel, who had founded the Heinkel-Flugzeugwerke bomber factory in 1929 and Dr. Willy E. Messerschmitt, the chief aviation designer and director of Heinkel-Flugzeugwerke. In addition, Adolf Baeumaker, chief of the German Air ministry research division was in attendance.

Although it was not known to Lindbergh, part of Ambassador Wilson's agenda for the dinner was to get Hermann Goering to support some of the U. S. State Department's concerns for easing the financial plight of the large number of Jews who were being driven out of Germany in a penniless condition by the Nazis.

Hermann Goering was the last of the guests to arrive that evening. Later Lindbergh remarked that when Goering arrived, he was standing in the back of the room. He noticed that Goering had a red box and some papers in his hand. After shaking hands with everyone, he approached Lindbergh. Goering shook hands with Lindbergh, then handed him the red box and papers, and spoke a few sentences in German. To Lindbergh's surprise he was informed by his interpreter that, by order of Adolf Hitler, *der Fuhrer*, he had just been presented with the *(Verdienstkreuz Deutscher Adler)* the Grand Service Cross of the Supreme Order of the German Eagle, the highest of German civilian decorations given to foreigners. Inside the red box was a golden cross with four small swastikas finished in white enamel. The accompanying proclamation on parchment was signed by Adolf Hitler.

Previously, Henry Ford who had been selling his custom-designed three-ton V-8 trucks to Germany received the medal from Hitler through the German consul in Cleveland, Karl Kapp, at his 75th birthday dinner in Detroit on July 30, 1938.

At the moment, the award given to him by Goering didn't faze Lindbergh. After all, for years following the *Spirit of St. Louis* flight, he had been collecting medals at a furious rate from countries all over the world from France, England, and Belgium to Japan to Guatemala and in- between. In fact, in its edition of September 21, 1941, the *Chicago Daily Tribune* printed a page displaying 28 of the 118 medals conferred on Lindbergh by the nations of the world that were currently on display in St. Louis. A reprint of the page was offered as a wall poster to Lindbergh fans for $1.50.

That night Lindbergh's wife Anne urged him to return the medal. However, Charles felt to do so would be cause for an international incident. He was convinced that Germany was simply playing catch-up in recognizing the achievement of his 1927 solo, trans-Atlantic flight with the award of the medal.

At first there was little mention of Lindbergh receiving the German Eagle in the American Press and he never wore it. However as Lindbergh's anti-war activities increased, not only would the medal from Goering become an everlasting albatross on his legacy, but it would also become a *cause-celebre* for his critics to question his patriotism and allegiance to the United States—even by the Roosevelt administration.

As World War Two began the U.S. Government was becoming increasingly anxious about the German's using their blitzkrieg tactics as they continued to occupy more and more of Europe. Former GM executive John Pratt who was now working for the U.S. Government asked Alfred Sloan to give GM's full support to the government. Pratt requested that Sloan not retool GM's auto plants for 1941 models and wait to see if they would be needed for war materials production.

Sloan ignored Pratt's requests. Looking at the success of the Nazis and the collapse of the countries they had over-run, Sloan was of the opinion that the war in Europe could soon to be over and that the U.S. would not be a combatant in the conflict.

In May 1940 GM President William Knudsen stepped down from his position to aide his native Denmark which had fallen under Nazi control.

Then President Franklin D. Roosevelt called Knudsen and asked him to come to Washington and head-up the industrial war mobilization. Before accepting Knudsen decided to speak with Alfred Sloan. It was a fact that Sloan while preparing for the war effort that GM would eventually have to make hated to see any GM executives working for the government or more plainly stated, in the Roosevelt Administration.

William Knudsen stated in his 1947 biography *Knudsen—A Biography* by Norman Beasley, that when he spoke with Alfred Sloan, he told him to decline Roosevelt's request because he was sure they would make a monkey out of him in Washington.

But Knudsen's values came to the fore and he decided that due to the fact that he had come to the United States with nothing and the country had been so good to him, he felt obligated to answer the president's call to duty.

As it turned—out Alfred Sloan was 100% right—William Knudsen would be treated shabbily by the Roosevelt Administration. In January 1942, without notice, William Knudsen was suddenly removed from his post. No one in the Roosevelt Administration had even bothered to inform him and he found-out about his dismissal on a news ticker. Deeply hurt by his dismissal, Knudsen continued to support the war effort by becoming a trouble-shooter for the U.S. Army with the rank of general.

In 1940 Alfred Sloan, now 65-years old, had planned to step-down as the CEO of GM. When William Knudsen left the company to go to Washington, Sloan had promoted Charles E. Wilson, casually referred to as "the engine" to the position of president. But with the uncertainty of war still looming, Sloan decided to stay on.

Charles Wilson would become a driving force in taking General Motors through the war and into the 1950s. Wilson was born in the Cleveland suburb of Minerva, Ohio on July 18, 1890. When he was 14 years old his family moved to Pittsburgh where Wilson would graduate from the Carnegie Mellon College in 1909. After graduating college, he joined Westinghouse Electric. During World Wat One he was in charge of designing and development of the Westinghouse radio generators and dynamotors for the U.S. Army and U.S. Navy.

Following the war Charles Wilson would join General Motors in April 1919. He would become Chief Engineer of the Remy Electric Company a GM subsidiary.

In 1926 when the Dayton Engineering Laboratories Company was added to the Remy Electric Company, Wilson was appointed as president and general manager of the newly organized Delco-Remy Corporation. At that time the company had about 12,000 employees.

Over the next two years Delco-Remy, under Wilson's direction would develop Lovejoy shock absorbers, industrial motors for refrigeration and washing machines, automobile lamps and Delco batteries. By the end of 1928 Delco-Remy was operating in four cities. The company's manufacturing operations for the production of electrical equipment for motorcars was concentrated in Anderson, Indiana; shock absorbers and industrial motors were built in Dayton, Ohio; automobile lamps in Anderson, Indiana and Cleveland, Ohio and Delco batteries in Muncie, Indiana.

In January 1929, Charles "the engine" Wilson was named assistant to the president of GM and was transferred to Detroit. In May 1929, he was made a vice president of General Motors. Wilson chain-smoked Chesterfields and often didn't realize that ash had fallen on his lap. In its cover story on January 24, 1949 *Time* magazine described Wilson as a "reserved blue-eyed boss who thinks fast, talks slow and never wastes time pounding on the desk."

While Detroit would become known as the Arsenal of Democracy during World War Two, Alfred Sloan had very little to do with the conversion of GM to war production. Sloan concentrated on planning for the post-war agenda of the company to regain its prominence in the automotive industry and associated products, both domestically and internationally. He had been concerned that GM building war materials would not be as profitable as automobiles or consumer products. Sloan was also concerned it might also hurt brand loyalty and the conversion of GM manufacturing facilities to making war materials would be a massive and expensive time-consuming task.

All the nonsense going on in Washington and Detroit stopped abruptly on December 7, 1941 with the Japanese attack on Pearl Harbor and the United States entry into World War Two. America's entry into World War Two quickly led to rationing of rubber, gasoline and steel, so automobile production was limited to military vehicles. Only replacement parts for private cars were allowed to be reproduced. Suddenly, auto manufacturers found materials unavailable and were forced to cut production schedules.

Right after Pearl Harbor GM President Charles Wilson lobbied in Washington to continue to manufacture automobiles but was turned down by of all people William Knudsen at the Office of Production and Management. In February 1942, all civilian automobile production officially stopped. Going forward all auto manufactures would be totally engaged in the production of war materials.

At Chrysler production was immediately curtailed and only 5.292 cars were produced in the 1942 calendar year.

GM under the direction of Charles Wilson converted its automotive plants to the manufacture of armaments. A total of 102 plants were involved, and from February 1942, to September, 1945, no automobiles were produced. The GM war manufacturing effort led by Charles Wilson was massive. The company produced enormous numbers of tanks, airplane engines, machine guns, armored vehicles and diesel-powered trucks for use by the U.S. Army and Navy. The Buick division under the direction Harlow Curtice built the M-18 Hellcat Tank Destroyer for the Army, the first mobile Allied weapon to prove a match for heavy German Tanks. By 1945 GM had produced one quarter of all tanks manufactured for use by U.S. Forces.

To accomplish the mammoth task GM spent $900 million building plants between 1940 and 1944 that were mostly paid for by the government. While GM did make a profit during World War Two of $673 million, that was a pittance of its pre-war profits.

Doing his part Alfred Sloan all during the war kept the public informed of what GM was doing by carrying-on a huge advertising campaign. Each ad carried the GM slogan "Victory is our business."

The rationing of such automotive essentials as gas, tires and steel so only military vehicles could be produced was a hardship for the country. But there was a great sense of sacrifice on the home front. People planted victory gardens Metal drives were held in cities all over the country. The Boy Scouts of America ran a well-managed scrap campaign collecting hundreds of tons of metal left at gas station depots. People brought anything metal they had at home, such as tin cans, pots, and car parts, to be melted down to make steel for the war materials. In Cincinnati the management of the Shillito's department store donated its 10-ton metal marquee to scrap.

There were no official governmental travel restrictions during World War Two. While the movement of essential war related passengers and war materials made it difficult for people to travel thousands of miles for recreation and tourism, they still did. The National Parks including Yosemite, the Great Smoky Mountains and the Grand Canyon remained open, workers still took vacations. In 1944 Mt. Rushmore situated in the middle of the country attracted 29,575 visitors. Some came by car and others by bus. The military also used the National Parks for various training and rest and recreation of troops.

The national importance of the Pennsylvania Turnpike other than being an efficient road for cars and trucks across the state came to the fore during World War Two when it became a high speed artery linking major industrial areas necessary for the movement of men and supplies for America's war effort.

During World War Two Route 66 would become a major artery for conveys of military supplies and troops. Because of the isolated location of most of the highway new military bases were constructed along Route 66, even a POW camp was built at McLean, Texas.

Lyricist Bobby Troup and his first wife Cynthia (Troup was later married to singer Julie London) were living in Lancaster, Pennsylvania at the end of World Two. Troup decided that if he were going to make it big as a songwriter then he would have to move to Los Angeles. So, Troup and his wife set out for California and as they traveled over Route 66 he began to write down various rhymes in regard to the highway. Upon reaching LA Troupe turned his rhymes into lyrics and wrote the music to "Route 66." He soon sold the song to Capital Records and later in 1946 it was recorded by Nat King Cole and became a huge hit.

Since then "Route 66" has been covered by dozens of artists in almost every popular musical genre including artists such as Asleep at the Wheel, Bing Crosby, Perry Como, The Manhattan Transfer, Harry James, the Four Freshman and the Rolling Stones.

Following World War One and into the early 1920s the focus for airplanes had been for military use and stunt flyers. Still the possibility of travel by air was being discussed by promoters and skeptics alike. It was in 1925 that air travel received a huge boost with the start of the Airplane Reliability Tours sponsored by the Detroit Chamber of Commerce. The mission of the tours was to prove that travel by air was safe. That year a tour involving sixteen planes completed a 1775-mile test that began at Ford Airport in Detroit. Eleven of the planes completed the tour.

In 1926 Henry Ford attempted to enter the new air transportation market. Along with William B. Stout who started one of the first regularly scheduled airlines, Ford developed the Tri-Motor airplane.

Then the interest in air travel became very popular following Charles Lindbergh's historic non-stop trans-Atlantic flight from Long Island, New York to Paris, France on May 20, 1927.

Henry Ford had first met Charles Lindbergh shortly after his trans-Atlantic flight. On August 11, 1927, Lindbergh making a three-month goodwill tour landed in Detroit, the city of his birth. There at Ford Airport to greet him was 64-year-old Henry Ford. After showing Ford the *Spirit of St. Louis*, Lindbergh took him up in the air for his first flight in an airplane. The flight lasted ten minutes, after which Lindbergh took off again, this time with Edsel Ford in the cockpit for another ten-minute flight. Although he manufactured tri-motor planes, Henry Ford refused to be flown in his own product, so it was surprising that he consented to go up in the air with Lindbergh. Before leaving Detroit, Lindbergh took a very nervous Ford and few of his officers for a ride in one of the Ford Motor Company's planes.

Nonetheless by 1931 after building about 100 Trimotors, Henry Ford lost interest in aviation and ceased production.

Now the U.S. was fighting World War Two and Henry Ford began to produce military aircraft. In 1941 Ford had begun construction of a huge mile long bomber plant at Willow Run for the purpose of manufacturing the Liberator B-24 four-engine bomber. Critics of Ford dubbed his new plant "Will-It-Run."

The Liberator B-24 bomber powered by four Pratt & Whitney twin R1830 WASP 14-cylinder radial engines had a maximum speed of 303 M.P.H. and a service ceiling of about 28,000 feet. It accommodated a crew of seven, had 11 machine guns and could carry a bomb load of 8000 pounds. It was a long-range bomber with a combat radius of 2,100 miles.

The Willow Run plant cost $165 million to build and had 70 assembly lines. Dormitories were constructed on site and a commuter line was expanded to the plant. It was Henry Ford's goal when production began in 1942 that with an estimated 100,000 workers the plant could produce one plane per hour. The actual production numbers were a little less. By mid-1943 there were 42,000 workers at Willow Run turning-out 230 B-24s a month. By the end of 1944 production increased to 650 planes per month.

Henry Ford, with the advice and consent of Harry Bennett, hired Charles Lindbergh to work as an advisor at Willow Run. Lindbergh due to his pre-war activities in opposing America's entry into a war against Germany while heading-up the America First Committee had been in disfavor with both President Roosevelt and the War Department. As a result, Lindbergh was denied employment by several aircraft manufacturers. But Henry Ford's hatred of Franklin Roosevelt was well known and he didn't care what the president or his administration thought about Lindbergh and put his expertise to work flight testing bombers and serving as a liaison between production employees and flights crews.

Production B-24E (Liberator) Bombers at Willow Run, (L) Joseph Clark Grew, Ambassador to Japan 1932–1941, (R) Edsel Ford. (Courtesy of The Library of Congress)

Within two days of arriving in Detroit, Charles Lindbergh was back where he had longed to be—in the cockpit of an aircraft. At Willow Run he went for an hour's test flight in one of the B-24-C planes built by Consolidated in San Diego. Upon landing, Lindbergh reported to Henry Ford that, there were many improvements that could and would be made before American fliers were sent to fight in the planes. Lindbergh would serve at Ford as a technical adviser and test pilot until 1944, being compensated at the rate of $666.66 per month. The amount was equivalent to the amount Lindbergh would have made serving as a Colonel in the U. S. Army Air Corps.

The U.S. Government was suspicious of Charles Lindbergh even before he was employed at Ford. In 1940, FBI Director J. Edgar j. Hoover sent one of his top chiefs John S. Bugas out to Detroit to investigate reports that someone in the War Department had been leaking classified information to Lindbergh. When Bugas interviewed Henry Ford he simply told him that when Lindbergh visited with him, they only talked about Jews.

The heavy demand for war materials brought a demand for additional workers to produce them. While many women moved out of the home and into the industrial plants of Detroit to fill the void left by the large number of men called to service in the military, large numbers of southern Afro-Americans started arriving in the city to also assist in the war effort. Suddenly there was racial tension in Detroit.

More than 50,000 Afro-American families quickly arrived in Detroit putting enormous pressure on the housing market. The first incident occurred in February 1942 when black families began to move into the Sojourner Truth housing project in the predominately Polish, all-white North Detroit area. The white residents quickly organized and resisted the influx of blacks in the area necessitating the mobilization of State troopers and local police to quell the disturbance.

Some of the racial tension had been caused by white dissatisfaction with Federal regulations of the Roosevelt administration requiring the hiring of blacks and other minorities in plants with government contracts resulting in several walkouts by white employees in automobile plants after blacks were put in upgraded positions.

Tensions continued to rise in the city and finally on a hot summer Sunday afternoon, June 20, 1943, the roof blew off as trouble started on Belle Isle, a recreation spot used predominately by blacks, but also by some whites.

The trouble on Belle Isle spilled over the bridge onto Jefferson Avenue. As fist fights escalated, rumors spread, and rioting began to spread through-out Detroit. Looting began in the predominately black area of Paradise Valley, latter it spread to other sections of the city. Then whites began attacking blacks as they left the city's all-night movie theaters in the downtown area. When whites attempted to enter black residential areas by car they were met by gunfire.

Finally, U.S. Troops were called in. When it was all over 34 people had been killed, 25 of them Afro-American, 9 were white, hundreds more had been injured, 1,800 were arrested and property damage was $2 million leaving an ugly aura of fear and hate to prevail over the city.

Detroit wasn't the only city to experience race riots during World War Two, similar disturbances had broken out in Los Angeles, Mobile, Alabama and Beaumont, Texas, but the riot in Detroit was by far the most destructive.

On May 26, 1943 Edsel Ford died at his home at Gaukler Pointe. Edsel, just 49 years old, died of undulant fever, a recurring fever also known as Malta fever. The disease is associated with transmission through milk. Henry convinced that unpasteurized milk would cure Edsel badgered him to drink it. At the time of his death Edsel had been ailing for more than a year. He had undergone surgery for stomach ulcers in January 1942 then recuperated in Florida for ten weeks, but failed to regain full strength.

In April after returning to Dearborn from Florida, Edsel although frail and weak, took on his father in a very bitter argument over an issue involving Harry Bennett. While Edsel was in Florida Bennett had fired A.W. Wibel a Ford employee who started as a machinist in 1912 and worked his way up to a vice president of purchasing position. The central issue in the argument between Edsel and Henry was a contract that Bennett had given to one of his cronies and that Wibel refused to honor.

As usual, Henry stood by his man Bennett and ignored the loud protests of Edsel about the Wibel firing. Henry even went a step further and told vice president Charles Sorenson that it was absolutely necessary for Edsel to change his attitude towards Bennett and furthermore it was to be known, despite how Edsel might feel, that Harry Bennett was in full charge of all labor relations issues and that he was in full accord with him.

The doctors at Ford Hospital thought another operation would be beneficial to Edsel but none of them wanted to perform the procedure because of Henry. Therefore an outsider was brought in to operate on Edsel. When Edsel was opened up it was apparent that he had stomach cancer, so he was quickly sewn back up and diagnosed as terminal.

Henry went into a rage! Convinced that Edsel's drinking had been the cause of his illness, he had Harry Bennett drive him out to Edsel's home at Gaukler Pointe where he entered the house and proceeded to channel Carrie Nation by smashing every bottle of liquor he could find.

A few days later a simple service for Edsel Ford was held at Christ Church at Grosse Pointe. There was no eulogy and there were no honorary pall bearers. He lay in state in a plain coffin between a couple of clusters of roses and a large circle of gardenias sent by Local 600 of the UAW.

The entire Ford family was discombobulated and divided by the death of Edsel. Benson Ford, the second oldest of Edsel's children blamed his grandfather Henry for his father's death and proclaimed that he wanted nothing more to do with him. Henry Ford II, the Edsel's oldest son at first blamed the doctors at Ford Hospital for the demise of his father, then soon after came to the conclusion that Edsel had died as a result of all the turmoil that his grandfather had put him through.

Henry II was also thinking about the fact he might soon be cast into a position in the family business where he would now have to confront the power of Harry Bennett. Eleanor his wife was concerned that with the death of Edsel, that his grandfather might make Bennett the next president of The Ford Motor Company.

The death of Edsel Ford who had been a popular executive left a huge void in the operations of Ford Motor Company and its war effort. The Roosevelt administration was so worried about the gap in leadership relative to the company's war production that it seriously considered nationalizing The Ford Motor Company. Suddenly the company was left without a president, treasurer and nominal general manager. Henry Ford had turned the title of president over to Edsel in 1919, now he was nearing his 80th birthday in July and while remaining on the board of directors made it well-known that he wanted no title with the company.

Edsel and his wife, the former Eleanor Lowthian Clay, had three sons by their marriage. Currently all three were serving in the U.S. Military. Lieutenant Henry Ford II was serving with the U.S. Navy as an instructor at the Great Lakes Naval Training Station, Private Benson Ford was in the officer's candidate training with the U. S. Army and William Ford was a naval cadet after just graduating from Hotchkiss.

Danish born board member and vice president Charles E. Sorenson who was now 61 years old had been the builder of many of Henry Ford's ideas. It was actually Sorenson who had originated the moving assembly line for mass production of automobiles and then adapted it to building bomber planes at Willow Run that he was overseeing.

Henry Ford and Charles Sorenson met to discuss the void left by the death of Edsel and they came to the conclusion that B. J. Craig who had been filling-in as treasurer should continue in that position and Henry should return as president for the duration of the war. To assist Ford, his 29-year old grandson Henry Ford II was discharged from the Navy.

The rest of the aircraft industry had opposed Ford entering aviation and had expressed their dissatisfaction to the War Department. They were skeptical about the company's ability to deliver high quality aircraft and hoped that their production schedule could not be met. But by 1945 Ford would produce an astounding 8000 Liberator B-24 bombers.

The Liberator B-24 was used by both the Royal Airforce and the United States Army Air Corp. to pound Nazi controlled targets in North Africa and across Europe, including oil fields in Romania. Furthermore, the B-24 played a large part in neutralizing Germany's U-boat threat in the North Atlantic as the planes were responsible for sinking 93 U-boats. The plane also was used to wreak havoc on Japanese shipping in the Pacific. However the B-24 was not particularly popular with crews who dubbed it the "flying coffin' due to the fact that it had one exit near the tail that made it difficult to escape a crippled aircraft.

Both Ford and Willys-Overland produced the most iconic American World War Two vehicle manufacturing 649,000 Jeeps. A total of 631,873 were delivered for military use with 51,000 Jeeps being sent to the Soviet Union. The word Jeep is said to be derived from combining two factors. The first, the code letters GP, the G meaning Government and the P which is a code letter meaning '80 inch wheelbase reconnaissance car' the name that was given to the Ford prototype and later adopted by Willys as their trademark. When these two are slurred together the letters GP tend to sound like 'Jeep.'

The Ford plant at Cologne, Germany had been seized by the Nazis during the war. In consideration of the damage to the Ford plant at Cologne as a result of Allied bombing, following the war Ford was paid $1.1 million by the U.S. Government.

Controversy involving the Ford plant in Cologne, Germany would come to the fore more than fifty years after the war had ended when on March 4, 1998, Elsa Iwanowa would file a suit in U.S. District Court in Newark, New Jersey (*Iwanowa v. Ford Motor Company, et al, New Jersey District Court, case No. 2:98-cv-00959*) on behalf of thousands forced to perform slave labor by the Nazis in building trucks at the factory between 1941 and 1945.

Although it has not been substantiated it has been historically alleged that Ford Motor Company (USA) owned from 55 to 90% of the shares of its subsidiary Ford Werke A.G. during 1933 to 1945. Furthermore, that Edsel Ford and Robert Sorenson high-ranking officials of Ford Motor Company, served as directors of Ford Werke A.G. throughout the Nazi Third Reich.

"The lawsuit filed by Iwanowa alleged the company made immense profits providing the German army with tracked vehicles and other trucks. This was because it worked at peak capacity for many years and did not have to pay wages to many of its workers. Unlike most American facilities in Germany, Ford was not taken over by the German government during the war."[2]

Elsa Iwanowa, who was 16-years old at the time, stated that she was one of the slave workers subjected to inhuman conditions at the Cologne Ford plant during the war and was seeking reasonable payment for her work performed.

The Ford Motor Company has stated that it categorically did not control operations at the Cologne plant during the war.

At trial Ford moved to dismiss Iwanowa's claim under the law of motions based on lack of subject matter jurisdiction, failure to state a claim and expiration of the applicable limitations period.[3]

On October 28, 1999 the suit against Ford was dismissed in its entirety, with prejudice.

Regardless of the controversy that surrounded Henry Ford, Edsel Ford and The Ford Motor Company, the company's war effort for the U.S. and its Allies was huge and its plants ran at the same pace in manufacturing war equipment as they had in peacetime production.

The Chrysler Corporation, led by J. T. Keller who had followed the late Walter Chrysler as president, also made significant contributions to the war effort. Keller had begun his automotive career as a general master mechanic with GM in 1911 and worked his way up to the position of vice president of Chevrolet in 1921 before joining Chrysler.

Chrysler was actually producing war materials before the entry of the U.S. into the conflict. In the spring of 1940 Chrysler began producing war materials for Great Britain, France and the Soviet Union.

Then during late summer 1940 Chrysler received a contract with the Department of Defense for $54.5 million to construct and provide staff for a plant to build tanks. Chrysler constructed the Detroit Tank Arsenal and by 1941 had already built 729 2-ton General Grant M-3 tanks. Chrysler would also produce the 32-ton Sherman M-4-A-4 tank between 1942 and 1945 that would be the primary combat vehicle of U.S. Ground Forces in World War Two. Overall, Chrysler would produce 25,000 tanks during the war.

Chrysler had also been extremely productive in building aircraft during the war. At their Chicago Dodge plant Chrysler built 18,413, 2200 hp Wright Cyclone 9-cyclinder radial engines for the Boeing B-29 Superfortress. On August 6, 1945 a B-29 Superfortress named the Enola Gay dropped the first U.S. atomic bomb "Little Boy" on the Japanese city of Hiroshima killing 140,000 people.

Chrysler also built 60,000 highly efficient 40 mm SCR584 radar-guided anti-aircraft guns. The weapon was so effective that it knocked down 96% of the German rockets launched to attack London. They were often referred to as Pom-Pom guns because of their alternating firing pattern.

The most famous of the war materials manufactured by Chrysler was the Dodge truck. At the beginning of the war Dodge trucks had a civilian reputation of running well over time without needing repairs. Both GM and Ford trucks and in particular, those with the Chevrolet 216 six cylinder "stave bolt" overhead valve engines had a tendency to break down.

The U.S. Army had brought all three makes, Dodge, GM and Ford, to Europe following D-day to provide supply efforts as American forces drove the Nazis out of France and beyond. Trucks were necessary for the logistics of getting food, fuel and ammunition to the front lines as allied bombers had destroyed all the French rail lines.

All the supply trucks in the rear areas were being run on low octane fuel because the high-octane fuel was diverted for aircraft. Consequently, GM and Ford trucks were breaking down with burnt-out valves; maintenance depots were filled with them and replacement parts were hard to get. But the Dodge trucks with flat head engines kept working and some lasted through-out the entire war without a rebuild.

General George C. Patton was using the Dodge trucks to resupply the 3rd Army. To expedite the resupply effort Patton had a large 12-inch bright red circle painted on the trucks and told his military police to give the trucks clearance on any road leading to the front. The convoys became known as the Red Ball Express. So swift and efficient were the Red Ball Express Dodge trucks that General Dwight Eisenhower told General Omar Bradley to slow down Patton's logistics so that they did not cause an embarrassment to the forces being led by British Field Marshall Bernard Montgomery.

The total war production by Chrysler was enormous. In total during the war Chrysler, including the Dodge, Plymouth and DeSoto divisions, produced 438,000 various sized army trucks, 18,000 engines for the B-29 Superfortress, 60,000 Bofors anti-aircraft guns, 1,000 railroad cars of precision machinery for the gaseous diffusion plant at the atomic bomb project at Oak Ridge, Tennessee, 3.25-billion rounds of small arms ammunition, 100 miles of submarine nets, 1,500 searchlight reflectors, 7,800 Sea mule tractors and tugs, 29,000 marine engines, 328,00 explosive rockets, 101,000 incendiary bombs, 1.99 million 20-mm shells, 20,000 land mine detectors and other implements of war.

Henry Ford had returned to take over the executive duties at Ford after Edsel's death, although a lot of the crucial decisions were made by Harry Bennett using a smoke screen by stating that he had discussed matters with Mr. Ford and this is how he wanted things done.

Following the war, The Ford Motor Company found itself in trouble—the company needed new leadership. The suggested appointment of Henry Ford II as president of The Ford Motor Company was a bitter pill for the elder Henry to swallow. He was afraid that if he gave his grandson complete authority to run the company that his friend Harry Bennett's days would be numbered. So, he resisted.

It took Clara Ford, the elder Henry's wife and Eleanor, Edsel's widow to make it all happen. Clara told Henry that if he didn't appoint Henry II the president and give him full authority it would further divide the family. Then Eleanor laid the knock-out punch on Henry when she announced that if her son was not appointed president with full authority, she would sell her 41% stock interest in Ford she had inherited from Edsel. Although smitten, immediately Henry Ford called a board meeting the next day. Henry Ford II was appointed president on September 21, 1945. Benson Ford still angry with his grandfather over the death of his father declined to attend the meeting.

Henry Ford II had a completely different personality than his teetotaler, tight-fisted, anti-Semitic grandfather and that of his introspective, even-tempered father who preferred to hobnob exclusively with the upper crust residents of Grosse Pointe. Henry II was impulsive in his business decisions, had nothing against raising a glass or two or more of booze and had a tendency to mix with a wider spectrum of society both in his business relationships and socially.

Bobby Lane the Detroit Lions Hall of Fame quarterback in the 1950s stated that once after a pre-season game he and linebacker Joe Schmidt and a few others went out for some after game drinks. After settling-in at a café and ordering a round of drinks, Lane recognized a portly gentleman sitting at the end of the bar alone. It was Henry Ford II. Lane went over and asked him to join his party and without hesitation Henry II immediately joined in the merry-making.

Henry Ford II inherited a company that was surprisingly near bankruptcy losing nearly $10 million a month and using faulty bookkeeping practices. His grandfather had never been much of a bookkeeper and often jotted down figures on the backs of envelopes.

It was Henry Ford II's task to rebuild the company. He gave the order to fire Harry Bennett but did not actually carry-out the act. That was left to John S. Bugas.

Edsel Ford had got to know John Bugas in 1941 after he had contacted him about a theft ring inside Ford that was taking millions of dollars of the company's properties each year. Some of Harry Bennett's cronies were suspects. Eventually Bugas would be hired as director of industrial relations by Edsel, although Harry Bennett took credit for the hiring. Bugas soon was witness to the turmoil at Ford and becoming aware of the struggle that young Henry Ford II was about to encounter, and he became extremely loyal to him.

On the morning that Henry Ford II told John Bugas to fire Harry Bennett, before going to his office to issue the order he put a .38 caliber pistol in his belt. As he entered the office Bennett pulled a .45 pistol out of his desk and shouted an obscenity at Bugas. The former FBI man retained his cool and told Bennett that if he pulled the trigger, he would put a bullet right through his heart. Bennett was informed of his termination and told to leave the premises. Bugas then left the office. For the next few hours Harry Bennett burned his personal papers and by the end of the day was gone.

Henry Ford II then hired many Harvard Business School graduates with M.B.A. degrees to clean-up the mess and implement sweeping changes by the introduction of modern management principles into the company's operations.

It was also a stroke of luck for Henry II that a group of talented men would seek him out. A group of ten Army Air Corps officers sent Henry II a telegram requesting a meeting. During the war all of them had worked together running the Air Corps office of Statistical Control and now they wanted to continue working as a team.

The leader of the ten was Colonel Charles (Tex) Thornton who told Ford that they could improve cost efficiency in the company just like they had for the Army Air Corps. None of the men had any experience in the automobile industry, but Ford agreed to hire them.

The ten would become known at Ford as the "whiz kids" and two of them, Robert McNamara and Arjay Miller would eventually become presidents of The Ford Motor Company.

To stabilize the company financially Henry Ford II hired Ernie Breech an accountant with 23 years' experience at General Motors. Subsequently, Breech was able to convince several talented GM engineers like Del Younger and Lewis Crusoe, who had worked at GM's Fisher Body for 32 years, to accompany him to Ford.

Charles Wilson actually endorsed the departure from GM of these talented men headed for Ford. By the end of World War Two, GM had become the largest, richest, most powerful company in the world. Wilson reasoned that helping Ford out was good for business as it created an illusion of competition and therefore would keep the U.S. Justice Department from building an anti-monopoly case against General Motors.

With a new management team in place, by the end of 1945 Henry Ford II was advertising the company's new cars featuring either a V8 engine with 100 horsepower or six-cylinder with 90 horsepower. Then he began to put production emphasis on pick-up trucks introducing the F-series. The design of the F-series was revolutionary in that these trucks were built on a car platform. The line came in eight sizes and weights from ½ ton to 3 tons. Soon Ford was back in the black.

Following the war Henry Ford's Willow Run B-24 bomber plant was sold by Henry II to Henry Kaiser who began the Kaiser-Frazier Corporation and began to produce a sub-compact car the Henry-J in the plant. In 1947 Kaiser merged his company with Willys, but by the early 1950s was out of the passenger car business.

During the war the War Labor Board had controlled wages and prices and also advocated expansion of unions. The UAW had agreed as did many other unions not to strike during the war. But with the troops returning home in 1945, labor sensed a post-war booming economy on the horizon and wanted an early piece of the pie. Four days after V-J Day the UAW asked GM for a 30% increase in wages. The union's goal was to keep peacetime take-home pay at the same level as during the war.

Nationally the UAW now represented 1.2 million workers including 350,000 women. On November 20, 1945 at the Barlum Hotel in Detroit 200 representatives of the UAW which now represented 320,000 hourly workers in 96 plants owned by GM voted to launch a nationwide strike against the automaker to begin the next morning. The union was holding firm to its request for a 30% increase in wages and also wanted a hold on raising prices on products. UAW vice-president Walter Reuther was exhilarated. Slapped on the back by an associate, Reuther blurted out "Just like old times, isn't it."[4]

The next morning at 11:00 a.m. at GM's Cadillac plant on Clark Street workers laid down their tools and walked off the job. That morning they had completed 35 cars. The same thing happened all over the GM automotive empire. Workers left the Fleetwood plant, Chevrolet Gear & Axle and others in Detroit. The labor action followed at the Fisher Body plant in Flint, Michigan, the Delco-Remy plant in Muncie, Indiana, warehouses in Los Angeles and at

80 GM plants in 50 cities. In all 175,000 workers put on their hats and coats and went home.

As much as Walter Reuther may have perceived that it was just like old times, the fact was that this was a new kind of strike; it wasn't about union recognition or starvation wages or working conditions. This strike was about workers demanding more money. Reuther was of the opinion that better wages in the auto industry would be cause for wage increases across the economy and benefit the country as a whole by increasing production and abundance of goods. It was a full-economy exercise.

As for the UAW demand to have a voice on price increases of GM products; company vice president Harry Anderson effectively stated that it was none of the union's business what the company charged for its products. Anderson stated, "When we sell our products at competitive prices, buy our materials in competitive markets and pay high wages to our employees by all of the usual standards of high wages, what we may make after taxes is a fair profit for our stockholders."[5] Anderson added the company did not even open its books to the 420,000 stockholders.

The UAW strategy was to pick off each of the big three, Ford, GM and Chrysler, one company at a time and play them off against each other. The union had high hopes that it could convince young and inexperienced Henry Ford II to agree to a 23% increase in wages, but that strategy failed when in mid-November Ford effectively told the union to go to hell. It was an attempt by Reuther and the UAW to begin pattern bargaining. But it would be a while before pattern bargaining among the big three would occur formally. In fact it wasn't possible to use the strategy until September 1955, when for the first time all three contracts at Ford, GM and Chrysler had the same expiration date, enabling the UAW to give equal consideration to each of the big three as a potential strike target.

The GM strike was actually one of a series of labor actions that followed V-J Day and the UAW's demand for a 30% wage increase began to lose footing when other unions began to settle for less. The United Electrical Workers settled their strike for a 17.5% increase and so did the United Steelworkers.

Alfred Sloan had stayed on the sidelines as GM president Charles Wilson negotiated with Reuther. The UAW strike against GM dragged-on for 113 days until March 13, 1946 when the union finally settled for a raise of 18.5 cents per hour or 17.5%.

In the end, Alfred Sloan, Charles Wilson and GM were the victors and the workers returned to the job of building cars. But that did not mean that the workers had not improved their standard of living with $5 billion compensation, a five-year contract including health insurance and pensions. Actually, it was a win-win contract for GM and the UAW. General Motors got a stable work force for several years and in an unprecedented move by Charles Wilson he guaranteed workers annual wage increases tied to the rate of inflation and quantifiable increases in productivity.

In 1946 Alfred P. Sloan stepped down from his management role in GM, but remained on the board. Although effectively GM was now under the operation control of Charles Wilson, Sloan attempted to keep him on a short lease. Regardless, it would be Wilson's vision that would lead GM into the second half of the twentieth century, not that of Sloan.

After facing public ridicule as a result of the Treasury Department allegations of not paying his fair-share of taxes for 1936, the following year Alfred Sloan began the Alfred P. Sloan Foundation by endowing the organization with a gift of $10 million.

The Alfred P. Sloan Foundation gave generously to Sloan's alma mater the Massachusetts Institute of Technology (M.I.T.). Gifts included a laboratory for study of automotive and aircraft engines and aeronautical engineering problems. In 1945 Sloan personally gave $350,000 for an industrial management professorship and four years later he donated $1 million for a metals processing laboratory.

In 1950 the foundation donated $5.25 million to establish the M.I.T. School of Industrial Management. In 1964 the name of the school would be changed to the Sloan School of Management.

Also, in 1945 the Alfred P. Sloan Foundation donated $2.56 million to Memorial Hospital in New York City which was the seedling money for the Memorial Sloan-Kettering Cancer Center. Charles Kettering a GM research scientist had raised Alfred Sloan's awareness of the need for cancer research so Sloan placed his name alongside his own on the organization.

Alfred Sloan was of the belief that if a search for a cure for cancer could be undertaken with the same intensity that was used to solve industrial problems then significant progress could be made.

Following the GM strike in 1945 the UAW membership took notice of Walter Reuther's leadership and elected him president of the union in 1946.

On May 12, 1948 the UAW authorized a strike at Chrysler that lasted for 17 days and resulted with the workers receiving a 13 cent-an-hour raise to $1.55 an hour.

By the fall of 1946 full production of private cars and trucks was back in operation at all auto plants in Detroit. While many consumers made the case that the 1946 and 1947 Fords, Chevrolets and Dodges were nothing more than warmed-over engineering of pre-war 1942 models featuring new grills and trims, by 1949 power and style in designing automobiles was in vogue.

Like Ford, Alfred P. Sloan also demanded that the U.S. Government compensate General Motors for the damage that occurred to the company's Opel plant at Russelsheim, Germany during the war. The Opel plant under German occupation had produced the three-ton Blitz truck for the Wehrmacht and also made parts for the Junkers Ju-88 bomber. Sloan in his demand asserted that all American personnel had been withdrawn from the plant by October 1939 and the parent company had no further contact with the company after 1941. Nonetheless a legal connection between GM and the plant at Russelsheim was never severed. In 1967 GM was awarded $33 million in reparations by the U.S. Government.

It is ironic that the damage done by the Royal Air Force and U.S. Army Air Corp to the GM plant at Russelsheim was carried out by B-24 bombers built by Henry Ford at Willow Run.

On the evening of April 7, 1947 Henry Ford died at the age of 83 at Fairlane his home in Dearborn. That day Ford had toured the River Rouge plant. When Ford passed the only ones by his side were his wife Clara and a member of the household. Torrential rains had recently disabled Fairlane's electric and heating system. So, the world's wealthiest man lay dying in his bed with warmth provided by a wood-burning fireplace in a room lighted by kerosene lamps and candles reminiscent of his boyhood farming days.

A half hour after Ford had died his physician Dr. John Mateer of the Ford Hospital staff arrived at Fairlane and stated that a cerebral hemorrhage was the cause of his death.

Three days later nearly 100,000 people filed by his body as it lay in state at St. Paul's Episcopal Church in Detroit and later at Greenfield Village, Ford's museum in Dearborn. Then the remains of Henry Ford were taken in a funeral procession to rest in a cemetery in Dearborn transported in a Packard hearse.

9.

The Volkswagen Beetle Comes to America

One of the most iconic cars to roll down the highways of America in the second half of the twentieth century was the Volkswagen (VW) Beetle (or Bug). Following World War Two major American automobile manufacturers such as Ford, GM and Chrysler weren't interested in building small cars. The prevailing attitude in Detroit was small cars meant small profits. Furthermore, it cost just as much to make a bumper for a big car as it did for a small car. So the VW Beetle was a misfit among the mass of big and powerful gas-guzzling cars being built and driven on U.S. highways and its rise in popularity was a rather strange odyssey that no gambler would have ever given more that even odds on succeeding in the American market—but it did.

The VW Beetle had its genesis in pre-war Nazi Germany. Adolf Hitler had always been fascinated with automobiles. In 1926 he had attended the German Grand Prix and met the esteemed engineer of racing cars and limousines Ferdinand Porsche at the event.

Although Hitler had been given a Mercedes when he was released from jail in December 1924 by a prominent dealer in Munich, he would never learn to drive. Nonetheless the world would soon see Adolf Hitler time-after time in news reels standing in the back of a Mercedes giving the Nazi salute as he was chauffeured through pageant-like rallies with tens of thousands German people cheering deliriously.

A year before Adolph Hitler had become Chancellor in 1932; the German automobile manufactures had only produced 42,000 cars. The German auto industry output of the time was dwarfed not only by the United States, but also the production of France and England.

The Volkswagen was to be born out of the desire of Nazi dictator Adolf Hitler to motorize pre-World War Two Germany with an inexpensive car that was simple, reliable and could transport a family of four. It was to be a car that could be mass-produced for the masses. He wanted Germany to have its own version of the Ford Model T.

The *Fuhrer* had been a great admirer of Henry Ford and he read his book *My Life and Work* which had become a best-seller in Germany. He even had a picture of Ford hanging on the wall of his office. Of course, Hitler was also very fixated with Henry Ford's anti-Semitism and also had read his hideous hate chronicles in *The International Jew*.

While Hitler's fascination with the automobile and the state of the German roads may seem ironic, he believed that new cars and highways for the German people would not only bring joy to them on Sundays and holidays, but would raise their stature in the world. To that end, beginning in 1933 and for several years thereafter Adolf Hitler appeared at the Berlin annual auto show and asked auto executives to manufacturer a people's car. In fact, it was during one of those appearances at the auto show that Adolf Hitler first used the term *volkswagen*.

But before the people's car would come to fruition there was the matter of building highways in Germany. When Adolf Hitler became chancellor, he inherited an SS colonel by the name of Fritz Todt. The colonel was a civil engineer and in 1932 he had developed a plan to construct a highway and road system in Germany calling for 3000 miles of *autobahns*. Todt estimated that the construction project would employ about 10% of those unemployed in Germany.

The plan was right down the *Fuhrer's* alley and he approved it immediately. Although construction of the highway had actually begun in 1932, the first spade of dirt for the expanded *autobahn* was turned by Hitler himself in September 1933. By the fall of 1935 the second link of the autobahn had been completed from Frankfurt to Darmstadt that included two concrete lanes in each direction separated by a grassy median. Six hundred miles of autobahn would be built in three years. In 1942 with Germany caught-up in its senseless attempt at world domination in the war, construction on the autobahn ceased after more than 2000 miles had been completed.

But in 1936 as the autobahn expanded so did German automobile production. The time was right for Hitler's desire to see the production of the people's car.

At the 1934 Berlin auto show Adolph Hitler met with Ferdinand Porsche. The two exchanged their vision for a people's car and Hitler presented Porsche with a small drawing expressing his vision for the car. Porsche had already developed a plan for a car with an air-cooled rear engine and torsion bar suspension. While the car only had about 25-30 horsepower and weighed about 1400 pounds it could travel up to 50-60 miles an hour and carry four passengers. The rear engine feature eliminated the heavy weight and bulky drive shaft of the engine over the drive wheels. The engine being air-cooled made it cost-effective for mass-production.

The only demands made by Hitler were that the car would be completely made with German parts. There has been some who have advanced the theory that this made the brakes on the car weak until production was resumed after World War Two.

The other demand by Adolph Hitler was that the car be manufactured with an interchangeable chassis to adapt it to military use with different bodies.

To the other automobile manufactures in Germany it now became clear that there was a national mandate to produce a people's car. Daimler-Benz, Auto Union, BMW and Opel (a division of General Motors) had formed an amalgamation called the Reichsverband der Deutschen Automobilindustrie (RDA). Although there wert a lot of skeptics among the members, including Heinrich Nordoff who was running Opel, they also knew that none of the companies could muster the tens of millions of dollars needed to produce the car. So, with Hitler waving a lot of government cash at Porsche, in early summer 1935 the RDA signed a contract with Porsche to be the lead agency in designing a people's car.

The idea for the design of a backbone chassis, rear-engine with air-cooling and a scarab like streamlines body was hardly new. A number of automotive engineers and designers were working on the concept at that time. According to Jason Torchinsky writing on *jalopink.com* in 2015, "Joseph Ganz, an automotive and car designer, had started building prototypes of very Beetle-like cars for companies like Adler and later a production car the Standard Superior."[1]

It was the Standard Superior in 1934 that was the first car to use the term volkswagen in advertising. Joseph Ganz was a German-Hungarian Jew. The Nazis were acutely aware of that fact and buried Ganz's input to the rear-engine concept on any German cars. In fact, in 1933 Ganz was arrested and the following year fled to Switzerland.

But the Standard wasn't the only German car to feature a rear-engine; the Mercedes-Benz 130H was already on the market with one.

At that time Tatra a Czech automobile manufacturer was designing a large, powerful V-8 rear-engine, air-cooled streamlined car. The company was also working on a volkswagen type car—the Tatra 97. Both Hitler and Porsche were very aware of these cars. The designer of the cars Hans Ledwinka had even presented a detailed drawing of the T97 to Hitler who in-turn gave it to Ferdinand Porsche.

In mid-1934 Adolph Hitler funded the volkswagen project under the direction of Ferdinand Porsche with 10 million marks. Subsequently, what would become Volkswagen was founded on January 4, 1937.

Ferdinand Porsche began to tinker with more than a dozen motor prototypes and finally came-up with one that was somewhat beetle-like and fit the specifications of a people's car. His final design for what would become the Volkswagen was based on the work of many other designers and automobile manufacturing companies.

The Munich agreement was signed on September 30, 1938 after a conference of European powers at Hitler's Bavarian Alps retreat near Berchtesgaden. The agreement signed by the United Kingdom, Italy and France allowed Hitler and the Nazis to occupy border areas with German-speaking populations. Hitler had threatened to invade certain areas if not permitted by other European powers to occupy them. Therefore with a mandate from several other European nations in hand, the Nazis occupied the Sudetenland and then in March 1939 crossed the Czech border. The border area of Czechoslovakia was of strategic importance to the Czech people as it was where most of their country's banks and industry was located. The Tatra plant was in that region and the Nazis quickly closed it.

Following World War Two Czechoslovakia was occupied by the Soviet Union and production of the T97 was resumed. Neither the Czechs nor the Soviets had forgotten about the work of the Nazis and Ferdinand Porsche on the Volkswagen that in so many ways resembled the T97. So, they sued Volkswagen. Porsche would admit that he had studied the plans for the T97 and in 1961 Volkswagen settled the matter with Tatra's successors by paying 3 million Deutschmarks.

Ferdinand Porsche designed the rear engine *Kraft durch Freude* people's car in 1938. After Porsche had completed his design for the car the S.S. then put it through a series of brutal tests including one road test of over a million miles.

The Wehrmacht tested the car's air-cooled engine and found it sound as it did not over-heat in the dessert sun and didn't freeze in the artic.

Writing in *The New York Times* in 1955, Melvin J. Lasky stated in regard to the Porsche's prototype, "He (Porsche) finally came up with a strange little beetlelike contraption a "people's car" of breathtaking ugliness," but one that stood every fanatical test which the S.S. experts put it through."[2]

In 1938 a one-tenth scale model with rubber tires of the forthcoming *Kraft durch Freude* (Kdf) people's car was presented to a very enthusiastic *Fuhrer* by Ferdinand Porsche. Immediately Hitler ordered his labor front to build a huge assembly facility and city to surround it.

Adolph Hitler as well as the majority of the Nazi Party and a great deal of the German people harbored a burning desire to catch-up with American's industrial might. Ferdinand Porsche even visited Detroit to see what he needed to do to produce the German Model-T using the American assembly line production method. When he returned Porsche had hopes of creating a facility based on Henry Ford's River Rouge Plant.

A new industrial settlement was planned that would have the rather odd name of "City-of-strength- through –Joy-Automobile." It all seemed a bit bizarre. The city would be built on a plain of the Ludenberg Heath almost in the middle of nowhere. There was a lot of disagreement about the location. The economists felt it was too far from steel and coal. Hitler's generals felt it was too vulnerable to air attack. Even the city-planners found it too swampy and mosquito-ridden.

To reach the site of what would eventually become Wolfsburg one would have to travel over winding roads and past sleepy farming villages. Despite all the skepticism the city rose out of nowhere.

At that time the German labor force was strained. The Germans were rearming, and a considerable amount of construction was taking place around the country. Italian dictator Benito Mussolini came to the rescue sending thousands of guest workers to Germany to work on the automobile plant. A huge factory was constructed then company homes for about 2400 workers with additional ones planned for a future date. After the war the town's name would be changed to Wolfsburg and the car manufacturing company would become Volkswagen.

The facility was to be run by the German Labour Front (DAF). The DAF was the National Socialist trade union organization. It had replaced various trade unions in the Weimar Republic after Hitler's rise to power. Subsequently, the DAF was the only union organization allowed in the Third Reich.

The first production model of the *Kraft durch Freude* (KdF or Volkswagen) was put on display at the Berlin Motor Show in 1938. Then to promote sales and raise consumer interest in the German people for the KdF, the following year a parade of the cars took place in Berlin.

Over 300,000 Germans participated in a savings plan to buy a KdF where a worker set-aside 5, 10 or 15 Reichsmarks a week until a total of 750 had been reached then a person would receive an order number for a car.

Fate would have it that only a few thousand KdFs were actually produced and they were showpieces for well-connected Nazi party officials. With about 280 million Reichsmarks on deposit for the cars Hitler expanded the war into Poland and Russia, consequently the factory was converted to produce war materials and orders for civilian cars were put on hold.

Starting in 1941 the KdF or Volkswagen plant using mostly Russian prisoners of war as a labor force began to build a few cars and nearly 50,000 Type 62 Kublewagens, a vehicle with a beetle chassis with 4 doors and 18-inch tires, rather than the 16-inch tires used in the KdF. Also manufactured at the plant was the vehicle's amphibious counterpart the Schwimmwagen Type 166. Field Marshall Erwin Rommel used a Type 62 as his staff car during his North African campaign.

However, the German manufacturing rate of the Kdf was not even in the same ballpark with the American production of the Jeep. By contrast, notwithstanding what the Ford Motor Company was producing, the Willys-Overland plant in Toledo, Ohio manufactured one Jeep every 80 seconds.[3]

With the German troops bogged down on the Russian front in the winter of 1941-42 and ill-equipped for the extreme weather, the KdF plant began to manufacturer 100,000 cast iron stoves for the freezing and frost-bitten troops.

Hitler's expanded war increased the need for additional workers at that plant, so slave labor began to be supplied by SS officer Fritz Saukel from concentration camps, prisons and occupied countries to meet the demand. Author Phil Patton states in his wonderful book, *Bug—The Strange Mutations of the World's Most Famous Automobile,* "Ordering up labor on demand became standard practice for almost all German industry, which used seven million slave and concentration camp laborers during the war."[4]

In 1944, 650 Jewish women were transferred from Auschwitz to work at the KdF plant to manufacture bazookas and mines. To provide housing for these workers a satellite camp was built at Neuengamme.

Living conditions for these workers was deplorable. Wooden huts were constructed without running water, heat or storage. The workers were locked in the huts at night and slept in three-tiered wooden bunks without bedding. The workers were provided with food that consisted of two paltry meals a day. Those workers who became ill were sent to Buchenwald concentration camp. Failure to meet production quotas led to beatings from SS officers or other plant workers.

At the Nuremberg trials in late 1945 and early 1946, Fritz Saukel, was found guilty of war crimes and would be hanged.

Later in 1943 the KdF plant began to produce the German's V1 rocket that would wreak havoc and terror on London.

Despite the highly efficient SCR584 radar-guided anti-aircraft guns built by Chrysler and put into action, the Nazi's V1 attacks killed 6,184 people and seriously injured 17,981 in London.

As a result of intelligence reports on the manufacturing of the V1 at the KdF plant it made the facility a priority on the Allies bombing list. The plant had been constructed in an open area and was an easy target for British Lancaster bombers. Production at the KdF plant was halted on August 7, 1944 due to increased Allied bombing.

Near the end of the war the plant was still attempting to produce war materials. But the supply of captured Russians that had been the major labor source had been exhausted as the war in the east turned against the Nazis. To provide a rag-tag labor force the plant was now being staffed by slave laborers from occupied countries, political prisoners and POWs from Poland, Ukraine, Romania, France, Belgium, etc., and also Jews who had been imprisoned in concentration camps at Auschwitz, Bergen-Belsen and Dachau. This included women and children. Some of the children at Auschwitz had been personally selected by infamous Nazi doctor Josef Mengele to be sent east to the KdF plant.

It all came to an end in early April 1945 when the U.S. 102nd Infantry Division captured the KdF (or Volkswagen) plant. The Soviet lines were only fifteen miles away. The S.S. guards at the plant had high-tailed it out ahead of the approaching Allies. So those prisoners and slave laborers remaining at the plant took out their revenge on whatever was possible attempting to finish the destruction the bombers had started. The fact was the plant was a mess by the time the Americans liberated it.

The French demanded that the Volkswagen plant be transferred to their country as war reparations. But they dropped the demand when French auto makers voiced objections to the move.

During the war Ferdinand Porsche was taken out of the car production business by Nazi minister of labor Albert Speer and made head of the Panzer

Commission. Under Porsche's direction a remarkable 49,777 Panzer Tiger I, II, III & IV, and Panzer V Panther and Type 205 Panzer tanks were manufactured. On May 30, 1945 Ferdinand Porsche was arrested by the French as a war criminal and held prisoner until 1947.

While in prison Porsche was persuaded to assist the Renault combine that the French had recently nationalized and worked on the design for the Renault 4CV.

After being released Porsche returned to Austria and with a small workforce began to assemble his own car by hand. Volkswagen agreed to sell Porsche's car the Porsche 356 through their dealerships in Germany. Ferdinand Porsche died following a stroke in January 1951 and never saw the success that his car would achieve on the world market.

In the 1980s Volkswagen would underwrite a $2 million, ten-year investigation into its Nazi past. Respected German historian Hans Mommsen would be commissioned to conduct the study. Mommsen would produce a 1000-page book titled *Das Volkswagenwerk und seine Arbeiter im Dritten Reich* (*Volkswagen and the Workers During the Third Reich*). Among the findings in his book Mommsen would state that Ferdinand Porsche who joined the Nazi Party in 1937 was a willing participant in Hitler's regime and was morally indifferent to the use of 20,000 slave laborers in creating munitions at the factory.

In 1996 Volkswagen although under no legal obligation would create a humanitarian fund to voluntarily compensate enslaved workers at its plant during World War Two. The company funded the organization with a $12 million compensation pool. By 2002, over 2000 recipients from 26 countries had claimed benefits from the fund.

Immediately following the war Heinz Heinrich Nordhoff would suffer a similar fate as Ferdinand Porsche. Nordhoff was an American-trained auto executive who prior to the war had ran General Motor's Opel division in Bradenburg, Germany. When the plant was taken over by the Nazis for war production Nordoff over-saw production of Opel trucks for the German Army. At the war's end Nordhoff fled west and associated himself with the Opel plant at Russelsheim. That put him in a position to surrender to the Americans.

But it turned-out to be a bad move as the Americans branded Nordhoff a Nazi and blacklisted him. That left him unable to secure any employment on a comparable level to that which he had held prior to the war. He eventually took a job managing a local garage.

After the war Germany was divided-up by the Allies into four sectors to be under the administration of the Americans, British, French and Soviets. The Wolfsburg KdF plant now called the Volkswagen plant was in the British sector and no one in post-war Germany was sure what to do with it. Approximately 58% of the plant lay in ruins.

British soldiers from the Corps of Royal Electrical and Mechanical Engineers arrived and began to dismantle salvageable parts of the plant and send them back to England as reparations. The Soviets had been doing that too with any manufacturing plants that were within their sector.

Colonel Gott of the British Army came to Wolfsburg to determine what might be done with the Volkswagen facility. After considering the Volkswagen he concluded that the car was "too ugly, too noisy, too tiny."[5] It would be a bad investment for the Brits; the car had potential to become a novelty, but never a major seller.

Eventually British Major Ivan Hirst of the Royal Electrical and Mechanical Engineers arrived at Wolfsburg. He saw potential in the car and under his direction production was started-up again. Workers in the area were starving and willing to work for potatoes, chocolate and cigarettes. Major Hirst put them to work and the first post-war Volkswagen beetle was produced in early 1946. By March 1946 with 6,000 workers at the plant1000 Volkswagens had been produced. By the end of the year that number had risen to 9,871 and the workforce now numbered 8,000. However, a lot of the cars were used by the occupation forces rather than put on the commercial market. In fact, 1785 cars had been made for the British Army and German post office.

By 1948 it was clear to the British that something had to be done with the Volkswagen facility. They could continue to pay occupation costs in running it forever or do something with it.

In March 1948 the Volkswagen plant at Wolfsburg was offered to the Ford Motor Company. At the advice of the Ford board chairman Ernie Breech, Henry Ford II turned-down the offer to operate the plant. Sir Patrick Hennessey, the head of Ford's British division was also adamant that Volkswagen had no future.

But during 1948 a dramatic change in the West-German economy would take place. After a new constitution was drafted the old worthless currency was cancelled and replaced by a solid Deutschmark which was put into place.

The British were not as stern as the U.S. about hiring suspected or confirmed ex-Nazis to assist with the post-war recovery of Germany. Heinz Heinrich Nordhoff was hired as the managing director at the Volkswagen plant in a complicated trusteeship. Of course, a little more than a decade before it had been Nordoff who was one of the people's car strongest critics and skeptics. Nordhoff had claimed that the Volkswagen "Had more faults than a dog has fleas."[6]

In 1949 the British transferred the Volkswagen facility to the control of the new West German government. That year under Heinz Nordhoff production at the plant hit 20,000 cars.

It was also in 1949 that the first German Volkswagen, beetle or bug, was delivered to the USA. At first Americans were cool to the idea of kick-starting German post-war industry by buying the Volkswagen and only 330 were sold in the USA in 1950.

Under Nordhoff expansion at the Wolfsburg plant took place rapidly. He introduced many American auto manufacturing principles and where in 1946 744 men were building 1000 cars, by 1955 just 100 men where producing that number and it was the year that Volkswagen produced its one millionth car. However, the VW plant now employed 20,000.

All the profits were invested in the plant for facility improvements, new machinery and the addition of a one-kilometer (0.621371 mile or 5280 feet) assembly line.

Priced at just 3,790 Deutschmarks ($902 in US dollars) by 1955 every second car in West-Germany was a Volkswagen. Heinz Nordoff was quick to criticize German bureaucrats for riding around in limousines pointing-out that he ran the largest auto plant in Europe and had no problem traveling in a Volkswagen beetle.

As might be expected the Volkswagen was a major player in the Cold War propaganda battle as its success in a free-enterprise system was put in juxtaposition to what the Soviets could produce. In 1960 Volkswagen became a public company.

In late 1954 Heinz Nordoff came to the conclusion that with a growing American market for the Volkswagen it might be cheaper to manufacture the cars in the U.S. rather than export them from West Germany. The Wolfsburg plant was manufacturing 335,000 cars a year and 50% were being exported. At that time Volkswagen had 100 dealers in five states on the East coast (New York, New Jersey, Pennsylvania, Delaware and Connecticut). So Nordoff began looking for a possible site for an assembly plant in America. Sales for the Volkswagen without advertising in the U.S. were projected to be 35,000 for 1955 and the company was planning on introducing its new sporty Karmann-Ghia coupe built on the Beetle platform during the year.

In 1950 Studebaker purchased a 165-acre tract in North Brunswick, New Jersey and begun construction of a $5,500,000 car assembly plant. At that time Studebaker was a profitable independent auto maker employing 25,000 persons and had its main assembly plant in South Bend, Indiana with other plants in Los Angeles and Hamilton, Ontario.

The New Jersey plant was scheduled to be open by March 1, 1951, but then the Korean War broke out. So, the plant was converted to the manufacture of components and spare parts for the J47-S23 turbo jet engine.

By the time the Korean War had ended the Studebaker had lost considerable popularity in the American car market so plans to build cars in New Jersey were scrapped.

In 1955 Volkswagen bought the New Jersey plant from Studebaker for $4 million. But suddenly Volkswagen cancelled its plans for the New Jersey assembly plant and sold the property to a cable manufacturer at a loss. Heinz Nordoff announced that further analysis had determined that production costs would be too high in the U.S.

In a press release Nordoff stated, "Rather than increase prices or sacrifice to the slightest degree of the high quality that had been largely responsible for the

Volkswagon Beetle. (www.Pexels.com)

success of our product, we will be compelled to continue our present system of operation."[7]

The Volkswagen gradually gained popularity in the U.S. and by the 1960s 100,000 Beetles were sold in America. In 1968 5% of all cars sold in the U.S. were Volkswagens. The Volkswagen Transporter or Microbus sold 65,000 vehicles in 1970. Sales of the beetle peaked at 570,000 sold between 1960 and 1970.

In 1967 Heinz Nordhoff was forced into retirement by the German government supposedly as a result of ill-health. He died the following year.

The first sports car produced in the postwar U.S. was a "clunker"—the Crosley Hotshot. The Hotshot was built by household appliances/radio manufacturer and Cincinnati Reds owner Powel Crosley, Jr. It weighed 1,100 pounds and was 145 inches long. It was possible for a person of average strength to lift the lightweight engine. Surprisingly the Crosley Hotshot actually won the "index of performance" which was an honor for speed for its displacement at the 1950 Six Hours of Sebring. But the Hotshot while being slow had major engineering flaws and was dangerous. In fact, a 1961 Drivers Ed film *Mechanized Death* featured a mangled Hotshot.

The Hotshot engine was a disaster; a dual–overhead cam .75-liter four cylinder, was brazed together with pieces of stamped tin (a process Crosley would use for his toasters), rather than cast in iron. Often the blazed welds let go and things got noisy and very hot quickly.

Still Crosley Motors, Inc. had made the first attempt by an American manufacturer to build a small car, one that might have competed with Volkswagen. Furthermore, if it had better engineering it might have been America's Mini Cooper.

The company was in operation from 1939 to 1952 with assembly plants in Indiana at Richmond and Marion. In 1939 Crosley introduced a 2-door convertible that weighed under 1000 pounds and sold for $252. In 1941 more body styles were introduced and the car could get 50 miles per gallon. In 1948 its peak year, Crosley sold 24,871 cars including its sedan, sport utilities sedan, convertible coup and the CC Wagon, the company's most popular car. In 1952 the last year of operation for Crosley it introduced its Super Station Wagon, a sub-compact SUV.

Surprisingly, among the notable Crosley owners were President Dwight D. Eisenhower, General Omar Bradley, architect Frank Lloyd Wright, Vice President Nelson Rockefeller, radio & TV host Art Linkletter, actress Gloria

1951 Crosley Super Station Wagon. (Photo by author)

Swanson, bandleader Tommy Dorsey and most recently English rock-star Boy George.

By 1959 American automobile manufacturers were starting to experience increasing foreign competition in the domestic market for rear-engine small cars. There were 15,000 dealers in the U. S. handling 81 foreign cars which accounted for 10% of the overall market.

In 1959 Volkswagen hired an American advertising agency Doyle Dane Bernbach to help gain a larger market share in the U.S. The company used unconventional tag lines such as "Lemon," "Think Small" and "Don't Laugh" under pictures of the VW Beetle that got consumer's attention. By 1962 sales of VW Beetle in the U.S. would top 200,000.

Volkswagen had been sold in Mexico since 1954 and in 1964 began assembly in Puebla, Mexico.

In Germany sales of the VW Beetle reached their peak in 1961 when the company reached a settlement with the pre-war KdF savers association. Then the Berlin Wall was constructed by the Soviet Union cutting the VW market in Germany in half.

While the Big Three mainly ignored the growing demand for small cars and in particular the Volkswagen, in the late 1950s, Studebaker-Packard attempted to meet the growing demand head-on by marketing the DKW a German car attempting to compete with the Volkswagen. Then Studebaker-Packard decided

1963 Ford Falcon. (Photo by Lawrence T. Hay)

to build its own compact car and introduced the Lark. As a result of the Lark, quickly the company went from having a deficit of $43, 318,257 in 1956 to earning a profit in 1958 of $13,314,164.

GM did make a half-hearted attempt to meet the challenge head on of producing a small car with the low-priced, but flawed Corvair.

Chrysler gave the matter a little lip service saying it might consider converting its new front-engine compact Valiant to a front-wheel drive car.

Ford which had just introduced the compact Falcon almost got into the small car, front-wheel drive market in the U.S. in 1960. Before leaving to join the Kennedy Administration as Secretary of Defense, Ford whiz kid Robert McNamara who was running the division authorized a development of a new car that was supposed to compete with the Volkswagen as a small and inexpensive car—the Cardinal. It was to be built in Ford's German plant in Cologne and be introduced to the American market in the fall of 1962.

Ford had been building cars in Germany since 1931. Originally the plant was in Berlin but was moved to Cologne that year. After the Ford *Werke* in Cologne was seized by the Nazis during World War Two, tracked vehicles and trucks for the army and turbines for V-2 rockets were built at the plant.

Lee Iacocca who took over the Ford Division when Robert McNamara resigned, decided to take a closer look at the plans for the Cardinal and went over to Germany to check on the progress of the car. He stated in his biography *Iacocca* that when he first saw the Cardinal he was underwhelmed. When he returned to Detroit Iacocca told Henry Ford II to forget about the Cardinal in the U.S., it was doubtful that it would find a young market. He wrote, "It was a fine car for the European market, with its V-4 engine and front-wheel drive. But in the United States there was no way it could have sold the three-hundred thousand units we were counting on."[8]

The car introduced in Germany in September 1962 as the Taunus 12M with a 50-hp V-4 engine had a top speed of 78 mph and delivered 31.4 mpg. While more than 2.5 million were sold in Europe between 1962 and 1970, the car was third in sales in Germany behind the Volkswagen and Opel.

Although the Beetle's horsepower had been increased to 50 in 1966, the following year Fiat passed Volkswagen in sales in Europe.

While the Volkswagen had the advantage of versatility and its chassis could be adapted to a dune buggy, it had a reputation of reliability problems and it opened the door for the Japanese imports such as Toyota, Honda and Nissan to enter the American market. These cars soon not only eclipsed sales of the Volkswagen but also started to move ahead of many American models.

Volkswagen fought back. Under Heinz Nordhoff the company had been restricted to producing one primary model—the Beetle or Bug. In 1975 Volkswagen introduced the Rabbit (sold under the name Golf in Germany) in the U.S. Worldwide the car sold 15 million by 1985.

By the 1980s American automobile makers were under siege by the increasing number of foreign cars entering the U.S. each year. When the first wave of Japanese imports began to hit the American market in mass during the 1970s no one in Detroit was impressed or worried about the boxy little Toyotas or Hondas. There was a certain arrogance that permeated the board rooms of Detroit. The Big Three, Ford, General Motors and Chrysler believed that they had a world-wide monopoly on the auto industry.

While both the American and German auto manufacturers had to answer to stockholders with quarterly reports, the Japanese auto makers didn't play by the same rules. The Japanese played a long game and their planning process for a market was just not the next year's model, they could take years to implement their plans. It ultimately forced Ford, GM and Chrysler to make sweeping changes in labor relations, collective bargaining and to form partnerships with Japanese, Korean and European manufacturers while downsizing their operations.

The Volkswagen Company officially gave the type 1 the name Beetle in 1968. Since arriving on the shores of America in 1950 the Volkswagen Beetle has become thoroughly immersed in American popular culture largely due to the baby boomers who adopted it.

In California during the 1960s the Beetle was stripped down, and the chassis used to create dune buggies. On the beaches it became more than common, it was a status symbol for Beetles to be seen arriving with surf boards hanging-out the windows.

The VW Beetle or Bug has appeared in scores of movies beginning with Walt Disney's production of *The Love Bug* in 1968. No less than five other Disney movies have given star status to the Volkswagen appearing in such films as *Herbie The Love Bug* in 1997 and *Herbie Fully Loaded* in 2005.

The Volkswagen, particularly the VW Micro Bus, even became the favorite car of the counterculture generation (aka the hippies) of the late 1960s and early 1970s. The Volkswagen had evolved from Nazi staff cars with a swastika emblazoned on them into a psychedelic mode of transportation with a peace symbol painted on them. To the hippies the VW was a form of transportation that screamed anti-establishment.

1966 Vokswagon Bus. (Photo by Lawrence T. Hay)

Perhaps the rise in popularity of Volkswagen among the baby boomers is summed-up best by just fifteen words written by Angus MacKenzie in the May 2016 edition of *Motortrend.com*, "VW became a pop-culture icon: an underpowered, flower-powered middle finger to Detroit's self-obsessed excess."

But over time the VW Micro Bus (or Van) would evolve into the prototype for the SUV which now dominates the American market and is a favorite among American middle-class families and a recreational class known as soccer moms.

Also, during the late 1960s the Volkswagen chassis became the foundation of the ominous dune buggies driven by the era's leading psychopath Charles Manson. Manson fanaticized his dune buggies would be a sort of Panzer corps that would lead his band of bummed-out societal misfits and hop-heads into battle in the California desert against what remained of conventional society following an apocalyptic uprising by African-Americans that he called "helter skelter."

In the early 1970s Volkswagen would have to withstand a fiery attack on the Beetle by consumer advocate Ralph Nader whose challenge to the engineering flaws in Chevrolet Corvair in the middle 1960s had caused sweeping safety change regulations for the automobile industry.

In September 1971 Nader attacked the VW Beetle in a 200-page report as "the most hazardous car currently in use in significant numbers in the United States."[9]

Now it certainly is a fact that when a larger vehicle hits a smaller vehicle the smaller vehicle is more likely to suffer more damage and its occupants more injuries. But Nader was being overly cautious in supposing that the Beetle was too small for the America highway. Nader also alleged that in a crash a VW fuel filter cap would emit gasoline ready to ignite with a spark from a shorted wire.

But according to John Totnerlin of *Road & Track Magazine* who took Nader to task on his findings in the magazine, Nader had inaccurately stated statistics in his report.

Nader had reported that the 1968 VW Beetle had the seventh highest rate of injuries to occupants in accidents with 15 cars studied. According to Totnerlin in the original report prepared by Dr. B. J. Campbell the rate for the Beetle was actually 31st in a study of 170 vehicles.

Totnerlin's also refuted Nader's fire allegations. According to John Totnerlin the data that Ralph Nader had used from a New York State Department of

Motor Vehicles survey showed the fire incidents in VWs were based on three fires and that two other U.S. car makers had higher rates.

By the mid-1960s with rising labor costs in Germany and rising demand in the U.S. the Volkswagen management team came to the conclusion that they had to once again consider a site for production in either North America or Central America. They chose a site in Puebla, Mexico a city approximately 100 miles south-east of Mexico City.

In 1971 1.3 million VW Beetles were sold in the U.S. Soon after on February 17, 1972 the Volkswagen Beetle became the World Champion moving past the Ford Model T "Tin Lizzy" in units produced with 15,007,034.

On July 11, 1974 the last VW Beetle rolled off the assembly line in Wolfsburg, West Germany. A few others would continue to be built in VW's Emden, West Germany facility until January 1978.

In 1978 Volkswagen finally began production in the U.S. after taking over an unfinished Chrysler plant near New Stanton, Pennsylvania (Westmoreland County) about 35 miles from Pittsburgh becoming the first foreign automaker to manufacture cars in the U.S. since Rolls-Royce built cars in Springfield, Massachusetts from 1921 to 1933.

Between 1978 and 1988 1.15 million VW Rabbits and Golfs were produced at the site. But they were judged to be of inferior quality compared to the German made cars. That fact and the consistent financial losses experienced at the plant forced its closing.

By early 1978 the Puebla, Mexico Volkswagen facility was the only one in world still manufacturing the original Beetle. Then throughout the 1980s and early 1990s demand began to shrink as competition from Japanese small cars from Toyota and Honda began to dramatically increase their market share. When only 30,000 Beetles were built at Puebla in 2002, VW officials reached the conclusion that it was time to shut-down the operation. In 2003 after nearly 70 years, production was stopped on the original rear-engine Volkswagen Beetle.

By July 31, 2003 a total of 21,529,464 Volkswagen Beetles (or Bugs) had been built around the world. In 39 years of operation the Puebla facility had produced 1.7 million Beetles. In Mexico the Beetles were used for taxis and police cars. So, the company decided to give it one more try with a redesigned version of the Beetle.

In 1993 when Volkswagen was close to insolvency, Ferdinand Piech an Austrian engineer and respected business executive as well as the nephew of

Ferdinand Porsche became chairman of the company. Piech began to modernize the company's manufacturing process and acquired new brands, even taking VW to new heights in engineering with the introduction of the 12-cylinder Phaeton. Over the next decade under Piech's direction Volkswagen's would become a global automotive group with more than 600,000 workers and poised to pass Toyota and General Motors as the largest auto maker in sales with 11 models.

It was decided that the Puebla facility would be re-tooled to produce a modernized successor to the original VW. It would be a high-performance model based on the Golf but the design would be distinctively Beetle. On December 1, 1997 production on the New Beetle 2-door sedan started at Puebla and the first cars hit the U. S. market in 1998. The New Beetle would have the engine in the front driving four wheels with luggage storage in the rear.

Meanwhile an original Beetle was added to the design collection of the Museum of Modern Art in New York.

New opportunities for Volkswagen had come about with the collapse of the Soviet Union and the reunification of Germany in the late 1980s. With the fall of communism in Czechoslovakia the Skoda car company was on the verge of bankruptcy. In 1990 the new Czech government asked Volkswagen to take over Skoda. By 2000 Skoda wholly owned by Volkswagen was using the VW platform and selling briskly, including in the United Kingdom.

Other German car manufacturers were quick to take notice of the job VW had done with Skoda and in 2005 Mercedes bought an 18.52% stake in Volkswagen.

Then in 2006 Porsche got in on the action and purchased a 25.1% of the company. A year later Porsche increased its share to 30.9%. By 2009 Porsche owned 50.7% of Volkswagen and in May 2010 the two companies merged.

With a new corporate structure in place in 2011 VW returned to the U.S. building a state-of-the-art assembly plant in Chattanooga, Tennessee. It was expected in 2016 the plant would start to build the long-awaited VW three-row SUV.

When the Great Recession took hold in 2008 Porsche found its company in deep financial trouble attempting to find a market for sports cars. The American car companies were in deep trouble too and asking the government for bailout money. In a twist of fate Volkswagen acquired Porsche and set a goal of becoming the world's leading car manufacturer by 2018 including tripling its sales in the U.S.

The New Beetle that was produced in 1998 had not been a success. The new Beetle had the engine in the front, but was known to be unreliable, a rare circumstance for a VW and a huge public relations problem when faced with the satisfaction of buyers of Toyotas, Hondas and Nissans. In car reviews the New Beetle had been dubbed as cute and it was widely spoke of as a girlie car. As a matter of fact, the car did seem to attract young female buyers as its primary market.

In 2011 VW decided it was time to design a retro version of the New Beetle. The prefix "New" was dropped and the next generation of the Beetle was larger based on the platform of the Jetta and more powerful.

Regardless of the retro Beetle, during 2014 Volkswagen struggled in the U.S. capturing only 2.2% of the market selling 408,000 cars including 43,000 Beetle hardtops and convertibles. VW had wanted to get into the diesel market in the U.S. in 2005 but the company was afraid that it could not meet the U.S. emissions standards; eventually they would enter the market and pay a price. Still in 2014 VW stood as the world's second largest car maker, continued to dominate the lucrative market in China and sold 10.2 million cars worldwide.

But suddenly there was trouble on the horizon for the company. On April 26, 2015 Ferdinand Piech resigned following a failed attempt to oust VW CEO Martin Winterhorn. Then a scandal of monumental proportions was revealed.

In 2014 a study by West Virginia University raised questions over Volkswagen's diesel motors and excess emissions. The incident would commonly become known as "dieselgate" as VW was caught red-handed violating U.S. emissions standards.

Oliver Schmitt VW's director of regulatory compliance in the U.S. based in Auburn Hills, Michigan during the period of 2012 to 2015 assured regulators that VW had made no attempt to deceive them and attempted to convince them that the problem with excess emissions were caused by technical problems.

Lawsuits were filed in New York, Massachusetts and Maryland by state attorneys general accusing Oliver Schmidt of playing a central role in Volkswagen's attempt to conceal emissions cheating from regulators. It stood to reason that with Schmidt's position in the company he was aware of the intent by Volkswagen to cheat on U.S. auto emissions standards.

On November 19, 2015, Oliver Schmidt and other VW officials acknowledged the existence of a defeat device that had been installed in VW cars for the U.S. market that allowed the cars to cheat emissions tests. The software associated with the defeat device enabled the cars to sense that they were being tested for emissions. That would be followed by automatic pollution control devices being turned-on to limit the cost of engine performance.

VW acknowledged that as many as 11 million cars could be affected world-wide, including all of its U.S. 3.0-liter diesel models since 2009 and agreed to pay $16 billion to owners of diesel vehicles. Also affected were 2.0-liter diesel models for the Jetta (2009-2015), Jetta Sportswagen (2009-2014), Beetle (2001-2015), Beetle Convertible (2010-2015), Golf (2010-2015) Gold Sportwagen (2015) and Passat (2012-2015).

On January 4, 2016, the U. S. Department of Justice filed a complaint on behalf of the EPA against Volkswagen and its subsidiaries, Audi A.G. Volkswagen Group of America, Inc. and others, for alleged violations of the Clean Air Act.

Meanwhile in California air quality officials working with the EPA had been investigating Volkswagen emissions. In February 2016 attorneys filed proposed class-action suits against Volkswagen on behalf of more than 500,000 U.S. car owners and dealers in a U.S. District Court in California alleging that the company had engaged in widespread fraud in marketing its vehicles in the U.S., citing various federal laws used to stem racketeering.

In the suit filed in the federal court in San Francisco the plaintiffs claimed "Volkswagen cheated its way to the top of the automotive food chain and spared no victim along the way. Furthermore, it was alleged that Volkswagen knowingly rigged diesel vehicles in the U.S. to pass emissions tests. The defeat device reduced emissions control during normal road use, allowing the company to spew toxic tailpipe emissions as much as 40 times the legal limit."[10]

This was all happening while VW was spending millions of dollars on advertising its so-called "clean diesel" technology that resulted with the company controlling as much as 70% of the nascent diesel-engine market in the U.S.

With Volkswagen facing up to $46 billion in regulatory fines in America while being under criminal investigation in Germany, sales among the 650 VW dealers in the U.S. were down 14% (about $1.2 billion) in July 2016 in the wake of the emissions scandal.

In August 2016 Volkswagen told a federal judge the company had reached a basic agreement to compensate its U.S. dealers for the troubles they have endured. That settlement was estimated in the range of $1.2 billon to offset the declining value of the VW franchises. Before final settlement is reached it is speculated that VW will also have to buy back unsold and unfixable diesels from the dealers that could cost as much as $1.85 million per dealer.

In September 2016 James Liang a former VW engineer who worked at the company in California pleaded guilty to charges of conspiracy to defraud the federal government and violating the Clean Air Act.

Then on January 7, 2017, Oliver Schmidt was arrested by the F.B.I. in Florida on a charge of conspiracy to defraud the United States. The significance of Schmidt's arrest was that it escalated the investigation into the VW executive ranks.

Just how VW will climb up out of the credibility hole it has dug itself in the American market is not known. Speculation is that the company will have to spend millions re-emphasizing the long-time VW boast of quality or attempt to gain a larger share of the SUV sales in the U.S. dominated by GM and Toyota.

The company is however hedging its bets with the Trump administration in Washington, D.C. It is not clear at this point what direction EPA standards will take in regard to VW's future in the U.S. President Trump's choice to lead the EPA transition team Myron Ebell is chairman of the Cooler Heads Coalition that is advancing a mission "focused on dispelling the myths of global warming by exposing flawed scientific, and risk analysis."[11] So it's possible global warming could go on the back burner in the Trump White House.

California has the strictest environmental standards in the U.S. and former Governor Jerry Brown had indicated that his state will continue to follow its guidelines. Current governor Gavin Newsom is likely to do the same. Nine other states follow the California emissions standards.

Regardless of the outcome of the emissions mess VW got itself into, one glaring fact that remains in regard to the legacy of Volkswagen in the U.S. market is that, from the time the first Beetle was unloaded onto a New Jersey dock in 1950 the car has never been understood by American car buyers. If VW is ever going to be successful in America it is going to have cross that hurdle.

10.
The 1950s:
Fins, Rock n' Roll, Suburbs
& Interstates

The 1950s would be an era of unparalleled prosperity for the American automobile industry. While the automotive industry had to cut production during the Korean War to comply with the manufacturing of war materials and limit production of autos due to a quota, compared to the all-out government restrictions imposed on the industry during World War Two it amounted to a minor inconvenience—a blip on the production radar screen. In 1953 the quota was allowing Ford to manufacturer 800,000 cars a quarter. For General Motors auto production in Detroit was barely interrupted as the company took over an abandoned factory in Cleveland to produce all the tanks necessary for the Korean campaign.

Competition among the Big Three was fierce during the early 1950s, but in 1954 GM was the clear winner placing five of its cars in the top ten. The ten most popular cars in 1954 were in order Chevrolet, Ford, Buick, Oldsmobile, Plymouth, Pontiac, Mercury, Dodge, Cadillac and Chrysler. It was in 1954 that Cadillac for the first time entered the top ten list passing Chrysler.

By 1957 GM was spending $90 million a year to advertise its cars through an account held by the Campbell-Ewald agency in Detroit. In 1950 there were 40 million registered vehicles that were private, commercial or publicly owned. By 1960 there would be 61 million such registered vehicles and GM was selling

1947 Cadillac Fleetwood. (Photo by Lawrence T. Hay)

nearly half of all the cars, while one in six workers in the country was employed in the automobile industry.

For the city dweller buying a new car in the 1950s was a community affair. When one pulled-up in front of his house or apartment building in a new Chevy, Dodge or Ford, neighbors instinctively sensed that something special had descended upon them and went outside to look the vehicle over. The tires were kicked, the hood was raised, and everyone commented on the advanced technology of the big six or eight cylinder engine. Gleeful neighbors getting a high on the luxurious new car aroma would ask if they could get in the front seat and hold the steering-wheel. It was a cultural event that exemplified the prosperity of the era. But by the 1970s all of that consumer euphoria would fade into history and the act of buying a new car would no longer be considered any different of a consumer purchase from that of buying a new refrigerator.

By the 1950s GM had become so prosperous under the leadership of Charles E. "the engine" Wilson that the company took the lead in labor negotiations with the UAW thereby setting the standard for what Ford and Chrysler could expect to pay its workers.

Popular TV hostess Dinah Shore boosted the sales of GM on her Sunday night variety show in the middle and late 1950s with the lyrics of a sales pitch that became her theme song "See the USA in your Chevrolet."

Desi Arnez and Lucille Ball got into the act too when in 1955 several epi-sodes of their weekly zany comedy series "*I Love Lucy*" chronicled a rollicking, laugh-filled trans-continental motor journey from New York to Los Angeles with their series landlords the Mertzs, Fred (William Frawley) and Ethel (Vivian Vance) in a 1955 GM Pontiac Star Chief Convertible.

Beginning in 1960 GM's Chevrolet also sponsored *Route 66* a popular TV program that dramatized the wanderlust of two free-spirited young men Tod (Martin Milner) and Buzz (George Maharis) driving a Corvette across the fabled highway seeking adventure.

At the beginning of the 1950s the Big Three were aware that a huge post-World War Two market was theirs for the taking. Competition among the automakers in designing cars would emphasize fuel efficiency, style and power.

The easy part for the automakers, although it would yield marginal results, was fuel efficiency because previously that aspect had been ignored. Still in 1950 cars were 30% more fuel efficient than those built in 1930. GM conducted a study that revealed that a car which traveled 9550 miles in 1930 would use 935 gallons of fuel (10.2 miles per gallon). By 1950 standards a car traveling the same distance would use just 720 gallons of fuel (13.5miles per gallon).

Style in automobiles during the 1950s would be inspired by the dawn of the jet age. It began in 1948 when GM stylist Harley Earl designed the Cadillac Sixty Special with tailfins inspired by the vertical stabilizers on the World War Two era twin-tailed Lockheed Lightning P fighter plane.

Then in 1951 Earl designed a show car for GM, the La Sabre, based on the United States Air Force Sabre jet fighter. The car featured many jet age inspired standards including a wrap-around windshield, built-in hydraulic jacks, dual gasoline and alcohol fuel systems, a 12-volt electric system, a torque convertor transmission with an air cooler and tail fins.

There was a weak functional component of the fins craze advanced by Plymouth which claimed that the tailfins were not fins, but "stabilizers" to place the "center of pressure" as far to the rear as possible and thus "reduce by 20% the needs for steering correction in a cross wind.

By 1957 tail fins would define the era's styling and be included on nearly every model of car coming out of Detroit. Chrysler stylist Virgil Exner in-cluded tail fins on the Chrysler New Yorker and De Soto between 1957 and 1959. Ford also followed suit producing models with fins such as the Lincoln Premier, Ford Fairlane and Ford Thunderbird. Even Studebaker-Packard got

1958 Packard Hawk Convertible. (Photo by Lawrence T. Hay)

into the act between 1957 and 1959 producing cars with fins such as the Hawk, Commander and President.

But the fins leader was GM. When the GM Buick division began commercial production on the Buick La Sabre in 1958 of course the model featured prominent tail fins. While between 1955 and 1959 fins were a prominent part of the design of the Chevrolet Bel Air and Chevrolet Impala lines, as well as the Buick Roadmaster, the most exaggerated example of fins was to be found on GM's Cadillac Coup Deville and Cadillac Eldorado.

The fins on the 1959 Cadillac Coup Deville were sharp enough to open a letter! The fins on the Caddy rose almost to the top of the rear window screen and at mid-point featured a bulge that resembled a rocket fuselage. Consumer advocate Ralph Nader would later allege that a motorcyclist in California had nearly been killed when coming to a sudden stop he became airborne and was impaled on a Cadillac tail fin.

Fins on automobiles in the 1950s went hand-in-hand with the decade's most defining cultural expression—the rise of rock n' roll music.

In a speech before the Society of Automobile Engineers in 1955 noted industrial designer Raymond Lowey said that Harley Earl's cars had become "jukeboxes on wheels."[1]

1959 Cadillac Coup de Ville tail fins. (Photo by Lawrence T. Hay)

To some degree Lowey's statement had merit. For America's youth in the 1950s nothing was more symbolic of the era as Rock n' Roll and the car/girl mythology. The two were synonymous and defined the popular culture of the times. The juke box, hamburger joint and sock hop were the social focal points, while hot rods, souped-up Chevys, Fords and other American cars with huge tail fins were the era's youthful status symbols. It was a period of pretty girls sitting in the front seat close alongside boys sporting a duck tail or crew cut hair with the radio blasting. It epitomized freedom and a new social order and Rock n' Roll music was the era's soundtrack.

It all began in 1949 when General Motors produced the first popularly priced car with a compressed V-8 engine the Oldsmobile Rocket 88. It was the first of class that would later in the 1960s be called muscle cars

The automobiles of the 1950s would inspire many singers and songwriters. One of the first was rhythm & blues singer Jackie Benston who in 1951 with his group the Delta Cats recorded "Rocket 88" which was based on a 1947 song "Cadillac Boogie." "Rocket 88" peaked at #8 on the Billboard rhythm & blues chart. Bill Haley and the Saddlemen (later to become Bill Haley & The Comets) recorded a cover version of the song.

1949 Oldsmobile 88. (Photo by Lawrence T. Hay)

The Oldsmobile Rocket 88 would later be worked into the lyrics of "Rip It Up" originally recorded by Little Richard and covered by Elvis Presley.

The most recorded hot rod song of all time is "Hot Rod Lincoln" written by Charles Ryan and first recorded by Arkie Shirley on Souvenir Records in 1955.

"Hot Rod Lincoln" is a Rock-a-Billy song that was written by Ryan as an answer song to Arkie Shibley's 1951 hit "Hot Rod Race." That song describes a race in San Pedro, California between two hot rods, one a Ford the other a Mercury. Both cars are roaring along at high speed neck-and-neck then suddenly both are overtaken by a kid driving a hopped-up Ford Model A with a Lincoln-Zephyr V12 engine, overdrive, a four-barrel carburetor, 4:11 gear ration, and safety tubes.

Since 1955 "Hot Rod Lincoln" has been recorded by Asleep At The Wheel, the punk rock group All, Chris Costello, Commander Cody, Lawrence Ramsey and many others.

At the same time another Rock n' Roll giant was frequently cutting a record with an automobile worked into the lyrics. In 1955 Leonard Chess founder of Chess Records located in Chicago, Illinois signed Chuck Berry after he listened to one of his recorded tracks tapped on a $79 mono recorder. One of those tracks by Chuck Berry was "Maybellene" and when Chess released the record it quickly reached number 5 on the pop charts and made Berry one of the most popular Rock n' Roll singers in the world.

"Maybellene" is a song about a hot rod race and a broken romance.

"Maybellene" would become a Rock n' Roll classic and also be recorded by the Everly Brothers, Jerry Lee Lewis and many other artists.

Chuck Berry would continue to write and record hit songs using automobile themes through-out his long musical career. Just to mention a few; in 1955 Berry recorded "No Money Down" and in 1964 "No Particular Place to Go." And of course there was the 1960 classic "Jaguar and Thunderbird" which describes in its lyrics a drag race in rural Indiana.

Elvis Presley, his manager Colonel Tom Parker and Chuck Berry all owned Cadillacs. Presley's first was his iconic pink Cadillac. Later Elvis owned a solid gold 1960 Cadillac 75 limousine. The gold came from an exterior sheen of 24 karat gold highlights. The car is currently on display in the Country Music Hall of Fame Museum in Nashville, Tennessee.

Chuck Berry's 1973 red Cadillac convertible is currently on display at the National Museum of African American History and Culture in Washington, D.C.

While the hot rod and car songs of the 1950s tended to have a rough edge in their lyrics and attracted slightly rebellious teenagers as their primary listeners, by the early 1960s hot rod cars songs would be mainstream with a broad sociological stratification of incomes and education levels among their followers led by clean cut, Southern California groups such as Jan and Dean and the Beach Boys.

Jan Berry and Dean Torrence, natives of Southern California, were pioneers of the surf and hot rod music sound that would be taken to an even larger popularity by the Beach Boys. In fact, the Beach Boys greatly influenced by Jan and Dean; had shared a common songwriter on some of their songs and also did a little studio back-up singing for them.

One of Jan and Dean's first major hits was "Drag City" which hit the charts in 1963. In 1964 the duo had a monster hit with "The Little Old Lady From Pasadena." The song was inspired by Kathryn Minners an actress then in her early 70s who had made a series of commercials for Southern California Dodge dealers promoting the company's popular muscle cars. The tag line of the commercials was "Put Dodge cars in your garage honey."

Also In 1964 Jan & Dean recorded "Dead Man's Curve" which was a song about a drag race with tragic consequences.

On April 12, 1966 life would imitate art for Jan Berry. When driving his Corvette Stingray in Beverly Hills Berry would slam into a parked gardener's truck. Berry would then go through a full decade of physical rehabilitation before he could resume his music career.

As popular as Jan and Dean were in the early 1960s the undisputed champions of Surf and Hot Rod music were the Beach Boys. Originally recording on the Candix label the Beach Boys didn't have much success with their release of "Surfin" in 1961. Then Murry Wilson father to Dennis, Brian and Carl Wilson, who along with their cousin Mike Love and friend Al Jardine who formed the group, shopped the group's demo records around that included "Surfin USA" and "409" a song written by Brian Wilson and Gary Usher about Usher's Chevrolet '409.' When Capitol Records offered Murry Wilson $300 for the master discs of the songs, he grabbed it.

In 1962 on the Capitol label the Beach Boys released a single that featured "Surfin Sarfari" on the A-side and "409" on the B-side. The record was a huge hit.

Going forward the Beach Boys decided to continue with the combination of the surfing and drag racing format as a standard modus operandi for recording and success followed with each record released. In 1963 "Surfin USA" on the A side and "Shut Down" on the B side was released. Then the combination of "Surfer Girl" and "Little Duce Coup" was released in August of the same year. In 1964 cars moved over to the A-side as the Ford Thunderbird was memorialized in American popular culture by the Beach Boys who used it as the central focus of the lyrics in their hit song "Fun, Fun, Fun." Then "I Get Around" and "Shut You Down" would soon follow.

As the Beach Boys established an international following they began to move away from surfing, open roads and drag racing themes and began to write and record songs about the idyllic life-style of California teenagers with hits such as "All Summer Long," "California Girls" and "Help Me Rhonda." By the middle 1960s the group was experimenting with psychedelic music with "Good Vibrations."

The Beach Boys had clearly made their mark as the vinyl kings of the surfing and hot rod craze and were more responsible than any other single artist or group for the creation of the genre.

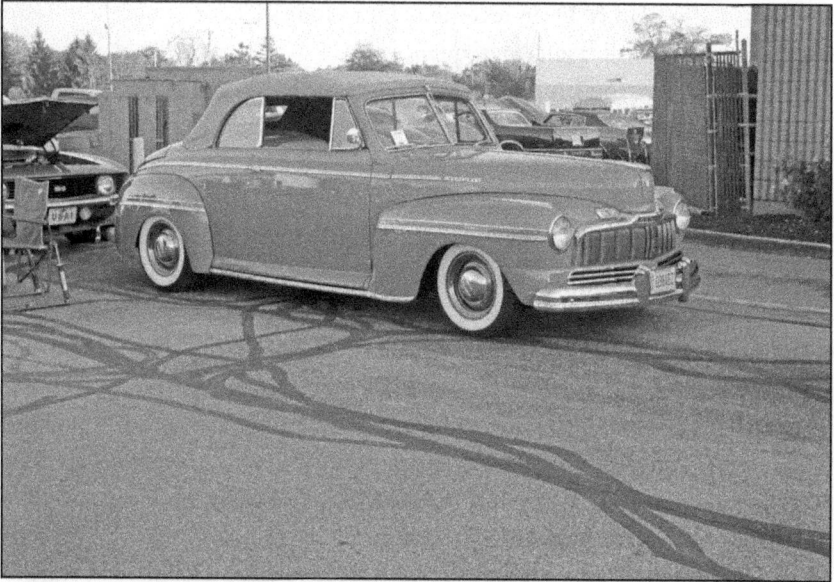

1947 Mercury Convertible. (Photo by Lawrence T. Hay)

While other artists would join in the hot rod craze, their contributions would be million seller one hit wonders such as the Rip Cords "Hey Little Cobra" and Ronnie and the Daytonas "Little GTO."

The artists and groups associated with the British invasion of the American pop and rock music of the mid 1960s made no attempt to make records with a hot rod theme. That was considered purely American and the Brits played it safe staying solidly within the traditional Rock n' Roll theme, although sometimes with a twist that became known as the Mersey sound.

Nonetheless there was an occasional headline made by an English rock group associated with the automobile. One of the more hilarious such incidents occurred in 1967 when Keith Moon, drummer for The Who, plunged a Lincoln Continental into the swimming pool of a Holiday Inn in Flint, Michigan.

Charles Wilson had led General Motors to the brink of becoming the world's first billion-dollar company when in 1953 President-elect Dwight D. Eisenhower tapped the GM CEO to become his Secretary of Defense.

Wilson's confirmation hearing in front of the Senate Armed Services Committee on January 15, 1953 became one of the most memorable such proceedings in American history. During the hearing Wilson, who would have to take a $577,500 a year pay cut to accept the job, was asked if was going to sell his stock in GM if confirmed by the committee. At the time Wilson owned 39,477 shares of GM estimated to be worth $2.5 million. Secretaries of Defense have the authority to sign-off on huge defense contracts with vendors, including GM.

Wilson replied that he intended to retain his stock in GM. Then Wilson stated "For years, I thought that what was good for our country was good for General Motors and vice versa.[2] Since that day Charles Wilson has become the most misquoted prospective cabinet member in U. S. history—as his words were turned around to suggest that he stated "what was good for General Motors was good for the country."

An additional committee hearing and an agreement by Wilson to sell his stock became necessary before he was confirmed. Charles "the engine" Wilson went on to serve in the Eisenhower Administration with distinction between 1953 and 1957. Then Wilson went into retirement and died on September 26, 1961 on his plantation in Louisiana.

GM had incredible executive bench strength in the 1950s and Charles Wilson was succeeded as president of the company by Harlow Curtice on February 2, 1953.

Harlow Curtice had been born on August 15, 1893 in Eaton Rapids, Michigan. He would graduate from Ferris State College in 1914 where he studied accounting and business.

In 1914 Curtice answered a blind ad in a newspaper for a bookkeeping position at AC Sparkplugs in Flint, Michigan. By 1929 he was president of the company.

Buick was the oldest of GM's divisions and in 1926 it had sold 266,733 cars, but by 1933 it was failing badly having sold only 49,000 cars. It was that year that Harlow Curtice was named president of the Buick division. Through the leadership of Curtice the Buick division would once again rise to a place of prominence in the GM brand selling 377,428 cars in 1941.

By 1948 Buick would be a major force in the automobile market with the introduction of "Dynaflow" which was a unique torque converter transmission which eliminated gears and the conventional clutch in the forward diving position.

By 1953 there was an air of pessimism starting to permeate the Detroit automakers as most had come to the conclusion that the post-war economic boom was about to bust. To the contrary, Harlow Curtice was full optimism. He wasn't content with GM having 49% of the market; regardless of the possible consequences of government anti-trust charges, Curtice wanted 75% of the market. On January 1, 1954 Curtice committed GM to a $1 billion expansion program. It was during 1954 that GM produced its 50 millionth car, a 1955 Chevrolet Bel Air.

In 1956 Harlow Curtice was named *Time* magazine's "Man of the Year." By the time Curtice retired on August 31, 1958, GM was selling 60% of the cars and trucks purchased by Americans and in one year had made a vault busting $1 billion in net profits.

Some of the automobiles produced in the 1950s became classics in engineering while others became classic busts.

In 1952 Henry Ford II convinced Louis D. Crusoe who had previously been the vice president of the Ford division to abandon retirement and return to work. While in attendance at the Paris Auto Show in 1953 Crusoe and a Ford designer saw the Chevrolet Corvette for first time. Crusoe was convinced that Ford could build a car to compete with the Corvette. He quickly gained approval and then combined his talents with that of Ford automotive engineer George Walker to design the Thunderbird.

The name Thunderbird came from a contest that Crusoe initiated among Ford employees in which the ultimate name accepted would win $250. More than 5000 names were submitted including Hep-Cat, Beaver, Tigre and Runabout. The winner Thunderbird was submitted by Alden "Gib" Giberson a young Ford stylist who took the name from native-American mythology.

The Ford Thunderbird or T-Bird as it would become popularly known was introduced in 1955 with a base sticker price of $2,695 equipped with a 292 CTP V-8 engine featuring such amenities as power seats and a clock tachometer, which personified style in automobiles. While the Thunderbird took time to find its market selling only 53,000 over the first three years of production the car outsold the Corvette in 1955 by 14,000 to 700. While the original T-Bird was a two-seater, in 1958 by request of Ford consumers a four-seater was produced.

With sales sagging behind the T-Bird, GM considered discontinuing the Corvette, but an engineer with the company appealed to Ed Cole to keep the car as he felt stopping production would be an admission of failure.

The 1953 "Vette" as it was to be commonly known had come in just one color, polo white. GM agreed to keep producing the Corvette and by 1962 were selling 10,000 a year and making a profit. The Corvette would continue to rise in popularity through-out the 1960s until it had reached iconic status as

1963 Ford Thunderbird. (Photo by Lawrence T. Hay)

America's classic sports car. When the Corvette ZO6 was chosen as the official pace car of the Indianapolis 500 in 2015 it marked the 13th time a Corvette had been the pace car and 26th time a Chevrolet had the honor.

Meanwhile the T-Bird went in a different direction and was no longer considered a competitor to the Vette. The original plans for the Thunderbird had been to build a car that weighed 2,575 pounds that could do 100 mph. But the car kept growing in engine size and by 1976 the T-Bird was a huge gas hog with a 400 cubic inch engine, 7.5-liter, V-8 that got 8 miles per gallon in the city and 11 on the highway.

The last Ford Thunderbird to roll off the production line occurred on July 1, 2005. Then in 2015, by popular demand, the Thunderbird returned to production.

The Oscar nominated George Lucas film *American Graffiti* released in 1973 staring Ron Howard and Richard Dreyfuss would feature a memorable white 1956 T-Bird convertible.

The 1956 Thunderbird convertible used in the film had been purchased by Clay Daily and his wife off a used Ford car lot in San Bernardino, California in 1964. At that time the T-Bird had been painted red and had about 55,000 miles showing on its odometer. A couple of years later the Dailys would move to Petaluma, CA. They would paint the T-Bird white.

In 1972 Clay's wife had parked the T-Bird in downtown Petaluma. When she returned to the car, she found a piece of a brown paper bag on the windshield. A note had been written on the bag and the message inquired if the T-Bird's owner would like to have their car in a movie. There was a telephone number written on the paper bag that said to call if interested. The Dailys thought it was all a joke, nonetheless, they called the number. The telephone number turned-out to be for Lucas Films and they were serious about using the car. So, the Dailys agreed and the rest is history; their white T-Bird appeared in *American Graffiti* rolling down the streets of Petaluma and on the highway beyond with Suzanne Sommers as the mysterious blonde behind the wheel teasing Richard Dreyfuss.

The Thunderbird would make an encore performance on the silver screen in the 1991 female bandits classic *Thelma & Louise* staring Geena Davis and Susan Sarandon. As the film concludes; the law is in hot in pursuit of the two outlaws so they form an impromptu suicide pact then drive their T-Bird over a cliff and free-fall 2000 feet down into the Grand Canyon at Dead Horse Ponte State Park in Moab, Utah.

Ed Cole the man at GM who prevented the Corvette from being taken out of production was a Michigan farm boy turned engineer who was a technological visionary.

In between marriages in the late 1950s Ed Cole dated movie actress Mamie Van Doren, aka "The Blond Bombshell." Mamie Van Doren was a former Miss Palm Springs who had listed on her dating resume a past relationship with eccentric billionaire Howard Hughes. Not to be outdone; to express his devotion for the actress Cole presented Mamie with a pink Corvette so that it would match her lipstick.

In the early 1950s Ed Cole created a new lighter 4.3-liter, V-8 engine at GM and made it standard in the 1955 Chevrolet. That year GM with Cole's V-8 engine sold 1.83 million cars in addition to 393,000 trucks with the new V-8 engine.

The 1956 Chevrolet featuring a 283 horsepower V8 engine, with fuel injection and dual exhausts was so powerful that some were still being used in NASCAR races into the 1970s beating all in their class until being grandfathered out of competition.

Some other cars coming out of Detroit in the late 1950s and early 1960s became automotive engineering disasters.

1956 Chevrolet Corvette. (Photo by Lawrence T. Hay)

In 1957 Volkswagen had sold over 70,000 cars in America and the American Motors compact Nash Rambler was also selling modestly well. So, GM decided to attempt to recover some of the low-end market from Volkswagen.

In one of the most paradoxical events in American automotive engineering history, Ed Cole who had overseen the development of GM's powerful V-8 engine in the 1949 Cadillac was charged with designing a compact car that could compete on the market with Volkswagen and the Nash Rambler. The car that Cole and his team built for GM would become one of the biggest automotive engineering disasters of all-time—the Corvair which is discussed in the following chapter.

By 1963 with lawsuits against Chevrolet reaching one hundred the company was forced to cancel production of further models of the Corvair.

The Corvair became the centerpiece of a 1965 book *Unsafe at Any Speed* authored by budding consumer advocate Ralph Nader. In his book Nader asserted that the Detroit automakers were not concerned with safety and wouldn't even include such fundamental life-preserving items as seat belts in their cars.

Another memorable automobile that was considerably safer than the Corvair but failed to find a market in the 1950s was Ford's Edsel. The car named after Henry and Clara Ford's only son was dead on arrival in the marketplace.

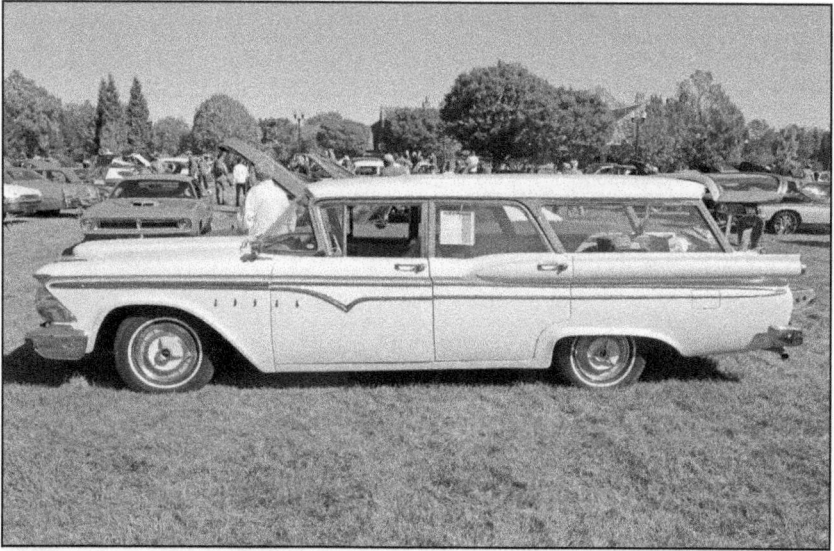

1959 Edsel six-passenger Villager Station Wagon with its 332-cubic-inch-V8 engine. (Photo by Lawrence T. Hay)

The reasons for the car's failure were varied. Some said that the Edsel just had too many gadgets. The car did feature such items as a push-button transmission and a speedometer that changed colors as the speed increased.

The shape of the Edsel's grill was a source of much controversy. Some said that it resembled a woman's lips puckered-up about to be kissed. Some offered a quasi-Freudian analysis saying that the Edsel's grill resembled a vagina. While still others said the shape of the grill gave the car the appearance that it had no power. While the Edsel was a very powerful car with a 346 horsepower V8 engine, it just couldn't stand up to the heavy competition from other manufactures' large cars such as the Chrysler New Yorker and GM's Pontiac and Chevy Impala.

In 1959 only 44,841 Edsels were sold and in 1960 production was cut after 2,846 had been built. By comparison the 1958 Chevy Impala with a 290 horsepower and V8 engine sold 55,989 convertibles and 125,480 coups. The Edsel venture had cost The Ford Motor Company a $250 million loss and brought an end to the company's Continental Division. Soon after the demise of the Edsel, Lincoln and Mercury were combined into one division.

But some good would also come out of the Edsel debacle for Ford. Robert McNamara who by that time had advanced to vice-president of the Continental Division (later controversial secretary of defense in the John F. Kennedy cabinet

1956 Chevrolet BelAir owned by Paul Welz. (Photo by Lawrence T. Hay)

over decisions relative to fighting the Viet Nam War) would put to use the plant and equipment that were used for the Edsel to create the Falcon, Ford's first compact car which in 1965 would morph into the Mustang.

Unfortunately, some car manufactures were not able to keep-up with the popularity of lines produced by Detroit's Big Three; Ford, GM and Chrysler, so they started to fold in the late 1950s.

Most notable was The Packard Motor Company which had been producing automobiles in Detroit since 1899. During the 1930s the Packard had been synonymous in describing American luxury cars right alongside Cadillac and Lincoln. In fact, during the period between 1925 and 1934 Packard outsold Cadillac by 2 to 1. That trend continued and in the pre-war period of 1935 to 1941 Packard increased its sales over Cadillac by 3 to 1.

But by 1950 Cadillac surpassed the sales of the Packard and never looked back. In order to compete with the Big Three, Packard merged with Studebaker, but production of the Packard ceased in Detroit in 1957. Studebaker then dropped Packard from its name plate and struggled on for a few more years before calling it quits.

Today, the massive former Packard plant in Detroit personifies the term "rust belt." The plant consisting of 3.5 million square feet sitting on 35 acres is the largest abandoned factory in the world and serves as the tombstone for the golden age of auto manufacturing in Detroit.

By 1950 America's over-populated post-war cities were busting at the seams; New York City had a population of 7,891,957, Chicago 3,670,962, Philadelphia 2,071,605, Los Angeles 1,970,358 and Detroit 1,849,568. It just wasn't the nation's largest cities that were cramped, mid-sized cities like Denver, Pittsburgh, Cincinnati, Houston, Indianapolis and Kansas City felt the inner-city pinch too.

From the time of the Great Depression through World War Two very little new housing had built. During this period new housing starts fell from a million a year to less than 100,000. In fact, prior to the war the average contractor built only two homes per year. Consequently, by the mid-twentieth century most people in the nation's inner cities were living in close proximity with each other in dowdy pre-1920 constructed apartment buildings and houses. The suburbs that existed outside of the city limits were for the most part small under-developed communities, more often than not, rural in character and a difficult commute into the downtown areas.

One of the most notable persons to take charge and change that condition was William Levitt. Born in Brooklyn in 1907, Levitt's father ran a real estate development company. During World War Two William Levitt served as a lieutenant with the U.S. Navy Seabees charged with constructing instant airfields.

William Levitt was very cognizant of a looming crisis involving housing in America's post-war cities. He knew an affordable housing crisis was eminent with the projected baby boom and the expected post-war booming economy.

Following the war Levitt along with his brother Alfred, an architect founded a construction company and began to produce low cost, quality housing in mass that resulted in the establishment of completely new communities. Prior to the war Levitt had taken out an option on a thousand acres of farmland near Hempstead, Long Island that had been mostly potato farms. Following the war Levitt would continue to add real estate to that which he already owned in the area. It was this land that would become Levitt's first planned and nearly self-contained community that he would call Levittown.

The homes designed by Levitt for his community were simple in design with lots of 60 by 100 feet with a living room that was 12 by 16 feet with two bedrooms, one bathroom and a kitchen in the back so women could watch their kids in the yard. The basic Levitt Cape Cod sold for $7,990 and later an expanded ranch-style house was added that cost $9,500. There were no down

1941 Packard One Twenty. (Photo by Lawrence T. Hay)

payments and no closing costs. It was noted by Kenneth Jackson in his book *Crabgrass Frontier* "that in their simplicity, durability, and value, the early Levitt houses were not unlike the Model T."[3]

While Levittown promised the good life, it was selective in that regard. At its beginning Levittown was a "whites only" community. William Levitt justified his segregationist policy stating, "As a Jew I have no room in my mind or heart for the racial prejudice. But . . . I have come to know that if we sell one house to a Negro family, then 90 or 95 percent or our white customers will not buy into the community."[4] By 1953 Levittown with a population of 70,000 constituted the largest community in the U.S. without any black residents.[5]

After the Long Island project William Levitt would build two more large housing communities, one in Levittown, Pennsylvania and another in Willingboro, New Jersey. Levitt's planned communities would become the model for nearly all subdivisions built in the U.S. between 1955 and 1970 with 10% of the builders putting up 70% of the new houses.

By 1970 there were more people living in suburbs than urban or rural areas in the country. Between 1945 and 1954 nine million Americans moved to the suburbs. By 1980 more than 60 million had migrated to former farmlands that surrounded cities.

The mass-migration to the suburbs was dependent on the automobile. So, during the 1950s the automobile would affect significant cultural and social changes.

The first drive-in movie theatre had begun operation on June 6, 1933 in Pennsauken, New Jersey, but following World War Two as more and more people relocated to the new post-war suburbs the drive-in became part of the suburban leisure landscape alongside the miniature golf course. The drive-in movie was widely popular with families who could bring the kids, including the baby. Young couples who wanted a place to cuddle and "make-out" found them highly conducive environments. At its peak of popularity in 1958 there were 4,065 drive-in theatres in the U.S.

The symbiotic relationship between the suburb and the automobile also created the shopping center that later morphed into the mall. The first planned out-of-town shopping center opened in Raleigh, North Carolina in 1949. The first enclosed climate-controlled shopping mall opened in Minneapolis in 1956. By 1980 there were 20,000 major suburban shopping centers and malls across the U.S.

Even McDonald's began as a suburban drive-in burger joint. Founded by brothers Dick and Maurice "Mac" McDonald in San Bernardino, California their restaurants would grow into a fast food behemoth under the direction of Ray Kroc after establishing a franchise agreement with the brothers in 1954.

Ray Kroc who lived in the Chicago suburbs once vowed that there would never be a McDonald's in the Chicago loop. In Kroc's mind McDonald's was a family restaurant; a lower middle class suburban burger environment with pickles, ketchup and onions on it and the only thing he could count on by putting one of his hamburger joints in an urban area were bums and rowdy teenagers who would damage the reputation of the establishment.

While McDonald's had started as a suburban institution; money talks and Ray Kroc listened. By the early 1970s McDonald's were sprouting-up in downtown areas of cities across the nation from San Francisco to New York. By 1977 McDonalds was grossing more than $3.2 billion a year and outselling its primary competitor Burger King by four to one.

With all the new post-war cars coming out of Detroit in the 1950s and suburbs sprouting up the need for an improved highway system was self-evident. President Dwight D. Eisenhower would address that need in a grand way. But there would be a considerable learning curve for Eisenhower before he was in a position to act.

In 1919 Harry Ostermann replaced Henry Joy, president of the Packard Motor Car Company as the Lincoln Highway Association's new president. That same year the Lincoln Highway project was resurrected.

Harry Ostermann had led a colorful existence being employed at various times as a New York newsboy, a sailor in the U. S. Navy, an employee of Buffalo Bill's Wild West Show, a drifter, orange picker, businessman and inventor.

In 1914 after a failed business adventure Ostermann had joined the Lincoln Highway Association as its Field Director. Ostermann was a skilled public speaker and advocate and led campaigns to urge citizens to speak out on behalf of better roads. In 1919 he persuaded the War Department to undertake a transcontinental convoy to study state of and efficiency of America's roads from a strategic military perspective.

The Army agreed and in 1919, the Secretary of War assigned 81 trucks and one tank to be under the command of Lt. Colonel Charles McClure to set out on a transcontinental convoy from Washington, D.C. to San Francisco along the proposed marked routes of the Lincoln Highway.

On October 14, 1918, Dwight D. Eisenhower's 28th birthday, he had been given a temporary war time promotion to the rank of Lt. Colonel. In 1919 he and Major Sereno Brett were assigned to accompany the convoy as observers. Because the two officers decided late to participate, they missed opening ceremony of the convoy which took place July 7, 1919 on the Ellipse of (a big patch of land) just south of the White House in Washington. Soon Eisenhower and Brett joined the party when it reached Frederick, Maryland where camp was made for overnight.

One of the fallacies in Eisenhower's military career is that during this exploratory journey he made some great contribution to America's highway system, but the truth is that Eisenhower had viewed the convoy as a vacation.

From Frederick, Maryland the convoy then headed for Gettysburg, Pennsylvania to access the Lincoln Highway and proceed west for San Francisco. The exercise turned-out to be an enormous undertaking and adventure. Along the way the convoy endured a large number of flat tires, broken axles and motor repairs. After driving over endless stretches of dirt roads, wagon trails and rivers with no bridges while enduring welcoming speeches and ceremonies in all most every town, borough and city along the way, sixty-two days after leaving Washington, D.C., the military convoy was carried across San Francisco Bay by ferry and paraded through the city to Lincoln Park where a final speech was made.

But the convoy had proved that long-distance motor travel was possible, that the gasoline engine had replaced the mule and the construction of the Lincoln Highway soon began in earnest.

Two decades later General Dwight David Eisenhower served as the supreme commander of the Allied Troops in Europe in World War Two. At the end of the war in 1945 General Eisenhower had the opportunity to view first-hand the German *autobahn*.

The first leg of the German *autobahn* had been completed in 1932 consisting of a 108-mile-high speed highway between Cologne and Bonn. When Adolph Hitler and the Third Reich came to power the autobahn was expanded and by the fall of 1935 the next link of the *autobahn* had been completed from Frankfurt to Darmstadt. Hitler would ultimately expand the *autobahn* to 1086 miles as an alternative to trains for moving military units around Germany.

By 1953 Dwight D. Eisenhower, aka Ike, was now president of the United States. The new president was deeply aware of the potential threat to America's population in urban centers created by the Cold War standoff with Joseph Stalin and the Soviet Union and the advent of nuclear weapons. Eisenhower saw the building of a high-speed interstate highway system as an efficient method of evacuating large American urban centers in the threat of nuclear attack.

Furthermore, different kinds of roads were now needed and needed in different places. In the early 1950s many of the nation's highways were completely obsolete having been constructed over old Indian trails and cow paths. Early road builders always took the path of least resistance and didn't even move boulders, land boundaries or many buildings.

A large number of local roads remained unsurfaced and main roads needed improvements, including divided highways for heavy traffic and expressways together with ample parking for metropolitan areas. But above all a modern interstate highway system was needed.

In 1948 the Federal government had completed a study for an interstate highway system without regard for future requirements. Consequently, by 1954 that study was obsolete as travel by automobile, bus and truck had increased by 40%. The next study done in the early 1950s would project road needs for a period of ten to twenty years.

President Eisenhower proposed to build an interstate system that would provide safe and speedy transcontinental travel, improve inter-city communication, farm-to-market movement and relieve metropolitan congestion, bottlenecks and parking, and of course provide evacuation routes from primary targets in the event of a nuclear showdown with the Soviet Union.

Congress had made half-hearted attempts over the years to plan a major interstate system but always seemed to face some unsurmountable obstacle. Until that point in time in the early 1950s highway construction had very much been a state affair with financial and research assistance from the Federal government through the Bureau of Public Roads. Highways built with Federal aid formed the U.S. roads through-out the nation.

Governors of various states had been arguing in the early 1950s for less, not more, Federal government participation in highway revenues and construction. If it were not the states quibbling about who was going to pay for the interstate highway system, it was the special interest groups like the American Automobile Association (AAA) and others that could not present a unified position to Congress. It was clear that if an interstate highway system was going to be built the Federal government would have to take the lead.

President Eisenhower knew both the public and Congress would see the inherent value in the project, not just from a transportation perspective of moving goods and people rapidly from city to city or a defense position to evacuate them, but also by the fact that the building of the system would employ millions of workers in an integrated industrial output for well over a decade to complete it.

In 1955 there had been 7.92 million cars sold, 2 million more than in 1954. In Detroit the auto manufacturing executives at Ford, General Motors, Chrysler and American Motors were nearly giddy with the thought of a huge new modern highway system crisscrossing America; together with the steel manufacturers at U. S. Steel, Bethlehem Steel and Republic Steel, they saw the building of an interstate highway system as a potential boom for business.

However, at first the oil companies were not in lock-step support of building the interstate system fearing that they would bare the major share of the burden for financing the system through an increased gas tax.

While the German *autobahn* may have sparked Eisenhower's interest in constructing an American interstate highway system the model for the system was the Pennsylvania Turnpike, the first state-run toll superhighway that by the early 1950s was carrying 10 million vehicles a year.

Eventually both Congress and the AAA began to support am interstate highway system. AAA urged its members to contact their congressmen and

Dwight D. Eisenhower, 1956. (Wikimedia Commons)

senators and began a "Program for Better Highways" that proposed a 15-year, three phase, pay-as-you-go financing plan through moderate, graduated increases in Federal automobile taxes with the Feds paying for 90% of interstate highway construction and maintenance.

Eventually congressmen and senators became cognizant of the fact that the existing Federal highway system ran through 403 of 435 of the congressional districts confronting them with reality that they all had a stake in the outcome of an interstate plan.

In a message to Congress delivered on February 22, 1955 President Eisenhower stated that, the nation's highway system was a gigantic enterprise, one of the United States largest items of capital investment. It consisted of 3,366,000 miles of road on which 58 million motor vehicles traveled on. Eisenhower said that the replacement costs of the system's drainage and bridges and tunnels works were incalculable and one in seven Americans made their livelihood and supported their family out of it. But in large part, the network was inadequate for the nation's growing needs.

Saying that the interstate system should be given top priority in construction planning, Eisenhower pointed out that when completed as planned the interstate system while it would only comprise 1.2 % of the total road mileage in the country, it would join 42 state capitals and 90% of all cities in the country with a population over 50,000.

In regard to the national defense component in the need to build an interstate highway system President Eisenhower stated, "In case of an atomic attack on our key cities the road net must permit quick evacuation of target areas, mobilization of defense forces and maintenance of every essential economic function. But the present system in critical areas would be the breeder of deadly congestion within hours of an attack."[6]

At the urging of President Eisenhower, Congress passed The Federal Aid Highway Act of 1956 and the president signed the bill on June 21. The passage of the bill began the construction of the Interstate Highway system on August 13. 1956.

The bill allocated $26 billion to pay for the system with the Federal government paying 90% of the new construction costs. The money came from an increased gas tax of 3 cents instead of 2 cents that went into a non-divertible Highway Trust Fund.

The longest Interstate Highway constructed in the system would be I-90 which runs a total of 3,020 miles connecting Seattle, Washington and Boston, Massachusetts.

While the building of the Interstate Highway System would increase commerce and mobility across the nation, the construction of the 42,000-mile system would come with social consequences.

While the Federal government provided financial aid to the states to build the interstate, each individual state's highway department was responsible for determining the route of each interstate highway through their respective state.

The system's planners universally routed the interstate wherever they believed it to be beneficial to the system as a whole. In almost every city in the system's path entire neighborhoods were destroyed. Some of the neighborhoods blocking construction of the system had been stable for over a hundred years. In these areas people were displaced from their homes, most were black people, who then began to integrate previous all-white neighborhoods setting-off a huge round of white flight to the suburbs. In other cases, the system led to abandonment and decay of many cities.

It all happened very quickly too. So quickly that in some urban areas displaced people barely had enough time to evacuate their homes and find another dwelling before the wrecking ball came through the walls.

In Cincinnati in order to clear the way for Interstate 75 an inter-city neighborhood designated as Kenyon-Barr by planners on the southwest corner of the core area of the city was demolished. Kenyon-Barr (now called Queensgate) was declared a slum by the city. At the time the area was inhabited by 25,737 people of which 25,155 were Afro-Americans. The area although deprived economically contained 10,295 dwellings, 137 food stores, 118 bars and restaurants, 86 barber shops and beauty parlors, 80 churches and missions, 24 dry cleaners and 6 funeral parlors.

Residents of Kenyon-Barr were informed that they had to move via a notice that came in the mail on city letterhead: "The building which you occupy has been purchased by the City of Cincinnati. [...] Now that you have received this letter you should start looking for another place to move immediately. [...] ALL OCCUPANTS OF THIS PROPERTY MUST MOVE." The message was signed, "Very Sincerely Yours, Wanda W. Dunteman, Supervisor of Relocation and Property Management."[7]

Even the late author/major league baseball pitcher Jim Brosnan felt compelled to mention in his 1962 book *Pennate Race* the circumstances of Afro-American residents in another part of Cincinnati's West End neighborhoods where Crosley Field was located as century old homes were being demolished that stood in the path of I-75. During Reds home stands Brosnan routinely took a city bus to Crosley Field and in his book, he wrote, "To get to (Cincinnati's) Crosley Field, I usually take a bus through the old crumbling streets of the Bottoms. Negroes stand on the corners watching their homes fall down."[8]

It just wasn't the urban dwellers that were affected by the encroaching interstate system, it affected rural residents too.

Rock/Folk singer John Mellencamp a native of rural Indiana often used the area for the backdrop in the lyrics of his songs. In his hit song "Pink Houses" Mellencamp made reference to an interstate running through the front yard of a black man adding that the man thought he had it good.

The planners of the interstate system also had little regard for preservation of national landmarks. While the interstate system was supposed to enable more tourist than ever before to see more historic sites in the country, little bits of Americana would disappear in construction of the highway.

In 1958 a fire storm of public backlash was created in Morristown, New Jersey by the planning of a stretch of I-278 that was to come within 100 yards of the mansion formerly owned by Colonel Jacob Ford used by General George Washington as his headquarters during the gloomy winter of 1779-80 where he reorganized and revitalized his depleted Army. The plan required taking some of the mansion's grounds for the highway and touched off a huge battle between local and state forces as well as some members of the New Jersey Congressional delegation.

When completed the Interstate Highway System actually consisted of 44,000 miles of highway crisscrossing the nation along with 82 tunnels, 55,000 bridges and 14,000 interchanges.

The construction of the Interstate Highway System during the late-1950s through the mid-1970s unified the American landscape like nothing had before it. Desolate beaches and mountain ranges gave way to new resort towns. Suddenly, a new term entered the American lexicon—the weekend getaway. Travelers began to speak of travel in terms of time rather than miles.

But with each mile of highway constructed in the system the country began to assume a homogenous appearance from north to south and from east to west as America entered the age of mass society.

Mass society in essence is a marketing concept more than a sociological circumstance where by the things that use to be considered unique to one area of the country or another, products, services, hospitality, etc., are repackaged and made available in the same format across the continent. In the process regional identity and tradition more often than not became compromised and even disappeared. No longer did you have to drive west of the Mississippi River to get a Coors Beer. At every exit on the Interstate System you would find the same accommodations, the Holiday Inn, the Days Inn and Howard Johnsons. It wouldn't be long before shopping centers were located at the foot of the exits, and they all looked the same.

Today the interstate system is formally known as the Eisenhower System of Interstate and Defense Highways. While for better or worse, depending on your point of view, the Interstate Highway System changed the way America did business; one fact that cannot be denied by all is that the Interstate made the entire country easily accessible.

In 2020 if you are in a hurry and have two people who can alternate between driving and sleeping, it is possible to cross the country via the Interstate
Highway system from New York to San Francisco in 2.5 days. Or those two
people could take a more leisurely journey, seeing a few sights such as a National
Park or some significant monuments while sleeping in motels and cross the
country in 5 days.

While the rise in popularity and convenience of airline travel following
World War Two had started the decline of passenger train travel in America, the
building of the Interstate Highway System was its death knell. Passenger service
went into a steep decline with each mile of interstate completed and nearly
passed into history as railroads merged and folded operations.

Also following World War Two, as highway construction increased, the
rural population's preferred mode of inter-city transportation changed from the
train to the bus and such companies as Greyhound and Trailways flourished
while the railroads were hard hit.

On May 1, 1971 Congress created The National Railroad Passenger
Corporation (Amtrak) to provide medium and long-distance passenger inter-
city service that today operates almost all the remaining passenger trains in
America. While Amtrak is government owned and partially government funded
it operates as a for-profit entity.

The legacy of the Interstate Highway System's creation is that it launched
a massive building and economic boom across America as communities were
expanded, the population migrated and new businesses were created as old ones
expanded due to the accessibility of markets created by the highway system,
thereby making America a global economic power.

All through the 1950s General Motors continuously dominated the auto
manufacturing industry. In 1956 following the death of his wife Irene, Alfred
P. Sloan stepped-down as GM's chairman-of-the-board. In retirement Sloan devoted himself to his foundation keeping regular hours in his Fifth Avenue office
in New York. The paneled office contained a portrait of his late wife and fresh
flowers were brought in each day. On those days when he had no luncheon
to attend, Sloan ate by himself in his office. His lunch always consisted of a
sandwich he had made at home and brought with him, neatly wrapped in wax
paper, in his coat pocket.

Until the time of his death in1966 the value of Sloan's gifts to his Alfred
P. Sloan Foundation and those of his wife, totaled $305 million, of which ap-
proximately $130-million had been given away.

On February 9, 1966 Alfred P. Sloan died at the Memorial Sloan-Kettering Cancer Center. He died of complications following a heart attack. He was 90 years old. Two days later he was laid to rest at St. John's Cemetery, Cold Spring Harbor, Long Island.

Alfred P. Sloan was the last of the great auto manufacturing pioneers and his passing brought to an end the golden era of the industry in America. Sloan had been out in front of building a company so big and powerful that its worst fear was not its competition, but fear that the government might break it up.

The decade of the 1950s had been all about Chevrolet and as the last seconds of the decade ticked away the Chevy was recognized as the American car, a brand so ingrained in the fabric of American popular culture that it was set right alongside mom, apple pie, baseball and rock n' roll as one of the true symbols of the nation.

Today all the classic cars of the 1950s live on in various venues. Many of the highly-stylized Chevrolets, Pontiacs, Buicks, Dodges, DeSotos, Fords and Studebakers of the era can be seen in pristine condition at the Henry Ford Museum in Dearborn, Michigan or in private collections, while in Havana, Cuba hundreds of the old 1950s classics somehow have been pieced together and still plod through the streets of the city daily amidst a back-drop of crumbling buildings and revolutionary memorials.

11.

Ralph Nader's Crusade - Unsafe at Any Speed

The number of deaths resulting from automobile accidents in the U.S. began to rise sharply after World War One going from 12,500 in 1920 to 33,000 in 1930 and have continued to rise annually ever since. The exceptions were the period during World War Two when gasoline and tires were rationed and in the early 1970s when a fuel shortage occurred, and the national speed limit was lowered to 55 mph at the suggestion of President Richard M. Nixon. Nonetheless, despite a drop of 17.5% in 1975 the number of auto fatalities that year was 45,853.

Despite the many safety innovations that have been implemented in automobiles over the past forty years such as seat belts, shoulder harnesses, airbags and steering wheel rims and spokes that bend rather than break upon impact, the carnage on America's highways still continues. The year 2015 saw the biggest percent increase in traffic deaths in the U.S. in fifty years with 38,300 people killed on U.S. roads, an 8% increase over 2014. Also 4.4 million were injured.

Until the 1950s the four largest automobile manufactures in the United States, American Motors, Chrysler, Ford and General Motors were afforded a unique position in the transportation industries as having a large measure of freedom from Federal regulation.

Though-out the first fifty years history of automobile manufacturing in America safety in the finished product had not been a high priority. The prevailing attitude of the automobile manufactures was that if their vehicles were operated by a good driver, were properly maintained, had good tires and good brakes, then they were safe to drive and for all the passengers. If there was a crash, it was the fault of the driver.

Robert S. McNamara had been one of Henry Ford II's post-World War Two whiz kids; by 1955 he was head of the Ford Division of the Ford Motor Company. In late 1955 General Motors began a campaign to get Robert S. McNamara fired at Ford for emphasizing safety in his company's 1956 models.

Although GM was confident that its re-styled 1956 models were superior in engineering to the Ford models, Harlow Curtice, GM's CEO was outraged by McNamara and Ford emphasizing safety in its cars. Curtice called Henry Ford II and told him to stop it. In particular, Curtice found the installation of padded dashboards, seat belts and innovative deep-dish steering wheels in Ford's cars suggested to buyers that they were safer than GM models.

GM was so brazen to suggest that with McNamara putting an emphasis on safety in Ford automobiles in their advertising campaign, they were changing the culture of buyers from one of a romantic connection to owning, driving and personal freedom in a car, to one of deep psychological concern of safety in their cars.

Robert McNamara and Ford did not back-down from their safety campaign and in fact they intensified the effort. Ford at the direction of McNamara put together brochures with comparative pictures of 1956 Fords and Chevrolets that had been in accidents. Irony was not a factor in that in these pictures the Fords always seemed to look as they had come out of the accidents with less damage. The brochures featuring these pictures were published bi-monthly and sent by Ford to all of its dealers.

At that time there were several former GM executives now serving in high places at Ford; Ernest Breech, the chairman of the board had been GM's chief financial officer and Louis Crusoe, executive vice-president of the car division had formerly been an executive in the Cadillac division of GM. Dale Harder, Ford's head of manufacturing, had also been with GM.

All of these former GM executives knew the company could make waves if it so desired. GM was capable of throwing a powerful punch in the automobile market. What would happen if GM suddenly lowered the cost of its cars $25 or even $50? It could possibly drive Chrysler or Ford into bankruptcy. But when Harlow Curtice began to question the wisdom of McNamara's safety campaign they eventually began to take heed.

Robert McNamara was forced to abandon his safety campaign and the bi-monthly brochures ceased being sent out to the dealers. The Ford Motor Company returned to emphasizing style and performance in its models. Then McNamara took a long vacation to a Florida while the board decided his future with Ford. When he returned, he headed-up a successful campaign that saw Ford out-sell Chevrolet in 1957. As a result, McNamara was now considered a rising star in the company.

Although Ford's safety campaign in 1956 had been a failure the company continued to offer seat belts as an option each year, even when other manufacturers stopped due to a lack of response from buyers. Most buyers simply believed that seat belts belonged in airplanes, not automobiles.

Nonetheless GM continued to build extremely powerful cars. The 1962 Chevrolet Impala SS 409 became the fastest US production car ever with a 0 to 60 mph speed in 4.0 seconds.

But the safety issue in automobiles that had been briefly raised by Ford did not go away. In fact, it raised the public's consciousness level about it. It was now a permanent part of the dialogue between buyers and dealers and within a few more years safety would take center stage in the marketplace. But before that would occur, a few epic events had to take place in Detroit.

It had not been the first time that the automobile safety issue had been raised. In October 1935, *Reader's Digest* had published a highly controversial article on auto safety written by a Harvard educated writer named Joseph C. Furnas. In his article Furnas documented the growing and horrific slaughter with bursting glass and body penetrating steel taking place on America's highways. His articles eventually ran in two thousand newspapers. The public outcry to the articles was met by Alfred P. Sloan, President of General Motors and Paul Hoffman of the Studebaker Corporation who donated $400,000 to start-up the Automobile Safety Foundation (ASF). Soon some of the gasoline companies and auto parts companies ponied-up donations.

Of course, there was a downside to Sloan's generosity as he held the belief that high performance in automobiles was far more important to buyers than safety features. He may have been right. It is a rather curious fact that in 1928 GM's Cadillac had been built with safety glass. Packard the Cadillac's primary rival did not include safety glass in its 1928 model and the result was that Packard outsold Cadillac by a wide margin.

The ASF neglected to focus on the safety of the automobile and advocated the safe and efficient use of streets and highways by drivers.

The first Congressional hearing on traffic safety took place in 1956 headed by Representative Kenneth A. Roberts (Democrat, Alabama), but regardless of how well intended the hearing was the automobile manufacturers controlled the agenda.

Another half-hearted attempt at legislating automobile safety occurred in 1959 when the House passed a bill requiring various safety standards to be included in Government purchased vehicles. However, the Senate took no action. Arguments against the bill included just what Detroit wanted to hear, that the industry could voluntarily build-in safety features without being required by law to do so. Also, there was belief by opponents of the bill that it would give the Government to much say on the design of automobiles. So, Detroit had won again.

There would be dabs and dribbles of legislation concerning automobile safety come out of Washington over the next decade. In fact, during the period of 1962-1964 Congress would enact three bills aimed at rudimentary auto safety issues. One bill would require that hydraulic brake fluid used in automobiles meet certain standards set by the Government. Another bill required seat belts installed in automobiles meet standards set by the Secretary of Commerce.

But it would take a major design blunder by General Motors to open the flood gates on motor vehicle safety. In one of the most paradoxical events in American automotive engineering history, Edward Cole who had overseen the development of GM's powerful V-8 engine was charged with designing a compact car that could compete on the market with Volkswagen and the Nash Rambler. The car that Cole and his team would build for GM was the Corvair one of the biggest automotive engineering disasters of all-time and would take center stage in leading Congress to enact safety standards in automobiles.

While the Corvair followed the Volkswagen's example of using an air-cooled rear engine and inexpensive swing-axle suspension, it was not designed on the concept of the VW.

The Corvair was a six-cylinder rear-engine drive model with smaller tires. On sharp corners if the Corvair was driven too fast it had a tendency to flip. Tested by experienced race drivers, they discovered to ensure safety in the Corvair, the front and rear tires needed to be inflated at different levels—a task that the everyday driver would never be concerned with.

Several high-profile automobile accidents involving the Corvair happened almost immediately after the car was introduced on the market.

On January 13, 1962 in West Los Angeles comedian Ernie Kovacs was driving his Corvair home from a baby shower given at the home of director Billy Wilder for the wife of fellow comedian Milton Berle. Kovacs lost control of the car and the impact with a utility pole caused the entire driver's side to cave-in on him. After being extracted Ernie Kovacs later died at a LA hospital. He was just 42-years old.

In Indianapolis the son of a prominent Chevrolet dealer was killed in a Corvair. Also, Carl Werner an executive in GM's Cadillac division was killed in a Corvair. After Chevrolet chief Bunkie Knudsen's niece was seriously injured in a Corvair, he demanded that the car be redesigned. By 1963 with law suits against the Chevrolet division reaching over one hundred the company was forced to cancel production of further models of the Corvair.

Then on November 30, 1965 Ralph Nader's book *Unsafe at Any Speed* was published by Grossman Publishers of New York and suddenly automobile manufacturing safety standards took center stage in Washington and Detroit.

Ralph Nader was a 31-year old bachelor that lived in northwest Washington, D. C. He was a Harvard trained lawyer and budding consumer advocate in his book Nader asserted that the Detroit automakers were not concerned with safety and wouldn't even include such fundamental life-preserving items as seat belts in their cars. He attacked almost every aspect of the automobile industry as negligent in consumer protection. Nader even went after the classic styling of various cars including the blade-like front fenders of the Lincoln Continental and the iconic fins of the Cadillac.

According to Ralph Nader the sharp, rising tail fin that had been introduced on the Cadillac in 1949 continued to rise at a grotesque rate until its designers started to recede it in 1960. Nader wrote that "in its greatest height, the Cadillac fin bore an uncanny resemblance to the tail of the stegosaurus, a dinosaur that had two sharp rearward-projecting horns on each side of its tail."[1]

Nader concluded that so unsafe were the Cadillac tail fins that in 1964 a motorcyclist in California was nearly killed by the fins. Apparently, the motorcyclist had been in a heavy line of traffic on a California freeway between Newport Harbor and Santa Anna when the road narrowed from four lanes to two due to construction causing traffic to swerve into the merging lanes. When the Cadillac in-front came to a sudden stop the motorcyclist found he was boxed and unable to turn aside. Consequently, he hit the rear bumper of the Cadillac at a speed of 25 miles per hour and was hurled onto the rear fin, which

Chevrolet Corvair. (Wikimedia)

pierced his body below the heart and cut him all the way down to the thigh bone. Luckily the motorcyclist survived.

But it was the Chevrolet Corvair that became the major thesis of Ralph Nader's 1965 book and his crusade for automobile engineering safety.

The Corvair was introduced in General Motors showrooms in September 1959 and Nader asserted that the hazards inherent in the model were already well-known. A couple of Ford test drivers had convinced a couple of GM dealers to let them test the cars in early September at the company's test track and lost control of them. But that wasn't the most shocking revelation that the Corvair was unsafe; it began according to Nader when the GM engineers led by Edward Cole, Harry Barr, Robert Schilling, Kai Hansen and Frank Winchell came up with the conception and design for the car.

By March 1966 Ralph Nader's book had experienced moderate sales with 27,000 copies in circulation. At that time two of the most popular books on the market were Truman Capote's *In Cold Blood* that had sold 279,000 copies and Jessica Milford's *The American Way of Death* which had sold 90,000 copies.

Referring to the books above, Nader tongue-in-cheek stated, "I could have used either title for my book."[2]

Traffic deaths in the United States had risen from 39,628 per 100,000 population in 1956 to 49,000 per 100,000 population in 1965.

In July 1965 the U. S. Senate convened a sub-committee (the Senate Government Operations Subcommittee on Executive Reorganization) to launch a full-scale investigation of automobile safety in earnest. The sub-committee was chaired by Senator Abraham A. Ribicoff (Democrat, Connecticut). The sub-committee studied the efforts of federal agencies in promoting and improving highway traffic safety.

The testimony from auto manufactures were conflicting views that in one way or another continued to blame driver failure for accidents more than the safety of cars they made.

James Roche president of GM testified that safety had always been a priority in manufacturing cars going all the way back to the 1910 models when doors were installed to prevent passengers from falling out.

While no measures were enacted, the comprehensive efforts of the sub-committee underscored a growing Congressional concern over traffic safety and determination to take stronger steps in 1966.

The outlook for Congressional highway safety advocates got a big boost when President Lyndon Johnson in his State of the Union address on January 12, 1966 called for the Highway Safety Act of 1966 to be enacted. To expedite the bill hearings were scheduled by the Senate Commerce Committee headed by Senator Warren G. Magnuson (Democrat, Washington).

Meanwhile in January 1966 Senator Ribicoff's Senate auto safety sub-committee reconvened.

On February 9, 1966, Alfred P. Sloan long-time Chairman of the Board and President of General Motors died at the age of 90. The next day on February 10, 1966 Ralph Nader testified in-front of Senator Ribicoff's sub-committee about the alleged unsafe practices in the automobile industry.

Nader stated to the Committed that the auto industry was sacrificing safety to emphasize power. As expected, Nader focused on the Chevrolet Corvair. He stated that the hazards inherent in the Corvair were well-known by General Motors as well as the other manufacturers before the car first came off the production line in 1959, particularly the car's propensity with its rear-engine design to roll-over.

In fact, in 1959 the Corvair had turned over in a J-turn test at less than 30 miles per hour. Nader went so far as to state that, according to Charles M. Rubly, the General Motors engineer responsible for the Corvair suspension, the stabilizer bar was then deleted from the car's production model in an effort to reduce costs and road noise.[3]

Suddenly Ralph Nader was a huge celebrity. He was featured in *The New York Times* and making appearances on late night TV with Johnny Carson on the "*Tonight Show*". Now everyone wanted to know more about Nader.

The public record showed that Ralph Nader had been born on February 27, 1934 in Winsted, Connecticut to immigrant parents from Lebanon. In Winsted his father had established a restaurant and bakery.

When Nader was a boy his mother had taken him for a nine-month visit to her native Lebanon. Then when Nader returned to school in America it was noted that he was speaking Arabic. So, it was suggested that he be put in kindergarten rather than the first grade. But his parents loudly objected and asked that the boy be given a chance. It all worked-out and Ralph finished first in his class.

Later when Nader enrolled at Princeton University it was suggested that he be placed in a special remedial English course. But once again he prevailed and was elected to Phi Beta Kappa in his senior year.

By the time Ralph Nader was in his early twenties he had grown to a lanky 6' 4" tall and weighed a slim 180 pounds. It was while attending Harvard Law School that his interest in automobile safety started to blossom. While attending Harvard Law Nader had owned a 1949 Studebaker, but he decided at the age of 22 that he really didn't need the car and got rid of it, but not because of safety concerns. It would be the only car he would own. None the less he retained his Connecticut driver's license.

While traveling around the country the many auto accidents that Nader saw started to concern him. He was president of the Harvard Law Record and wrote a lengthy paper on auto safety design and its legal implications. At Harvard a study of auto accident injury cases convinced Nader that the law was not fair and placed too much emphasis on driver failure and neglected automobile designs.

After graduating from Harvard Law School Nader worked as a research assistant to law professor Harold J. Berman then did a six-month stint in the U.S. Army. He then joined a law firm in Hartford. It was then that he started to campaign for safer cars. He started his crusade by writing magazine articles and

Ralph Nader, 1975. (Photo by Thomas J. O'Halloran, Wikimedia)

letters to editors and took auto negligence cases. He was attempting to influence state legislatures in Connecticut, Massachusetts and New York to require auto manufacturers in Detroit to make safer cars. All of his efforts fell on deaf ears and in 1964 he left Connecticut and went to Washington, D. C. to work for Labor Department in the Office of Planning and Research.

Then in 1965 his book *Unsafe at Any Speed* was published. At first the automobile companies laughed at Nader's book and refused to even read a page. But as the book gained popularity suddenly the Detroit auto establishment had to respond by attacking it.

It was particularly irritating to General Motors that their loudest critic didn't even drive a car and was some sort of self-appointed engineer. Suddenly, GM wanted to know all about Ralph Nader and the tactics the company used to get its information were tantamount to harassment. In response to Ralph Nader's Congressional testimony and his book, GM hired private investigators to report on him from mid-January to the end of February.

In late January as he prepared for his upcoming Senate Committee hearing, Nader began to receive bothersome telephone calls at home despite having an unlisted number. The callers were never obscene or abusive. According to Nader when he answered the telephone a voice would ask if it was he, and he would respond yes. Then the caller would suddenly as if reprimanding a child told him, "Cut it out now. Cut it out. You're going to cut me off I tell you! Cut it out!"[4] Then the connection would be broken.

The investigators began to trail Nader. On February 11, 1966, the day after his Congressional committee appearance Nader went to the NBC television studio in the new Senate Office Building for an interview. Two men who had been following him asked a guard for directions to the television studio. They described Nader's appearance to the guard and asked if he had gone in. Then they waited outside. But the investigators botched their assignment by mistaking Bryce Nelson, a *Washington Post* reporter for Nader and following him. The mix-up was discovered by the Capital Police and the two men were told to leave the building.

A week later Nader flew to Philadelphia for another interview and was shadowed by investigators. Then he was followed in Des Moines, Iowa.

The investigators began to interview friends and associates of his in an attempt to discredit him. On February 21, Vincent Gillen a former FBI agent and New York attorney working in the investigation of Nader interviewed Frederick Hughes Condon.

At that time Frederick Condon was an assistant counsel and assistant secretary of the United Life and Accident Company of Concord, New Hampshire. He had been paralyzed in an auto accident and Nader's book had been dedicated to him.

Condon was interviewed by Gillen at his home in East Andover, New Hampshire. He kept notes of the meeting and wrote a detailed memorandum. Condon remarked that Gillen was dressed in sport coat and slacks and wore glasses with heavy black frames. During the interview Gillen kept a tan attaché case on his knees that led to speculation that that the case contained a recording device. During questioning by Senator Ribicoff's sub-committee, Gillen denied that he had any such equipment with him when he interviewed Frederick Condon.

Gillen asked Condon about Nader's political affiliations to determine if he was a member of any left-wing organizations. He also inquired if Nader's middle eastern background had made him anti-Semitic.

Ralph Nader was a bachelor and Gillen asked Condon if he knew any reason why he wasn't married. Condon replied, "Are you asking me if he is a homosexual?"[5] Gillen replied, "I've seen him on TV and he certainly doesn't look like...But we have to be sure."[6] Gillen later defended his agenda of asking such personal questions by implying that an employer would want to know such things.

The detectives and investigators interviewed more than a half-dozen of Nader's friends, and some demanded complete identification before they would participate. They even questioned his stockbroker.

The investigators even tried entrapment in order to discredit Nader.

Nader was to say that on February 20 and again on February 23, he was approached by attractive young women in their twenties. In one instance Nader was in a pharmacy leafing through an automobile magazine when an attractive young woman approached him and asked if he would like to participate in a foreign affairs discussion at her apartment.

In another instance Nader was in a supermarket selecting a package of cookies when a young woman approached him and asked, he would help her move some heavy articles in her residence. While Nader refused, he later stated that the woman did not ask any other man to help her.

There had been unsubstantiated rumors circulating that the auto industry had employed several former FBI agents and one company even had a special investigations bureau that had contacts with police departments and private detectives. Supposedly, such a unit was in place to investigate backgrounds of executives the company was considering hiring so assigning a unit to investigate Ralph Nader was just a telephone call away.

As soon as news releases started to appear that the auto industry had undertaken an investigation of Nader, two Democrat Senators took quick action. Senator Abraham A. Ribicoff of Connecticut who was the chairman of the subcommittee that investigated the auto industry and Senator Gaylord Nelson of Wisconsin called for the Justice Department to investigate the auto industry.

The alleged harassment of Ralph Nader occurred during the time when he was a witness in a Senate sub-committee hearing, so Senator Ribicoff was quick to point-out on the Senate floor that Federal law provided for a five-year prison term and a fine of $5,000 for anyone who attempted to intimidate a Congressional witness.

The actions of the two law makers prompted a quick response from John S. Bagas, vice-president of Ford Motor Company who sent a telegram to Senator Ribicoff stating that Ford had not been involved in any alleged investigation or intimidation of Nader and had no knowledge or connections with the alleged incidents concerning him.

Subsequently Chrysler and American Motors followed suit denying any connection to an investigation of Nader. So that left General Motors holding the bag.

On the direct order of company president James M. Roche, late on the night of March 9, GM fessed-up to its involvement in the plot against Nader. GM stated it had initiated an investigation of Ralph Nader through a reputable law firm, but categorically denied any involvement with alleged intimidation or harassment of him reported in the press.

GM stated that the reason the company had initiated the investigation of Nader with his continued attacks on the Corvair and its rear-suspension system, an automobile that the company has stated is safe, was to determine if he was acting on behalf of litigants or their attorneys in Corvair design cases against General Motors.

When Nader was asked by the press if there was any credibility to the accusation of GM that he might me working for attorneys or litigants in Corvair cases, he stated that he had been questioned by lawyers about the Corvair because, "I am one of the few attorneys with any knowledge of automobile products liability."[7] But he quickly added that he had never received any fees in the matter.

Furthermore, Nader pointed-out that he was not the only critic of the Corvair pointing-out Senator Robert F. Kennedy (Democrat, New York) "who cited the Corvair in a public statement last month as an example of irresponsible manufacturing design."[8]

As soon as General Motors admitted that they had investigated Ralph Nader, Senator Ribicoff invited the company president James M. Roche to testify before the sub-committee. Smugly, GM hinted that they could provide proof that Ralph Nader was connected to lawyers handling Corvair suits against the company. It turned-out to be wishful thinking.

On March 22, 1966, in a nationally televised session of Senator Ribicoff's subcommittee, GM president James Roche testified. He publicly apologized to Ralph Nader for his company's investigation of him. While Roche accepted responsibility for the actions of GM, he stated that the investigation had been initiated, conducted and completed without his knowledge or the consent of GM's governing committee. Roche went as far as to state that the General Motors inquiry "was unworthy of American business."[9]

The investigation had cost GM $6,700 and produced a useless ream of reports that were submitted to the GM legal staff.

Senator Ribicoff read all the detective reports and said the investigation had failed to turn up anything detrimental to Mr. Nader. Addressing Nader who was in the hearing room, Senator Ribicoff stated, "You and your family can be proud. They (the detectives) have put you through the mill and they haven't found a dam thing wrong with you."[10]

Lee Iacocca had begun working at The Ford Motor Company in 1955 and was part of Robert McNamara's team that worked on Ford's 1956 safety campaign. Later he was to state, "Here I find myself in rare agreement with Ralph Nader; the Corvair really was unsafe. The (Chevrolet) Vega, with its pancake aluminum engine, was another disaster."[11] Iacocca then added that GM is so big and powerful that it could withstand a couple of disasters without suffering any real corporate damage.

But Ralph Nader wasn't through putting the auto industry on notice. He testified in front of the Senate Commerce Committee headed by Senator. Magnuson, that was in the process of preparing President Johnson's traffic safety legislation.

Suddenly General Motors was taking every precaution to ensure that its cars were safe. On April 4, GM sent out a recall for 1.5 million of its cars on America's highways to correct a throttle that stuck under certain conditions. The recall involved 1965 standard-sized Chevrolet models of the Caprice, Impala, Biscayne and Bel Air—with Power Glide transmissions. The recall also applied to the 1964 and 1965 Chevelle, Malibu with the Power-Glide transmission.

Nader continued to criticize the automobile industry head-on in the press. In an article published in *The New York Times*, April 15, 1966, Nader charged that the Chevrolet Division of General Motors had paid just $2 plus delivery for its tires.

Nader didn't just direct his criticism at GM; he also stated that it was very hard to find a more dangerous car on the American market than the German-made Volkswagen.

At the time there were 1.8 million Volkswagen cars and buses on American roads. While Nader did not get specific in regard to safety issues with the

Volkswagen when reporters pressed for more detail, he maintained that the door latches on the VW did not adequately guard against the tendency of the doors to fly open during accidents. Also, he alleged that the VW's stability in high speed highway travel and in turning corners was impaired by the design of the car's rear axle suspension.

However sincere the GM mea culpa extended by James Roche may have been it didn't stop the auto industry's criticism of Nader.

Henry Ford II, president of the Ford Motor Company was quick to respond to Nader's criticism of the Volkswagen, "He (Nader) even says that he doesn't think the rear axles are well engineered. Well I say we've got jobs for rear axle engineers and if he is that good, we'll be happy to give him a job. But frankly, I don't think he knows very much about automobiles."[12]

In his State of the Union address on January 12, 1966, President Lyndon Johnson stressed the need for a national highway safety act. Johnson called for the need to "stop the slaughter on our highways." Citing statistics showing substantially more Americans died on the highways than all the casualties in all American wars. The President even described the carnage as the gravest problem before the nation- next to war in Viet Nam."[13]

While President Johnson had been the catalyst in proposing a safety package to Congress in the end, he did little to support it financially requesting only $26 million in fiscal 1967. Congress had in fact authorized $91 million in the first year. An Administration spokesperson put a spin on the weak appropriations request stating that it represented the time already passed in the 1967 fiscal year. But it was a start as virtually nothing had been done before.

It would be Ralph Nader that had the last laugh not only with James Roche and General Motors, but the automobile manufacturing industry in general. The issues he had raised in regard to automobile safety put the manufacturers in an unfavorable position with the public and they were instrumental in the passage by Congress of the National Traffic and Motor Vehicle Safety Act of 1966 signed into law by President Lyndon Johnson.

On November 16, 1966 Ralph Nader would file a $26 million invasion-of-privacy suit against GM and be awarded $425,000 in an out-of-court settlement.

Ralph Nader would run for President of the United States three times. In 1992 he would run unsuccessfully as an Independent and in 1996 as the Green Party candidate. Nader would run one more time as the Green Party candidate in 2000 and the impact of his candidacy on the results of the election has been much misunderstood.

While Al Gore received more popular votes in the 2000 presidential election 51,999,897 than George W. Bush 50,456,002, he lost the election by a slim margin of electoral votes. The total electoral vote count of 271 for Bush as to 266 for Gore was decided by the U.S. Supreme Court.

The battleground state of Florida was critical in the outcome. The final vote total for George Bush in Florida was 2,912,790 and for Al Gore 2,912,253. Ralph Nader received a total of 97,488 votes in Florida. But since 2000 it has been widely believed that Ralph Nader took Democrat votes away from Al Gore in Florida thereby costing him the presidency. But the facts are that Ralph Nader really had nothing to do with the outcome of the 2000 presidential election; George W. Bush received 308,000 votes from Democrats in Florida that put him over the top in the state's popular vote.

12.
AMC Attempts to Run with the Big Dogs

At one time there had been hundreds of automobile manufacturers in the US, but the herd began to thin during the depression and continued in the aftermath of World War Two. By 1970 the American auto industry was nearly completely dominated by The Big Three—General Motors, Ford and Chrysler. Still one American company refused to run up a white flag and surrender the market to The Big Three, the American Motors Corporation, aka AMC.

AMC had been formed on January 14, 1954 with the merger of the Nash—Kelvinator Corporation and the Hudson Motor Car Company. At the time it was the largest corporate merger in US history.

The architect of the merger was Nash-Kelvinator CEO George Mason who wanted to build an automobile manufacturing company big enough with the necessary resources to compete with the Big Three. Within a year of the merger Mason died and his assistant George Romney was named the new president.

Under George Romney the company focused on building a small car line and by the end of 1957 the Hudson and Nash names were phased out from badging. AMC got off to a rocky start under Romney's leadership losing money in both 1956 and 1957 as dealers defected from the company's network and fought-off a takeover by corporate raider Louis Wolfson. But with Rambler sales remaining steady by 1958 Romney had turned the company around with AMC posting a quarterly profit, becoming the first American auto company to show a profit during the recession that year.

1957 Nash Ambassador Series 80. (Photo by Lawrence T. Hay)

By 1960 AMC had become the third most popular brand of automobile in the US, led by the sales of the subcompact Rambler. As a result, the company continued to grow and AMC stock went from $7 to $90 a share making George Romney immensely rich from stock options.

George Wilcken Romney born July 8, 1907 was the son of American parents, Gaskell Romney and Anna Amelia Pratt, who at that time were living in a Mormon colony and doing missionary work in Chihuahua Mexico. While Romney's parents were monogamists, they had moved to Mexico along with many other Mormons when Congress outlawed polygamy in the 1880s. Later the family was forced to flee the country due to Mexican Revolution and re-settled in Idaho and Utah while Romney was a child.

George Romney grew-up a devote member of The Church of Jesus Christ of Latter-Day Saints. While Romney attended several colleges, he did not graduate from any of them. Married in 1931, he and his wife Lenore would have six children, including son Mitt born in 1947 who would grow-up to become Governor of Massachusetts and the Republican candidate for president in 2012. Currently Mitt Romney is serving in the US Senate.

During the early part of the depression George Romney had worked in Washington, D.C. as a speech writer for Democratic Senator David T. Walsh of Massachusetts. In 1939 the Romneys moved to Detroit where George joined The American Automobile Manufacturers Association as a Washington lobbyist. In 1948 he joined the Nash-Kelvinator Company.

Despite being chairman of the board and president of AMC while making millions of dollars in the auto industry George Romney had a calling for public service. In 1962 after an agonizing 24-hour prayerful fast Romney resigned from AMC to run for Governor of Michigan. Elected by a margin of 78,000 votes over incumbent John B. Swainson, Romney would become the first Republican Governor in Michigan in fourteen years. He would be re-elected by wide margins in 1964 and 1966.

George Romney represented the liberal wing of the Republican Party in regard to social issues and civil rights and was opposed to the war in Viet Nam. He also had considerable labor support which was unusual for a Republican. In 1968 Romney would run for the Republican Presidential nomination before dropping out of the race prior to the New Hampshire primary. The eventual winner of the presidential race in 1968 Richard M. Nixon would name Romney to his cabinet as Secretary of Housing and Urban Development.

When George Romney became Governor of Michigan the AMC board of directors in an unprecedented move split the chairmanship and the CEO position. Vice President of Sales Roy Abernethy was named president and legal counsel Richard Cross became Chairman of the Board.

Previous to joining AMC Roy Abernethy had been vice president of Willys. As vice president of sales with AMC Abernethy had rebuilt the AMC sales and distribution network having set a goal to convert every Hudson and Nash dealer into an AMC dealer.

Abernethy believed that the biggest obstacle for the company to overcome was its image problem. It was his opinion the primary problem with AMC was that American car buyers conceptualized AMC as a manufacturer of plain, simple, little cars. So, he set about to change that by replacing the company's advertising agency and building bigger, more prestigious cars.

The first model fitting that description by Abernethy was the upscale Ambassador introduced in 1965. The Ambassador had been produced in various styles since 1958, but the new Abernethy edition was a stretched Ambassador built on a new platform with a more powerful engine and even came in a convertible. At first Abernethy's strategy seemed to work as sales of both the 1965 and 1966 Ambassador improved, when AMC's overall production decreased from record levels.

Still Roy Abernethy had considerable critics who had felt comfortable with the conservative approach of George Romney and steadily maintained that AMC should continue doing what The Big Three were not doing. Those critics and more specific investors had their opinions reinforced when the AMC 1966 annual financial report was delivered to them in a plain brown wrapper instead of the glossy format, they had received the previous year. Inside the figures revealed that corporate earnings had fallen to 27 cents a share, the lowest since the company had rebounded in 1958.

Roy Abernethy's response to the meager earnings report was to introduce completely new designs for 1967, a strategy that added $60 million in retooling costs and put a strain on the AMC financial resources. Sales of the Ambassador had been trending up the past few years having increased from 18,647 in 1964 to more than 64,000 in 1965 and 71,000 in 1966. Now Abernethy was attempting to position the Ambassador and Rebel designs on an equal basis with the economy lines of Chevrolet, Ford and Plymouth.

The 1967 AMC Rambler Rebel was a mid-sized car that would replace the discontinued Rambler Classic. The car would come in a variety of styles, the 770 sedan, SST hardtop and a station wagon. Yielding to the concerns of safety advocate Ralph Nader, the Rebel also featured an enhanced safety feature with a steering column designed to collapse under impact.

The 1967 AMC Ambassador and Rebel models were slightly souped-up too, equipped with "GEN-2" AMC V-8 engines. Furthermore, the engines and drivetrains were covered under a ground-breaking 5-year or 50,000-mile warranty.

But to develop these new cars and engines meant that AMC had to borrow money for working capital to keep the day-to-day operations going. Then AMC sales dropped in the first half of 1966 and the company reported a loss of $4.2 million on sales of $479 million.

Robert B. Evans saw the downturn as an opportunity. He saw that AMC's stock was selling for 60% of the company's net worth, so he invested over $2 million making him the largest stockholder and was subsequently, named chairman of the board.

In 1966 AMC recorded a loss of $12,648,000 before Tax Credits and Tax Assets. The hard facts were that Roy Abernethy was spending so much money it was becoming difficult for the company to turn a profit. Being the super salesman that he was Abernethy had made a presumption that AMC could compete with The Big Three in the compact car market if they gave the buyer more choices. AMC simply did not have the resources and market position to do that.

After five years with Roy Abernethy as its president AMC had gone from being a profitable company to one that was hemorrhaging money. On January 9, 1967, Roy Abernethy was forced to resign as president by taking an early retirement.

Roy Abernethy was replaced as president by Roy D. Chapin, Jr. who would take AMC on a decade long roller coaster ride in sales, twice bringing the company back from being on the verge of bankruptcy.

Roy D. Chapin, Jr. was born in Grosse Pointe, Michigan on September 21, 1915 and was educated at Yale University. Like Edsel Ford and Henry Ford II, Roy Chapin was born with motor oil in his veins being the son of Roy D. Chapin, Sr. one of the co-founders of the Hudson Motor Car Company. In fact, in 1936 Roy Chapin, Jr. started his career in the business with Hudson.

His father had become the stuff of legends in the automotive world when in 1901, he drove one of the country's first high volume' cars, the curved dash Oldsmobile, from Detroit to the second annual National Automobile Show in New York. Eight years later he helped found Hudson.

During the early years of Chapin's tenure as president of AMC the company prospered again as a result of expanding its international operations and increased sales of its compact cars due to rising oil prices. Also, in 1967 AMC received a federal tax credit that resulted in a $22 million cash rebate.

One of the key events that would be crucial to AMC's survival until 1987 took place in 1970 when Roy Chapin sat down to have lunch in California with Henry J. Kaiser, the well-known industrialist who owned Jeep. Kaiser informed Chapin that he would be interested in selling the Jeep brand to AMC for $75 million.

However, the AMC board was not sure what the benefit of buying Jeep would be to the company. Some felt that sport utility vehicles were a rather obscure market and felt the company would benefit far better by updating its aging lineup of cars.

According to Iain Anderson who was a group president and executive vice president and CFO at AMC from 1963 to 1978, "He (Chapin) was the primary proponent of the Jeep acquisition, the strongest voice for it. It was very controversial at the time. But he was much more familiar with the international arena, and he was much more familiar with Jeep."[1]

Going forward the AMC brand would experience modest success as it produced some of America's best-known cars in the late 1960s and 1970s, including the Javelin, AMX, Gremlin and Pacer.

AMC was even going where it had never been before. The 1975 AMC Matador Coup won three high profile NASCAR races.

The late Jerry Grant who died in 2012 was the first racecar driver to go faster than 200 mph in an Indy style racecar. He was versatile driver who drove open-wheeled cars seen in the Indy 500; long-distance endurance cars for sports cars; stock car races and Can/Am races. He drove in the California 500, the 12 hours of Sebring and in the Indianapolis 500 ten times.

From 1976 to 1979 Jerry Grant drove the most powerful car to ever appear in Indy car racing, "a turbocharged 209 cu in (3.41.) stock two-valve AMC Gen-2 block V-8 engine producing 1,100 hp (820 kW; in his Eagle chassis."[2] The Indy 209 was very fast on the straightaways, but the huge engine's weight made corners more difficult to handle.

AMC started to build smaller more fuel-efficient cars just as the cost of gasoline started to rise in the early 1970s. As a result, AMC made a profit of $44 million in 1973 which sent a shock wave through the corporate headquarters of The Big Three.

While the leadership of Roy Chapin, Jr. was key to moving AMC forward towards solvency, the vision of designer Richard A. Teague kept the company's products competitive, innovative and sometimes controversial. Teague's designs for AMC models attempted to challenge Ford and GM for the subcompact market.

Richard Teague designed several Jeep vehicles and AMC's compact platform for the Concord, Sprint and Eagle models. He also designed the Gremlin and worked on the design for the 1975 Pacer which was a rather weird looking car, but AMC's top seller.

The Pacer was the first car with a cab forward design. It was a small automobile that was wide and gave drivers and passengers the impression that they were driving and riding in a conventional large American automobile.

Born on December 26, 1923 in Los Angeles, California, Teague's mother worked in the motion picture industry during the silent film era. At the age of five Teague would also appear in movies being featured in five episodes of *Our Gang*, playing Dixie Duval, a girl.

A year later tragedy struck when Teague was seriously injured in an auto accident near Pasadena caused by a drunk driver. Teague lost several teeth, suffered a broken jaw and was left unable to perceive depth in his right eye. His mother was as an invalid. A year later Teague's father was killed in another auto accident caused by a drunk driver.

His grade school classmates included Ed Iskendarain (who became a drag racer) and Stuart Hilborn (who became a land speed racer). It was through association with those two that his interest in automobiles began when he participated in time trials on a dry lake northeast of Los Angeles.

After graduating from high school in 1942 and being declared exempt from military service as a result of his sight impairment, Teague worked as an aircraft technical illustrator for Northrop Corporation. At the suggestion of his boss, Paul Browne, a former designer for GM, Teague enrolled in night classes at the Art Center College of Design.

In 1947 Teague joined GM as an apprentice stylist and eventually was assigned to the Cadillac advanced design group. He also worked on the 1950 Oldsmobile.

After being let go by GM in 1952, Teague joined the Packard Motor Car Company as chief stylist. Among his accomplishments at Packard was working on the design of several show cars, including the Balboa. His last car designs

1964 Nash Rambler American 2-door hardtop, designed by Richard A. Teague. (Photo by Lawrence T. Hay)

for Packard before the company collapsed were for the show car Predictor and 1957 Clipper.

Richard Teague then joined Chrysler as chief stylist for a brief period before leaving due to management conflicts. Nonetheless Richard Teague now had the distinction of having worked for two of Detroit's Big Three auto makers.

In 1959 Teague joined AMC as a member of Edmund E. Anderson's design team and became the principal designer when Anderson left in 1961. The first AMC cars that included Teague's influence were the 1963 Rambler and Ambassador, AMC's first all-new models since 1956. In 1964 Teague would become vice president and serve in that capacity until his retirement in 1983.

Richard Teague's original design for the Gremlin was drawn on the back of an American Airlines sickness bag. The car was released on April 1, 1970 and remained in production until 1978.

While the Gremlin was much maligned by critics, it was a new design targeted at a youthful market. The Gremlin featured a six-cylinder engine, with a hatchback and came equipped with factory air conditioning for about $2,700. The 1973 Gremlin featured a "Levi" model with blue jean material upholstery. While the gas shortage in 1974 caused the Javelin and AMX to be discontinued, sales of the Gremlin and Hornet soared.

The 1979 AMC Spirit-hatchback would be a redesign of the Gremlin.

By the end of the 1970s hard times had returned to AMC as a result of poor timing, buyer's interest in imports and a weak economy. The Ambassador Brougham which was AMC's only full-size car had been introduced on the market right as the oil crisis was occurring.

The company lost $27.5 million in 1975 and $46.3 million in 1976. But thanks to strong sales of Jeep in 1977 AMC recorded a profit of $8.3 million along with a successful request granted from the EPA for a two-year wavier from the final emissions standards for oxides and nitrogen.

With the popularity of the Pacer, AMC redesigned the 1978 model with a new grill and an optional V-8 engine, but it proved too costly to manufacturer.

The writing was on the wall of the finance department, Jeep was going to have to pull the load to make the company financially stable and that looked like an impossible task.

There were also operational problems. The main AMC factory was in Kenosha, Wisconsin, it was the oldest such facility in the industry and furthermore assembly points were scattered across the city.

Once again AMC was having trouble borrowing money and it looked like the company might be heading for bankruptcy.

The only answer was for AMC to start looking for a foreign investor. In December 1980 the French state-owned auto manufacturer Renault acquired a large portion of AMC and took over the company. Renault, France's largest manufacturing company had been nationalized at the end of World War Two. It was the intent of Renault to keep AMC intact as an American subsidiary. The company was also helped by the US Government with a loan of $135 million so that it could assemble cars in the AMC Wisconsin plant.

But as the economy improved in the 1980s Americans once again wanted bigger cars. This presented a problem for Renault as most of AMC's cars were small. Now the French began to consider selling AMC.

In 1985 George Besse was named the fifth president of Renault by the French government then led by socialists and AMC had once again dodged a bullet and appeared to have an advocate to keep its assembly lines rolling.

George Besse was born on Christmas Day 1927 in Clermont-Ferraru, France and educated at Ecole Polytechnique. Besse was a European corporate turn-around guy. Previously he had turned heavy losses into profits within two years heading-up Pechiney Ugine Kuhlmann, the state-owned aluminum and chemical corporation. Also, he had executive experience in French telecommunications and uranium production for power plants.

At the time of his appointment with Renault the company was losing more than $1 billion a year. Besse's turn-around plan for Renault angered the French unions as it included the layoffs of 21,000 workers over a two-year period. Previously Besse had laid off 30,000 workers at Pechiney Ugine Kuhlmann. Besse also believed that Renault was top heavy and in order to strengthen production he replaced many top executives.

Immediately, Besse began to pour money into AMC. He began the production of front-wheel drive cars with the Alliance. Nonetheless, a lot of his critics believed that the Alliance was nothing more than a Renault produced in Wisconsin.

Besse also invested in the 4.0-liter six-cylinder engine that was still in production in 2006. Furthermore, he began heavily promoting the Jeep brand, believing that a huge demand for SUVs was just over the horizon.

These were turbulent times in Europe, the Soviet Union was beginning to crumble, and leftist groups were starting to spring-up, some of them were violent and promoted terrorism in the name of the worker and proletariat. The German Red Army faction had been carrying-out assassinations in West Germany and in October 1986 had taken credit for the assassination of Gerold von Braunmuhl, political director of the West German Foreign Ministry.

In France, Direct Action had taken credit for several bombings and gun fire attacks on various "capitalist targets" such as employers' association offices and factories, and various public targets such as police stations. The group had also taken credit for the shooting and killing of General Rene Audran, a senior official in the French Corp of Engineers in January 1985.

In January 1985, the German Red Army faction and Direct Action had announced they were forming a common front against NATO (the North Atlantic Treaty Organization) in Europe and others symbolic of what they termed as "capitalist imperialism."

In the French general election on March 16, 1986, the two major opposition parties gained a narrow majority, ending five years of Socialist rule. Four days later Socialist Francios Mitterrand was out as prime minister, replaced by rightwing Jacques Chirac.

Now George Besse with his sweeping downsizing plans and layoffs of workers in French industry had become a target for the discontent of leftist radicals and their agenda. Consequently, his fate came to the fore in the fall of 1986. When police warned Besse that threats were hanging over various targeted personalities … in alphabetical order, he simply shrugged his shoulders.

On the evening of November 17, 1986, George Besse left the Renault headquarters in Paris and was driven to this residence on the boulevard Edgar-Quinet. After being dropped off Besse was about fifteen feet from his front door when suddenly a young woman approached him. She stared at him briefly and then without a word opened fire on him with a handgun shooting him in the chest. Just to make sure she had completed her task, she leaned over the fallen Besse, his body covered in blood, and shot him again—in the head.

Immediately the woman with an accomplice who had covered the gun in her hand, rushed into the Raspail subway. As one of them entered the train, she threw a handful of Direct-Action leaflets on the platform. Direct Action would take credit for the killing of George Besse in retaliation for his layoffs and the killing of a Direct-Action member by a Renault security guard.

In 1986-1987 twenty members of Direct Action were arrested and eighteen members of the group were convicted in 1988 on charges of criminal conspiracy.

With the killing of George Besse, the future of AMC was uncertain. Raymond Levy was named the new CEO of Renault. Many in the French government believed that AMC was draining Renault of its financial resources. Within six months of the killing of Besse, Levy would cave-into the governmental pressure and Renault would be sold to Chrysler.

On March 9, 1987 all other remaining shares, were purchased by Chrysler leading to the end of the AMC brand. Chrysler now under the leadership of former Ford Motor Company vice president Lee Iacocca then combined all of the AMC design, engineering and manufacturing operations into its own. Then it created the Jeep-Eagle division.

18.
John Z. DeLorean, A Maverick Entrapped

By the end of the 1970s American automobile makers were under siege by the number of foreign cars entering the US each year. It forced the surviving Big Three manufacturers Ford, General Motors and Chrysler to make sweeping changes in labor relations, collective bargaining and to form partnerships with Japanese, Korean and European manufacturers while downsizing their operations.

It was about at that this point in time that a brilliant engineer at the GM Pontiac division by the name of John DeLorean decided to go out on his own.

John Zachary DeLorean was born in Detroit, January 6, 1925 and was the oldest of four sons born to a foundry worker at the Ford Highland Park plant. His father had been born in Central-Europe and emigrated to the United States on his own when he was just 14-years old. His father was big man, six feet, 220 pounds and he liked to drink and brawl when he got his paycheck on Fridays. According to John DeLorean, his father on occasion abused his mother Katheryn and his brothers. This led to periodic separations of the couple.

DeLorean grew-up partly in Los Angeles and partly in Detroit as a result of the divorce in which he spent time with both parents. In Detroit he lived in a racially mixed neighborhood at the corner of Six Mile Road and Dequindre at 17199 Marx.

Despite his father's shortcomings in having a penchant for the bottle, brawling and spousal abuse, he taught young John DeLorean how to work with his hands and he always believed that to be the genesis of his love for engineering.

DeLorean's father was a hard-core union man when the Ford Motor Company behind Harry Bennett was hell-bent on destroying organized labor. When Harry Bennett's goons beat Walter Reuther and other union men bloody on the bridge at Ford's River Rough Plant, DeLorean's father was among those standing his ground. In fact, his father was dead-serious about taking a stand for the union cause at Ford. To that end, DeLorean noticed one day that inside the large pocket on the driver's side of his father's Ford Model A, there was a loaded revolver.

DeLorean would become estranged from his father in his teenage years after he attempted to intervene when his father was beating his mother and got beat-up pretty good himself. His father eventually died suffering from the effects of alcoholism while living in a boarding house.

John DeLorean attended Cass Technical High School in Detroit. Other notable Cass Tech graduates besides DeLorean include singer Diana Ross and comedian Lily Tomlin. Evangeline Lindbergh, the mother of famed aviator Charles Lindbergh, taught chemistry at Cass Tech from 1922 to 1942 and was one of DeLorean's teachers.

DeLorean enrolled in an electrical course at Cass Tech and received a very thorough education. He actually won a music scholarship to attend the Lawrence Technological Institute of the University of Michigan in Detroit. In his junior year with World War Two in progress, he was drafted. After the war, honorably discharged and having never seen combat, DeLorean returned to Detroit and got his first job as a draftsman for the Public Lighting Commission and worked there for a year and a half.

Then he returned to Lawrence Tech and took a bachelor's degree in mechanical engineering from the school graduating in 1948. At the age of 24 at the suggestion of his uncle who was a foreman in the engineering garage at Chrysler, DeLorean applied and got his first job in the automobile industry joining the company as a staff engineer. But he felt the corporate culture of Chrysler was oppressive; it didn't stress individual achievement, but rather you were a cog in a big machine. So, DeLorean applied and was hired as an engineer by the Packard Motor Car Company.

His first assignment at Packard was to work on the development of an automatic transmission called the Ultramatic. His design was installed in the final product almost unchanged from his final draft.

Still Packard was in trouble and declining in market share rapidly. DeLorean's boss at Packard, Forest McFarland, a very brilliant engineer, saw the writing on the wall for the future of the company, so he resigned and took a job as director of advanced engineering for the Buick division of General Motors. John DeLorean, not yet 30-years old was chosen to replace McFarland as the department head at Packard.

It wasn't long before General Motors contacted DeLorean and convinced him to join the company. He was offered jobs in five different divisions of GM—he chose Pontiac and was paid a salary of $16,000 a year. One of the first innovations that DeLorean put in place on Pontiacs at GM were recessed window wipers. Until then the wipers on all cars, not just Pontiacs, were bulky and stuck out on the windshield. Ultimately, they would be torn-off in car washes. The concealed wipers solved the problem.

John DeLorean moved up the ranks rapidly at GM and by the 1960s he was urging the company to start building smaller cars.

But DeLorean's best work at GM was done when he went after the youth market with muscle cars and designed the Pontiac GTO introduced at the end of 1963 as a 1964 model. It was a brilliant innovation in both design and engineering. The GTO offered speed, performance and handling in a total package that younger buyers could afford.

The GTO became so popular with young people that a rock n' roll group Ronnie and the Daytonas had a hit million selling record when they recorded a song called "Little GTO."

DeLorean would follow-up with the Pontiac Firebird and Grand Prix for GM

In the early 1960s DeLorean told a reporter that in order to keep in touch with changing trends he listened to rock music. "These rock stations, "the things they say, what they discuss, that's what counts," he said. "It's the cheapest education you can get."[1]

The success of the GTO did cause some internal squabbling at GM. The sales of the GTO cut into the sales numbers of the Corvette and Chevrolet division and president Ed Cole was not happy about it. He contended that the design did not go through the Engineering Policy Group. But due to the GTO's success the matter never reached a high climax.

In 1965 when Pete Estes moved from being president of the Pontiac division to the Chevrolet division, John DeLorean was promoted as the new president of Pontiac. In a few years going forward he would become president of the Chevrolet division.

DeLorean urged GM to be proactive in installing catalytic converters in its cars to cut down on air pollution before it was mandated by Federal law. He would also streamline the administrations of the Chevrolet and Pontiac divisions. . He worked tirelessly and never slept more than four hours a night.

In 1972 DeLorean was promoted to group executive for the Car and Truck company and moved into an office on the 14th floor of the GM World Headquarters in Detroit. He was the youngest GM executive to hold the prestigious position. His responsibilities included heading-up five American car divisions (Buick, Cadillac, Chevrolet, Oldsmobile, and Pontiac), the GMC Truck and Coach Divisions and all Canadian truck and car operations.

But DeLorean found the 14th floor to be a different world filled with infighting and mind-boggling lack of concentration on ethical business practices and total disregard for supporting the civil rights struggle. General Motors was not run by executive engineers, the finance department had the power and the bean counters made the critical decisions for the company. One event led to DeLorean beginning to question whether or not he fit into the culture of the 14th floor.

DeLorean had been aware as most every engineer in the company had been of the problems in the Corvair and later the swing axle on the Tempest. Suddenly, he was confronted again with a personal ethical tug-a-war between best practice by the company and profits.

Beginning in early April 1972 a strike had occurred at the GM assembly plant in Norwood, Ohio (a satellite community of Cincinnati). The strike had left hundreds of 1971 Camaros unfinished on the assembly line. New Federal standards for pollution and safety compliance were to begin with 1972 models.

When the strike ended on September 28, 1972 it had lasted 174 days, the longest labor dispute in the history of GM and the cars left on the Norwood assembly line had been in the process of being manufactured for 1971 models and safety standards. Consequently, they could not be sold without modifications. So that left GM with just a few alternatives; it could rebuild the cars to 1972 standards, they could scrap them, or they could give them away to trade schools and high schools that offered courses in auto mechanics and repair. Whatever the decision, GM was going to suffer a financial loss.

The decision was made by Richard Terrell, John DeLorean's boss on the 14th floor, it was to complete the cars to 1971 pollution and safety standards and ship them to Canada where those standards were still a little more liberal than those in the US. But the Canadian scheme didn't work—it was leaked to the public by an employee at the Norwood plant. GM got a black eye on its public image and ultimately wound-up giving the Camaros to trade schools and absorbing the financial hit. But the episode left a very bad taste in John DeLorean's mouth. When it seemed that John DeLorean now making $670,000 a year was in reach of becoming president of GM, on April 2, 1973, at the age of 48, he resigned.

DeLorean considered becoming an owner of a Cadillac dealership in Florida that would have ensured his personal wealth. Instead he became the head of the National Alliance of Businessmen (NAB). The organization based in Washington, D. C. had been founded by former president Lyndon B. Johnson and the Ford Motor Company and was supported by General Motors to the point of paying John DeLorean's salary while he served. It seemed like a good fit for the civil rights minded executive as it would allow him to spend time promoting job opportunities for ex-convicts, black people and others with special needs. DeLorean would spend a year in the position.

John DeLorean was not your father's automobile manufacturing executive. He was tall, handsome, read extensively, rode horses, played tennis and golf; liked race cars, fine homes, hanging out with celebrities and beautiful women. DeLorean even played the jazz saxophone, sculpted, owned 10% of the San Diego Chargers and in 1973 became one of George Steinbrenner's group that bought the New York Yankees from CBS.

In 1969 DeLorean was divorced from his wife of 15 years. Then he married Kelly Harmon, the 20-year old daughter of former Michigan All-American football player Tom Harmon who at that time was working as a sports broadcaster. But DeLorean divorced her too, then was married for a third time to fashion model Christina Ferrare. At that time DeLorean was 48, Christina 23 years old.

In the mid-1970s DeLorean had told former colleagues at GM that he intended to build his own cars. It had been a personal dream he had been harboring for years. These cars would be sleek and sporty models that could compete with European models. Eventually he came-up with a concept for a sleek futuristic sports car that featured gull-wing doors and an innovative fiberglass chassis and underbody structure, along with a brushed stainless-steel body.

DeLorean did not have visions of grandeur; he knew that in the late 1970s it was impossible to compete with the major companies in the USA like General Motors, Ford and Chrysler and in Europe and Asia with BMW, Volkswagen, Toyota, Nissan and Honda. He was aware of the fact that regardless of how good a car you could manufacture, you would have to form dealerships and have an effective advertising campaign for several years to become established. What he wanted to build was a sports car that would attract a small portion of a very large market that would be attractive to existing car dealers. He wouldn't design a car with planned obsolescence built in, it would be a life-time car like the Rolls Royce. It would also be a high-performance durable car and safe.

In attempting to design a safer car DeLorean found-out what he already knew, most of the manufacturers weren't overly interested in safety. When GM learned that DeLorean and his engineers were working on an air-bag study financed in part by All-State Insurance, the company cancelled a $600,000 unearned bonus he had been promised.

In October 1975 the DeLorean Motor Company was established which would be followed by the DeLorean Manufacturing Company that would be responsible for the production of the new cars.

DeLorean began to raise money and lined up thirty-five American investors including celebrities such as Ira Levin, Johnny Carson and Sammy Davis, Jr., whose average investment was $100,000. The development partnership was put together in 1978 by Oppenheimer & Company of New York and was intended to be a limited partnership designed as a tax shelter. The limited partnership allowed investors to take a tax deduction while their money was being used for research.

John DeLorean set up operations for a manufacturing plant in a depressed area of Dunmurry just west of Belfast, Northern Ireland. He was welcomed by the British government for bringing 2500 jobs to a community struggling with unemployment, notwithstanding religious and civil strife. The British government invested $136 million in the venture. In fact, the conservative government of Prime Minister Margret Thatcher was so enthusiastic about the DeLorean venture that it had provided $50 million after the company had overran its cost projections.

The result was the first DeLorean DMC-12 came off the assembly line in March 1981. The car was equipped with a P-R-V-6 engine that was capable of going from 0 to 60 in eight seconds. For operating and closing the gull-wing doors a Grumman "cryso-twist" torsion bar was used. The heating- air-condition unit was produced by the Harrison division of General Motors. The fiberglass technology used in the car had been invented by Colin Chapman of Lotus and according to John DeLorean, "the chassis engineering we adopted was to have been the next model of the Lotus Esprit."[2]

The year 1981 had been productive and profitable for the DeLorean Motor Company. The first year's profits had been $6.5 million after stumbling production and having nothing but overhead for the first six months. A backlog of orders existed too that could potentially ensure a profitable year in 1982.

Following their final meeting of 1981, the DeLorean board members got together for a Christmas dinner celebration at the 21 Club in New York City. DeLorean said that the event was the happiest day of his life.

The DMC-12 appeared to be a great car, but at a sticker price of $25,000 it struggled to find a market in the US where car sales were sagging and the average car cost about $10,000. Then there was the Chevrolet Corvette that sold for $18,000. When DeLorean's company had been started the Corvette was out of production for a while being redesigned. Now it was back on the market and DeLorean never realized that Corvette would be his biggest competitor. It cut deeply into his sales and when the British pound suddenly surged in the foreign exchange market by 40% it made the DMC-12 financially unattractive to American buyers.

By 1982 only about 9000 DMC-12 cars had been produced and half that number had been sold and DeLorean's company was $175 million in debt. As a result, the company filed for bankruptcy and the British government seized the factory. Not only did the British stand to lose a lot of money, so did various private companies such as the French car company Regie' Nationale des Usines Renault which was owed $17 million.

John DeLorean tried everything possible to save his company. He had been friends for years with Lee Iacocca who was now heading-up a struggling Chrysler. When Iacocca was featured on the cover of *Time* in 1964 for the introduction of the Ford Mustang, DeLorean asked Iacocca why he was not on the cover of the magazine for the Pontiac GTO. DeLorean would eventually make the cover of *Time* in 1982 but it would not be for an automotive engineering achievement, but rather for a drug bust.

DeLorean went to see Lee Iacocca and asked him if Chrysler would be interested in merging with his company. As much as Iacocca would have liked to help DeLorean, he couldn't see how one automobile manufacturing company losing money could help another that was also losing money.

After the merger idea was rejected DeLorean came to see Iacocca again; this time he proposed a R&D tax shelter, which later became commonly known as the "DeLorean Shelter." Along with a couple of his associates John DeLorean had developed a plan whereby selling off limited partnerships that could be written off against the government could save a company tens of millions of dollars, maybe even billions. DeLorean's plan actually got considerable publicity in *Fortune* magazine.

DeLorean had prepared a huge, very costly study for Iacocca and proposed to him that Chrysler would benefit by going with an R&D tax shelter. But Lee Iacocca saw a bigger picture, one that might not be favorable for Chrysler in the long run. Even if DeLorean's plan worked on a limited basis, Iacocca was sure that the IRS would go ballistic over what they might perceive as being taken for a couple billion dollars. As Chrysler had been considering as one of its options seeking a government bailout to keep operating, Lee Iacocca had no choice in the matter but to once again turn-down a proposal by John DeLorean.

Then in early fall of 1982 with his company in receivership by the British government, John DeLorean made the worst and most irrational decision in his life. In an attempt to save his company, he made a deal to place the enterprise in the hands of men associated with organized crime, or so he thought.

The fact was that John DeLorean was about to become a victim in a government plot of entrapment engineered by an obsessed fame-seeking former drug trafficker turned DEA informant James Hoffman. Earlier Hoffman had been employed by GM and on the side began selling illegal drugs. When Hoffman was arrested, he avoided jail time by turning informant for the DEA.

The Federal government's War on Drugs was started in June 1971 by President Richard M. Nixon. To combat the drug trade the DEA was created replacing a smaller less effective agency, mandatory sentences were started, and no knock warrants used by law enforcement agencies.

By the early 1980s first lady Nancy Reagan had begun the "Just say no" anti-drug campaign and Los Angeles Police Chief Daryl Gates had created the DARE program for drug education that was exported from LA to national status. It was all well-intended, but the War on Drugs eventually got out of hand.

The DEA had become a very powerful, over-zealous agency, even dangerous to individual liberty in some respects. So, it wasn't surprising that in the case of entrapment they hatched against John DeLorean that it would be one of the most blatant non-homicidal miscarriages of justice committed in the USA during the twentieth century.

In 1982 the DEA wanted to build a case against 50-year old Morgan Hetrick a pilot and the owner of Morgan Aviation Company. At the time the police in Ventura, California were curious as to how Hetrick was accumulating such large amounts of cash. They thought maybe he was running a high-stakes

Adelaide, Australia, John De Lorean with DMC-12. (www.dreamstime.com)

illegal gambling operation. They didn't know he had been flying large amounts of cocaine into the United States. So they contacted the IRS and the Customs Service.

When the Ventura police finally contacted the DEA, they stated that they had been watching Hetrick and his twelve plane fleet for some time. Then James Hoffman told the DEA that he knew Hetrick. In fact, he had stolen money from him.

By that time Morgan Hetrick had retired from flying in drugs, but he still needed a place to launder money. The DEA had with the cooperation of the organization taken over the Eureka Federal Savings and Loan in San Carlos, California and they planned to use the bank to build cases against drug traffickers laundering money. The DEA installed as president of the Eureka S&L, special agent Benedict Tisa, who took the undercover name of James Benedict.

In May 1982 James Hoffman arranged for Morgan Hetrick to launder money through the Eureka S&L. In fact, Hetrick had met with James Benedict and told him he hauled large amounts of drugs into the USA. Unbeknown to Hetrick the conversation was recorded.

James Hoffman was on the DEA payroll and doing quite well. He began to brag that he could bring down a celebrity. The one he ultimately chose was John DeLorean. At the time John DeLorean was in the newspapers regularly. Hoffman convinced the DEA that DeLorean had been in drug trafficking business for some time and that he had known Morgan Hetrick for some time. Immediately the plot would thicken rapidly.

John DeLorean didn't know James Hoffman personally. James Hoffman had rented a house in Panama Valley, California. Ironically, John DeLorean had a vacation home in Panama Valley and his son Zachary had gone motorcycle riding with Hoffman's son. DeLorean had only met Hoffman once in that community when he spoke briefly with him in his driveway.

In June 1982 Hoffman began making telephone calls to DeLorean's New York office. At first, he only reached DeLorean's secretary. Then one day he hit pay dirt and got DeLorean on the line. Hoffman asked DeLorean if it was too late to save his company. DeLorean said that it was not, and Hoffman told him he could arrange for some investors.

On July 9, DeLorean sent Hoffman a package of information about his car company addressed to a post office in Escondido, California. It was the usual information that investors would obtain from any other company- financial statements, programs, etc. Then a few days later DeLorean was at his vacation home in Panama Valley when he received several calls from Hoffman. He told DeLorean that his investors were ready to go and that he needed to meet with him immediately.

DeLorean told Hoffman that he was planning to meet a friend and business associate in the company, Roy Nesseth, at the Marriott Hotel that day and suggested that he come up to his room. He told Hoffman that way Nesseth and he could meet him. But Hoffman was reluctant to meet with DeLorean with Nesseth present. He said he wanted to discuss the investment one-on-one. All of sudden the potential transaction took on an aura of a cloak and dagger affair. Hoffman told DeLorean to meet him in the hotel bar alone. He agreed.

During the meeting held in a dimly lit booth in the back, Hoffman told DeLorean that his investors were willing to put up $15 million. It was just what DeLorean needed. But Hoffman insisted that he acting as middleman get a 15% commission of $1.5 million and $300,000 for expenses. DeLorean considered Hoffman a little weird, but hardly that much different than all the other middlemen he had met recently. So, he agreed to the terms. Later DeLorean wondered if Hoffman had led him to the remote booth in the bar because it was bugged with a DEA hidden microphone to record their conversation. But he could never prove it.

James Hoffman was working with a DEA agent by the name of John Valestra who used the cover name John Vicenza. He had told the DEA agent about his telephone call to John DeLorean at his New York office, but the call was not recorded. However, DeLorean was later convinced that his conversation with Hoffman at the Marriott bar was recorded but later destroyed because it would have proved his innocence.

DeLorean stated that he was somewhat suspicious of Hoffman, so he called the Eureka Federal Savings and Loan and was told by James Benedict that he had an account on deposit in the range of eight figures.

James Hoffman had told DeLorean that Eureak could arrange for some financing of cars he had inventory in the US. DeLorean asked Benedict if he could finance perhaps nine cars or the entire 1300 that he had in the US at about $13,500 each. It was supposed to be a rather routine transaction that car dealers use to obtain loans for cars in their inventory.

Between July and September 1982 DeLorean received about 200 calls from Hoffman and Benedict assuring him that they would get the money for him.

On September 4, Hoffman called DeLorean and told him to meet him at L'Enfant Plaza Hotel in Washington, D.C. When DeLorean met with Hoffman, he told him that he could have all the money he needed, maybe $30 million. Hoffman said that he had run into delays arranging financing but, in the interim, had put together a deal with some Colombians. Somehow it evaded DeLorean's thought process of what the connation of dealing with Colombian businessmen might entail.

Then Hoffman told DeLorean that he had another idea. He would be willing to invest his $1.8 million commission in arranging financing in a drug deal and then use the profits to buy stock in his auto company.

Shocked! DeLorean told Hoffman that the interim deal was a better way to go. Now he began to wonder what he was getting himself into. DeLorean now had doubts about James Benedict and Eureka S&L too. How deep did this organization go—was it mafia controlled?

Back in New York DeLorean kept getting telephone calls from Benedict telling him to put up the $1.8 million commission for Hoffman as he was putting him in a bad spot. Finally, DeLorean told Benedict to kill the deal.

About two weeks later Hoffman called DeLorean and asked him if the deal was dead. DeLorean said that it was. He had no collateral. The banks had a lien on his personal property and the British Government had control of his assets.

Then in the middle of the night DeLorean received a threatening call from Hoffman. He told DeLorean he knew too much—he couldn't get out.

According to John DeLorean, Hoffman then said, "It you get out there'll be a bloody mess—I'll send your baby daughter's head home in a shopping bag."[3]

The alleged drug deal that James Hoffman was going to make was to involve Morgan Hetrick. The next morning James Benedict called DeLorean and told him he had spoken with Hoffman and that he had a plan to enable him to put up the collateral needed. Benedict said that he would tell Hetrick that DeLorean had put up some money.

On September 28, John DeLorean went to Los Angeles and met with John Vicenza who Benedict had said was associated with the Eureka S&L. The meeting was held in the Bonaventure Hotel and Hoffman was present.

DeLorean gave Vicenza an overview of the current state of his company and mentioned that he needed about $30 million to have a comfortable range for operations.

Then Hoffman began having a sidebar conversation with Vicenza and according to DeLorean they were discussing all the money they were getting from various drug deals and how much they would have to invest in the company. DeLorean could not believe that he was sitting in possible consort with criminals.

Hoffman said all the money would be available in hours, but he wouldn't bother Morgan Hetrick until everything was in place.

DeLorean stated that any money invested in his company should come from a legitimate source like the Eureka. Still at one-point Hoffman asked about laundering money through DeLorean's car company.

Then DeLorean was asked to call Morgan Hetrick. Actually, DeLorean had met Hetrick a week earlier at a meeting arranged by Benedict at the Bel Air Sands. He was told to tell Hetrick that deal was on and he had the cash available. He was being set-up as the middleman.

DeLorean now wanted out more than ever. He said in retrospect in his 1985 biography *DeLorean,* he was ready to give them 100% of his company. That way he would ensure the safety of his family while Hoffman, Vicenza and Benedict would find attempting to work with the British Government that they would gain nothing.

On the evening of October 18, 1982 John DeLorean boarded a plane in New York bound for California where he believed he was going to make a deal with men who were willing to invest $10 million plus in his company and save the jobs of the workers in his DeLorean Motor Company plant in North

Belfast, Northern Ireland. He would discover that he had been set-up by the DEA and a former cocaine dealer.

DeLorean had a hunch that his new partners were mobsters. It was risky business and he felt if the deal went wrong it could cost him his life. The mobsters were in effect donating $10 million that would give them control of an auto plant that the British government owned in a region of Northern Ireland that was war torn and war weary as Catholics and Protestants battled over political control of the six counties under British rule. To give him some cover and counterbalance his fear of physical harm, DeLorean told Hoffman and Benedict that there were IRA (Irish Republican Army) connections to his plant's ownership. But when the mobsters put $10 million into the Eureka S&L and Benedict wire transfers it to Ireland, they will own $10% of DMC, Inc. If they believed that they had just purchased an enterprise that could assist them in moving and laundering money, they will be wrong. Their ownership will be little more than symbolic.

DeLorean was so concerned for his life that he wrote a letter to his attorney believing that when the mobsters learned the truth in their investment and if they tried to harm him, he would tell them of the existence of the letter and they would fear killing him would blow their cover.

As John DeLorean arrived in Los Angeles on October 19, 1982, all of his ducks seemed to be in row.

The day before DeLorean left for California federal officials had arrested Morgan Hetrick and Lee Arrington of San Diego after Arrington attempted to sell 27 kilos of cocaine worth $6.5 million on the street to a DEA agent.

The next night John DeLorean arrived at Los Angeles International Airport (LAX) and he was met by James Hoffman. DeLorean was immediately being taped as the two went to a nearby hotel where without knowing it he was meeting with two DEA undercover agents who were supposed to sell him cocaine and then help distribute it. DeLorean brought no cash with him to pay for the 27 kilos of cocaine which was presumed to be that seized by agents in the arrest of Lee Arrington. DeLorean was allegedly offering the agents a big stake in his failing auto company.

James Benedict and John Vicenza were waiting in the hotel room and DeLorean wondered if they were going to kill him. But Vicenza asked DeLorean about his auto company. He told Vicenza that it had sold about 1000 cars and that British Government were going to lay off all the workers at the end of the week because $10 million had not been put into the company's account as working capital. Then Vicenza asked about the money laundering scheme that had been proposed by Hoffman. DeLorean replied that it had not been done.

DeLorean kept talking business in an effort to bore everyone. Then Benedict went to a closet and brought out a suitcase. It was full of cocaine. Then they ordered champagne to have a toast to their new partnership with DeLorean.

All at once the door opened and another man came into the room. The man announced himself as Jerry West with the FBI and told DeLorean that he was under arrest for violations of the narcotics laws. John DeLorean had been framed by the US Government. DeLorean was read his rights by West. He was then informed of the rights waiver and asked if he understood everything. He said that he did and asked to see his lawyer.

The sting had been video-taped and was highly orchestrated. Immediately following DeLorean's arrest, the media got the story with pictures and it quickly spread around the world. John DeLorean the wonder boy of General Motors, the automotive Maverick had been charged by the US Government with trafficking in cocaine when 55 pounds of cocaine was found in a room registered to him near Los Angeles International Airport. Speculation was that the cocaine worth an estimated $24 million was an attempt by DeLorean to rescue his faltering auto company.

The following day John DeLorean was in court and prosecutors submitted an affidavit charging that DeLorean was to "arrange to finance the delivery of the 100 kilograms load of cocaine by certain valuable properties in an account under control of another party."[4] DeLorean was also charged with having several pounds of cocaine in his possession when he was arrested.

Soon after DeLorean's arrest James Hoffman was cut from the DEA's payroll. Then when the trial was delayed, the Federal prosecutor James P. Walsh Jr., decided something needed to be done with Hoffman so he would disappear. To keep him on the payroll, Walsh obtained information from the FBI and British government stating that John DeLorean had no ties to the IRA in Northern Ireland. Nonetheless, Walsh decided to exploit DeLorean's claim of ties to the terrorist organization and used it as the primary reason why James Hoffman had to be entered into the Federal Witness Protection Program.

On August 16, 1984 John DeLorean was found not guilty.

In his autobiography *DeLorean,* written with Ted Schwarz and published in 1985, he states that upon his unanimous acquittal on the jury's first ballot, he had the opportunity to meet the jurors in their deliberation room. DeLorean states that several of the women jurors had tears in their eyes and so did he.

They told him that through their verdict they wanted to send a message to the government that such a misuse of power would not be tolerated by the American people.

The DMC-12 went on to achieve iconic status when a modified version of the car was featured in Steven Spielberg's 1985 modern sci-fi cult classic film *Back to the Future* starring Michael J. Fox and Christopher Lloyd.

John DeLorean would gracefully fade from the public spotlight and die on March 19, 2005.

14.

Lee Iacocca - Visionary Engineer or Opportunist

Lee (Lido Anthony) Iacocca the son of Italian immigrants, Nicola and Antoinette, was born on October 15, 1924 in Allentown, Pennsylvania. His father used to remark that upon arrival in New York harbor at the age of 12 in 1902, that the only thing he was sure of was that the world was round.

Growing up Iacocca's parents always made him and his sister Della, feel they were special. His interest in cars began when his father Nicola bought a Ford Model A. His father was always tinkering with cars and was one of the first persons in Allentown to learn how to drive.

Nicola Iacocca was interested in the food business and in 1921 he opened the Orpheum Weiner House in Allentown. He reasoned that when times were tough people still had to eat. In fact, that prophecy turned-out to be true as all during the Great Depression the Orpheum Weiner House remained open. Later Nicola would bring Lee's uncles Theodore and Marco into the business. The business was still operating in Allentown into the 1980s under the name Yocco's by two of Lee's cousins.

In 1952, Lee Iacocca seriously considered leaving the Ford Motor Company to enter the food franchising business. He had taken notice how Ford dealers operated as independent franchises and for the most part were very successful businesses. Long before Ray Kroc with McDonald's or Dave Thomas with Wendy's began operating as franchises, Lee Iacocca had a plan to operate ten fast food outlets with one central buying location. In fact, Iacocca did open a small sandwich shop in Allentown called The Four Chefs that specialized in Philadelphia cheese steaks.

His father had set up the business and it was intended to act as tax shelter for Lee. Then in the first year he made $125,000 which raised his tax bracket to the point where it made sense to get out of the business.

Iacocca's father also got into the early car rental business buying into a company called U-Drive-it. After a time, he built up a fleet of thirty cars—mostly Fords. Nicola Iacocca had been friends with Charley Charles whose son Edward worked for a Ford dealership. Later Edward Charles would buy his own Ford dealership and introduce Lee Iacocca to the retail car business. By the time Lee was 15-years old through the encouragement of Edward he had decided that his life's work would be in the automobile business.

Regardless of the entrepreneurial skills of his father, Lee Iacocca always maintained that his mother was the real backbone of the family. For several years the family was very well off, but when hard times hit some of his father's business during the depression, Antoinette helped out in the family's restaurant and also went to work in a silk mill, sewing shirts to add to the family's income. The family always had enough to eat Antoinette was an excellent Neapolitan cook and even made a great pizza!

While growing-up in Allentown Iacocca had on occasion been subjected to some passive prejudice being called a "wop" or a "dago" by schoolmates and it left a minor mark on his personality. He didn't even see a black person in Allentown until he started high school. However, as he climbed the corporate ladder he began to experience some overt signs of prejudice.

Henry Ford II disliked Italians and had a penchant to stereotype all of them as being connected to organized crime. Iacocca was shocked to learn that when he appointed Gerald Greenwald, a Jew, vice-chairman of Chrysler in 1981, that it was an unprecedented move. Until then no Jew had ever reached the top ranks of the Big Three.

On August 27, 1946, Lee Iacocca joined Ford as a college graduate trainee from Lehigh University and came to the company with big .plans Iacocca was extremely ambitious, and his goal was to be a vice president of The Ford Motor Company by the time he was 35 years old. He missed it by 25 days.

But in the big picture Iacocca was aiming much higher than being a VP. His wife Mary had once stated to reporters that at home Lee kept a piece of paper on which he graphed his executive future with Ford. The graph included target dates for promotions, salaries and perks. His ultimate goal was to run the company when Henry Ford II stepped down.

On September 29, 1956 Lee Iacocca married Mary McCleary, the daughter of an Irish-Catholic plumber. Mary had been a receptionist at the Ford assembly plant in Chester, Pennsylvania. The two met each other at a Ford conference in Philadelphia. They would have two daughters, Lia and Kathryn.

While a trained engineer, most of Iacocca's career at Ford had been in marketing and sales in which he excelled. Shortly before Robert McNamara resigned at Ford in late 1960 to join the Kennedy Administration, he recommended the promotion of Iacocca to vice-president and general manager of the Ford Division.

John Dykstra was appointed as president of the Ford Division after McNamara left for Washington. But the ever ambitions Lee Iacocca had his eye on Dykstra's job.

In 1964 Lee Iacocca would gain national attention when the Ford Division launched the Mustang. The Mustang would help Ford gain 27.1 percent of the American car market in six months.

Lee Iacocca has always maintained that the Mustang was a product of his imagination, although most auto historians credit the product's development to Hal Sperlich. Nonetheless Iacocca had always wanted to see an American four-seat sporty car. So, when he became the Ford Division general manager it put him in a position to investigate whether building such a car was feasible. His instincts told him that there would be a market for such a car with the baby boomer generation.

At the time Iacocca presented his idea for the Mustang to Henry Ford II he wasn't interested in launching a new unproven line of cars. The company had just lost $250 million on the Edsel.

But Iacocca kept visiting Henry's office and pushing for approval to build the car. Finally, Henry relented, he authorized $45 million to develop and build the car. He told Iacocca "if it wasn't a success, it would be his ass and he might be looking for a new job elsewhere."[1] While the money allotted was considered a very low amount to design and push a new car through into production—Iacocca got the job done.

In early 1964 the Ford Mustang, a new sports car, was the most talked about—and least seen—auto of the year. The company had been guarding the Mustang for public introduction on April 13. Thus, it was little wonder that

Fred Olmsted, the automotive editor of Detroit's *Free Press*, stopped in astonishment when, in a Detroit parking lot, he spotted a red convertible emblazoned with the insignia of a galloping stallion. Olmsted recognized the car as the top-secret Mustang, rushed to a telephone to summon a photographer. Within less than ten minutes, the *Free Press* had the first public image of the car.

Before the Mustang hit the dealer showrooms in mid-1964 Ford began a massive pre-sale publicity campaign and received thousands of orders from consumers who had never seen the car. In a stroke of marketing genius, the Ford Mustang was featured at the New York World's Fair in April 1964.

When the design process for the Mustang began Lee Iacocca realized that the World's Fair was about 18 months away and that it would be a great venue in which to introduce the car with its intrinsic free advertising. Furthermore, since the car would be introduced as a 1964 ½ model, there would be a captive audience without any distractions from other car manufacturers who introduced their new-model cars in the fall.

The Mustang wasn't the only car exhibited at the Fair, Chrysler featured cars with turbine engines and GM showcased concept cars, but it was the most popular car on display.

Everything went right for the Mustang. The April 17, 1964 edition of *Time* featured Lee Iacocca and the Mustang on the cover. Three days later the Mustang was featured on the cover of *Newsweek* making it the only car to appear simultaneously on the cover of those two popular news magazines.

Later in early October 1964 Ford scored a huge marketing victory over GM during the World's Fair when Bill Fugazy a New York limousine travel company owner and friend of Lee Iacocca arranged for Pope Paul VI to ride in a Lincoln rather than a Cadillac during the pontiff's motorcade from Kennedy Airport to St. Patrick's Cathedral then to Yankee Stadium and for a brief visit to the World's Fair before returning to Kennedy Airport for his return to Rome. The motorcade, numbering 35 vehicles with a Lincoln at the head had traveled along the thoroughfares of Queens to Manhattan and the Harlem and Spanish Harlem sections of New York City.

The dealers loved the Mustang. While Ford company executives were hoping to sell 100,000 Mustangs in the first year, on the first day the car was officially available four million people went to dealers to see the car and sales topped 22,000. In the next six months sales would top 500,000.

In 1966 the Mustang hit the pop charts when Rhythm & Blues singer Wilson Picket's "Mustang Sally" was released giving the car yet another free boost in publicity. The song was extremely popular in both the US and UK. In 2004 the *Rolling Stone* listed "Mustang Sally "at number 434 on its list of the 500 greatest songs of All Time.

While the Chevrolet Monza had previously featured an interior with bucket seats and a floor shift, according to Iacocca, with the Mustang "We gave Detroit something they didn't have—a four-seat sporty car with European styling. It was 1967 before either GM or Chrysler could get a car on the market to compete with the Mustang. We gave it a hot new V-8 with sports car handling, and introduced it successfully to the race circuit, where it did well"[2]

Lee Iacocca believed that the market for the Mustang with a sticker price for the basic model of $2,368 was driven by the fact that the car offered consumers status for low costs.

The basic model was a hardtop, straight six with three speed manual transmission with a long list of options and consisted of sheet metal, glass, bumpers and new moldings

But the chassis, engine, suspension and drive-train components were in fact copies of the Ford Falcon and Ford Fairlane prompting some critics to refer to the Mustang as s souped-up Falcon.

Popular belief is that the Ford Mustang had been named for the P-51 fighter plane, but that is in fact an urban myth. At the time animal names for cars were becoming very popular. An ad man at the Walter Thompson Advertising Agency presented a list of animal names to Iacocca. Iacocca along with Gene Bordinat, vice president of styling, sat down and reviewed the list, ultimately settling on the name Mustang because the running horse connotation suggested moving fast through the countryside.

Due to the enormous success of the Mustang, in January 1965, Henry Ford II appointed Lee Iacocca head of both the Ford and Lincoln-Mercury Division. Later in the 1960s Mercury would launch the widely popular Cougar. Iacocca was appointed to the board of directors, now he had his eye on the prize, the top job at Ford—Henry Ford II's job.

Lee Iacocca believed that Ford needed to attract younger buyers. He was aware of the fact that European sports cars were starting to appear on American highways in larger numbers and to meet that challenge American automakers would have to create a sports car, a coupe that was practical, modestly priced, but still appeared sexy.

Gene Bordinat was the Ford Motor Company's vice president and director of styling. Bordinat's philosophy in regard to styling was consumer driven,

1965 Ford Mustang Hardtop. (Photo by Lawrence T. Hay)

"Styling serves to make the public aware that here is a new product, with improvements in materials, components and mechanical design—features that might be hidden to anyone but a mechanic or an engineer."[3] Bourdinat was in essence saying consumers didn't want these features hidden, they wanted them blatantly visible. The Ford Mustang which he and Iacocca would launch would create a new fad in the automobile industry—the Pony Car.

By automotive definition a Pony Car is an American class of automobile inspired by the Mustang that is affordable, compact, highly styled with a sporty or performance-oriented image.

From 1964 until 1967 Ford had a monopoly on the Pony Car; then in 1967 all the other manufacturers with the exception of American Motors started to produce various models. In 1967 the same year that Ford launched the Mustang GT, General Motors rolled the Chevy Camaro Z2B off the production line and it was an instant success in sales.

Other classic Pony Cars that would follow included; GM's 1969 Pontiac Trans AM and Chrysler's 1970 AAR Plymouth 'Cuda and 1970 Dodge Hemi Challenger. American Motors finally got in the game with its first Pony Car in 1970 when the 1970 AMC AMX hit the market.

Then in 1971 The Ford Motor Company laid an automotive engineering egg as large as the one that GM had laid with the Corvair when the company introduced the exploding Pinto. The Ford Pinto was a front-engine, rear-drive subcompact car manufactured and marketed by Ford for model years 1971–1980.

At that time Ford needed a subcompact car to compete with German and Japanese import models that were starting to flood the market. Ford president Lee Iacocca also wanted a low-cost car, one that could sell for under $2,000. When the Pinto was rolled-out on the market in 1971 it was a success selling 400,000 that year thereby putting it in the sales class of the Falcon and Mustang. Inside the company the Pinto was referred to as "Lee's car."

But there was a problem with the Pinto. The fuel tank was located behind the axle. This condition was a factor of the Pinto having a filler neck on the fuel tank that sometimes was ripped out in a low-impact collision allowing gas to be spilled out that frequently ignited causing the car to burst into flames. Several drivers and passengers had been burned to death in such collisions. Ford resisted making any changes. Lee Iacocca and other Ford executives were worried that lawsuits might bankrupt the company, so they kept their mouths shut. It took Ford until 1978 to issue a recall for 1.5 million Pintos built between 1971 and 1976.

One analysis of the Pinto fiasco suggests," There were various ways of making the Pinto's gas tank safer. Although the estimated price of these safety improvements ranged from only $5 to $8 per vehicle, Ford evidently reasoned that the increased cost outweighed the benefits of a new tank design."[4]

There were between 27 and 188 deaths attributed to the exploding gas tanks in the Pinto that resulted in 117 lawsuits. The two most significant of those cases were *Grimshaw v. Ford Motor Company* and *State of Indiana vs. Ford Motor Company.*

In the case of *Grimshaw v. Ford,* in May 1972, Lily Gray was traveling with 13-year old Richard Grimshaw in a 1972 Pinto when their car was struck by another car traveling approximately 30 miles per hour. The impact of the collision ignited a fire in the Pinto which killed Lily Gray and left Richard Grimshaw with significant physical injuries. At trial a judgment was rendered against Ford and the jury awarded the Gray family $560,000 and Matthew Grimshaw $2.5 million in compensatory damages. The jury also awarded $125 million in punitive damages which was subsequently reduced to $3.5 million.[5]

In the case of State of Indiana vs. Ford Motor Company, on August 10, 1978 three teenage girls of the Urlich family of Osceola, Indiana were killed when the 1973 Pinto they were riding in was involved in a rear-end collision. The driver of the Pinto had stopped in the road to retrieve the car's gas cap which had been inadvertently left on the top of the car and subsequently fell onto the road. While stopped the Pinto was struck by a Chevrolet van.

The Ford Motor Company sent the Urlichs a recall notice for the Pinto in 1979. A Grand Jury proceeded to indict Ford on three counts of reckless homicide. *State of Indiana v. Ford* was a landmark in product liability law as it was the first time a corporation faced criminal charges for a defective product, and also the first time a corporation was charged with murder. If convicted, Ford faced a maximum fine of $30,000 under Indiana's 1978 reckless homicide statute.

Ford advanced a legal defense that was vastly more ambitious than its effort mounted in the Grimshaw case. The Ford legal effort was led by James F. Neal with a staff of eighty and a budget of about $1 million, whereas the Elkhart County state's attorney had a budget of about $20,000 and a staff that consisted of volunteer law professors and law students. A former head of the NHTSA, testifying on Ford's behalf, said the Pinto's design was no more or less safe than that of any other car in its class. In 1980 Ford was found not guilty. In 1980 a civil suit was settled for $7500 to each plaintiff.[6]

In 1980 the last Pinto rolled off the Ford assembly line. By that time 3.2 million of the cars had been built. While Ford was never held criminally libel for the design, the car nearly took Ford's reputation with it.

As for Lee Iacocca, he maintained a defensive position about the fiasco that was the Ford Pinto. In his 352-page autobiography *Iacocca—An Autobiography* published in 1984 Iacocca wrote a mere eight paragraphs in regard to the Pinto, about 480 words. Iacocca stated that there was absolutely no truth that Ford attempted to save a few bucks and knowingly made a dangerous car. While he admitted that the auto industry had often been arrogant, it was not callous. "The guys who built the Pinto," said Iacocca, "had kids in college who were driving that car. Believe me, nobody sits down and thinks I'm going to deliberately make this car unsafe."[7]

In the winter of 1974 Ford announced a fourth quarter loss of $12 million. It was the first quarterly loss for Ford since 1946 when the Whiz Kids were brought in to implement policies to make the company solvent. As a result, Henry Ford II began to show some intense concern with the company. Lee

Iacocca and a few others at Ford would describe that concern as more like paranoia.

Although Ford was enjoying success with Lee Iacocca as the head of the Ford and Lincoln Mercury Division, Henry Ford II didn't personally care for him. Ford thought that Iacocca was becoming too big for his corporate britches. Rather than just fire Iacocca outright, Ford decided to attempt to build a case against him. To that end, in 1975 Henry Ford II authorized $1.5 million of company funds to investigate Lee Iacocca's business and private life.

Lee Iacocca began to notice strange things happening at the office. His secretary told him that as his desk was always a mess at the end of the day, she would take the liberty of trying to organize everything for him. But the next morning she would find that everything had been moved around.

On July 11, 1975 Henry Ford II called a meeting of his top five hundred managers. Assembled together in the auditorium they listened to Henry proclaim that he was the captain of the ship and that the company's management was going about business all wrong. Henry had a habit of settling arguments by reminding those involved that his name was on the building. Lee Iacocca of course was the company's top manager, so he interpreted Henry's remarks as being directed personally at him.

Later Lee Iacocca would state in his book *Iacocca—An Autobiography,* "After the meeting, we all started to wonder if Henry was losing his mind. The whole company was frozen. Nobody was doing a thing. Instead, people were busy trying to figure out what Henry was up to—and whose side to take."

As the news of Henry Ford's discontent with the management of his company began to leak outside of corporate headquarters the dealers seemed to be siding with Lee Iacocca. In early 1976 the Ford dealers held a national meeting in Las Vegas and made a mass declaration that Henry Ford was not offering the quality of leadership that they expected of him in keeping pace with General Motors.

It was about that time Iacocca received a telephone call from his friend Bill Fugazy who was the person who ran the dealer incentive plans for Ford in the New York area. He had also been the one who arranged for Pope Paul VI to ride in a Lincoln during his historic visit to the city eleven years ago. Fugazy told Iacocca that files had been removed from his office and he believed that his telephone had been tapped. While nothing incriminating came out of whatever this covert operation had been Iacocca became convinced that the object of it all was not an investigation of Fugazy, but rather it had been Henry Ford II attempting to uncover evidence of wrongdoing by him.

The investigation of Iacocca's business and private life by Henry Ford II turned-up nothing. When the investigation became known by Iacocca and other top Ford executives they began to fear Henry and became afraid that everything they said was either being taped or reported. The bottom line was that the Iacocca investigation had a very bad effect on the *esprit de corps* of the management of the company.

Iacocca felt outraged and believed that an apology was due him. His wife Mary wanted him to go public and sue Henry Ford II. When Iacocca confronted board member Frank Murphy asking why no one on the board got involved when the investigation was going on, he was told to forget about it. "You know Henry. Boys will be boys. Anyway—he came in with a cannon and went out with a peashooter."[8]

Henry Ford II had acquired a penchant for play. For a while in the 1970s he had grown a beard and become a jetsetter and was seen frolicking from Acapulco to the Riviera. Henry liked to drink and jump into a swimming pool fully dressed. His brother William "Bill" Clay Ford who owned the Detroit Lions said, "He has a darn good time when he has a good time."[9]

At that point in time when Henry Ford II was becoming concerned with Lee Iacocca, he had some health issues and he was drinking a lot. He had even brought his brother William Clay Ford into the business to maintain a family presence should he experience a protracted illness. After Henry was arrested for driving under the influence (DUI) in Santa Barbara, California with his then girlfriend, Kathleen DuRoss of Detroit, in the car, his second marriage started to come apart.

Henry and his first wife Anne McDonald the mother of his children had divorced in 1964 with a large settlement involved. He then married Cristina Austin, the divorced wife of a British naval officer. They were divorced after a decade; Henry then married Kathleen DuRoss in 1980.

He wanted his son Edsel, then 28-years old, to take over the company. Although his investigation of Lee Iacocca had turned-out to be a frivolous affair, Ford was still concerned about his overly ambitious personality. In 1978 he decided it was in his best interest to have Iacocca report to another Ford executive, Philip Caldwell.

Soon after the Nixon Administration had normalized diplomatic relations with China in 1972, Henry Ford II was invited by the government of the

People's Republic of China to come for a visit. In June 1978 Ford finally got around to taking the long-delayed junket. Ford knew in time China was going to be an important market. He also wanted to block the Japanese automobile manufactures as best he could. The visit was valuable and resulted in the sale of 700 heavy Ford trucks to China.

While Ford was in the far-east, Lee Iacocca decided to make his move and launch a corporate coup. Iacocca did not like reporting to Philip Caldwell, so he decided to test his strength with his fellow board members for a higher position. He was even so brazen as to board a company plane and fly to Boston and New York and present his case to fellow board members. He told a least two board members that Henry Ford II was senile and not up to the job anymore.

On July 10 when Henry Ford II returned from China, he was quickly informed of what had been transpiring by Arjay Miller who had succeeded John Dyksta in the Ford and Lincoln Mercury Division. Iacocca wanted to take the company away from Ford.

The matter came to a head on July 13, 1978 when Henry Ford II called Lee Iacocca into his office and with his brother William Clay Ford present as a witness, promptly fired him. While he was given $1.5 million in severance pay, Henry Ford II also had attempted to put a restrictive covenant clause in the discharge papers that if Iacocca went to work for another car manufacturer, he would forfeit the amount.

Lee Iacocca had been president of The Ford Motor Company for 7½ years, he had served longer in that position than anyone outside of the Ford family. Now 54-years old and after serving for 32 years at The Ford Motor Company, overnight Iacocca had been moved from the penthouse to the outhouse. On October 15, 1978 he was ordered to vacate his corporate office in the Ford world headquarters in Dearborn and move into the parts depot on Telegraph Road where he was permitted to begin a job search.

No longer did Iacocca have the luxuries inherent in the corporate head-quarters; gone was his private bathroom and an office the size of a luxury hotel suite with white-coated waiters on-call 24-hours a day to serve him. The last office for the man who had given the auto industry and the world the Mustang at Ford would be in a cubicle in an obscure warehouse with a cracked linoleum floor and two plastic coffee cups on a desk.

Iacocca sat down at his new desk while his long-time secretary Dorothy Carr stood by him with tears in her eyes. Then after a few minutes the depot manager entered the cubicle and offered to get the former president of Ford a cup of coffee from the machine in the hall. At that moment it seemed to be all gloom and doom for Iacocca.

But Lee Iacocca had brought these circumstances upon himself. He had discredited Henry Ford II and there was a piper to pay. As controversial or impulsive as Ford may have appeared or acted on occasion, he was not some guy that had simply been born into the automotive business with a silver spoon in his mouth that had no talent and was an executive in name only.

Henry Ford II knew the automotive business from A to Z. As a young man after being pushed by his mother he took over The Ford Motor Company operations following World War Two from a grandfather who had become visibly senile and was leading the company toward destruction. He proceeded to turn the company around and lead it into becoming the second largest automaker in the world.

While Henry Ford II didn't like small cars, he approved the development of the Fiesta for the European market. Cognizant of the fact that Japanese imports were here to stay, Ford also purchased 25% interest in The Mazda Motor Company. This move provided Ford with access to Japanese technology and low-cost parts and the development of hybrid Ford-Mazda cars that sold overseas and notwithstanding the popularity of Ford trucks, provided the company with a huge International presence and influence.

Unlike his bigoted grandfather who would have done nothing following the devastating 1967 racial unrest and riot that occurred in Detroit, Henry Ford II advanced proactive inter-racial action. He forced the creation of a National Alliance of Businessmen that was tasked with an agenda to find ways to change hiring practices, promotions and dealer selection practices that had quietly kept blacks out of Ford plants, offices and showrooms.

On October 1, 1979, the 71st anniversary of the Model T, Henry Ford II stepped down as CEO of The Ford Motor Company and became chairman of the finance committee of the board. He was replaced as CEO by Philip Caldwell.

Ford's finest hour occurred in 1986 as he watched those he had selected to run The Ford Motor Company, including many who had done well in overseas assignments, report profits of $3.3 billion to GM's $2.95 billion. It was first time since 1924 that Ford had exceeded GM on the bottom line.

Later in 1978 Lee Iacocca became president and CEO of Chrysler. He agreed to work in the position for $1 a year in salary with stock options. In a few years he would become chairman of the board.

At the time of Iacocca's departure from Ford to Chrysler the USA was in a deep recession. Even New York City was on the verge of bankruptcy. In July 1977 Mayor Abraham Beame went to Washington to beg President Jimmy Carter for assistance. The previous administration led by President Gerald Ford had refused any assistance to New York City. President Carter and his Treasury Secretary Michael Blumenthal worked-out a federal loan for the beleaguered city.

The Chrysler Corporation that Lee Iacocca had just taken over was the 10th largest corporation in America and in debt $4 billion which amounted to 10% of all U.S. Corporate debt.

Chrysler, an important government defense contractor employed 160,000 workers and was on the verge of bankruptcy. The company was also being threatened with a foreign take over by aggressive Japanese automakers. Just as Mayor Beame had done, Lee Iacocca went to see President Jimmy Carter. Once again, the Carter Administration was willing to come through giving Chrysler a guaranteed loan of $1.5 billion if approved by Congress.

It wasn't unprecedented for US automakers to request financial assistance from the US Government. AMC teetering on the verge of collapse had been doing it for years receiving tax credits, EPA emissions waivers and a designation as a small business to give the company preferential treatment on requests for government contracts.

The Chrysler request for Federal financial assistance was not entirely popular with the taxpayers and politicians alike. Both Ford and GM had incurred recent losses and were not asking for government assistance. At the time Iacocca was walking into the White House, hat-in-hand, hundreds of thousands of American workers were beginning to see their jobs disappear as Japan became the world's largest steel manufacturer and the term rust belt was commonly being used to describe the shrinking American industrial base that had spread along the Great Lakes for generations.

While US Steel, Bethlehem Steel and others began closing mills, other companies began outsourcing the manufacturing of everything from sneakers to televisions to rubber dog bones to foreign countries. Therefore a large number of people in the US held the opinion that there was nothing special about Chrysler and that the US Government should let the company die a natural industrial death.

Consumers held the opinion that during the 1970s Chrysler continued producing poorly built huge gas-guzzling cars in the face of two Arab oil embargos and made no attempt to compete with foreign competition from Toyota and Honda. All most overnight the percentage of consumers who were willing to consider a Chrysler product fell from 30% to 13%.

There were committee hearings in the Senate and House and high-profile politicians such as Senator William Proxmire of Wisconsin, Senator Barry Goldwater of Arizona and Congressman Richard Kelly of Florida felt the same way as many in the general public.

Representative Kelly often appeared on the evening news chastising Chrysler and accusing Lee Iacocca and Chrysler of attempting to con the government in seeking a bailout.

Senator Proxmire felt a bail out of Chrysler was a very bad precedent—believing that going forward Congress would be forced to bailout many more failing corporations.

Senator Goldwater had voted against the bailout of New York City and was poised to also vote against the Chrysler bailout for the same reasons as Senator Proxmire.

"Where do such subsides stop," asked Goldwater? "I am against subsides. Congress is not a bank or loan agency. In general, the feds should stay out of state and local government as well as private enterprise. Otherwise, as we have seen it will largely take over both. Neither state and local government nor business should operate on the notion that Uncle Sugar will pay for their mistakes."[10]

At that time the Chrysler public relations department felt the best strategy was to ride out the storm of controversy—eventually everything would be all right.

But Lee Iacocca decided that Chrysler should fight back. When Iacocca had left Ford, he convinced Ronald DeLuca an ad man from the agency of Kenyon & Eckhardt to abandon a $75 million account with Ford and take the Chrysler account.

It would be DeLuca along with Leo-Arthur Kelmenson, the Kenyon & Eckhardt chairman, who would create an advertising campaign that would ultimately convince Congress to approve the $1.5 billion loan guarantee for Chrysler.

The strategy developed by DeLuca and Kelmenson was for Chrysler to put together an ad campaign that would assure the public that Chrysler had a future. Instead of the usual advertising that Chrysler did featuring text and pictures of its new models, it mounted an aggressive editorial campaign using full page ads telling the public why the federal loan guarantees were necessary and what the company's long-range plans were. In short, Chrysler was telling America that it

President Bill Clinton meets with Lee Iacocca at the White House in 1993. (Wikimedia Commons by Ralph Answang, archived in the Clinton Presidential Library 9/23/1993)

was making the kind of cars they needed and that it had no intention of going out of business. The ads even refuted the common charges that Chrysler cars got lousy gas mileage, they were building the wrong kind of cars and that Chrysler's management wasn't strong enough to turn the company around.

All the ads carried Lee Iacocca's signature. The company wanted to tell the public that a new era had begun. Suddenly, Lee Iacocca became the most famous car salesman in America, but not by promoting Chrysler's cars, by promoting the company's future.

Some saw the Chrysler ad campaign as ridiculous. Ralph Nader called it a multi-million-dollar advertising campaign for welfare buying newspaper ads. He also pointed-out that Chrysler had retained Washington lobbying firms headed by Democrat Thomas Boggs and Republican William Timmons.

Meanwhile additional pressure on Congress to approve the bailout was coming from Chrysler dealers who were swarming Capitol Hill as well as the UAW whose membership still packed a considerable punch at the ballot box.

But Iacocca and Chrysler had a huge ally for the bailout bill in the House with Speaker Tip O'Neil of Massachusetts. When the House vote was taken it passed by 271 to 136, a two-to-one margin.

On the evening of December 19, 1979, the Senate voted on the bill and it passed 53-44. Many Senators simply rationalized their "yes" vote by saying they were in a no-win situation.

On January 7, 1980 President Carter signed the legislation (P.L. 86-185).

However, the bill came with strings attached. First Congress required that Chrysler obtain private financing for the $1.5 billion. The government was simply signing the note, not printing the money.

Second, Chrysler had to obtain $2 billion in commitments or concessions that could be arranged for the financing of its operations. It was suggested that the company attempt to reduce its employee's wages. The UAW agreed and wages were cut $3 an hour.

Lee Iacocca would use the bailout money wisely and the loan would be repaid on July 13, 1983, five years to the day that he had been fired by Henry Ford II. To celebrate the loan repayment a ceremony was held at the Waldorf-Astoria Hotel in New York with the media on hand and Lee Iacocca posing in front of an exaggerated blown-up four foot by 8-foot replica of the loan repayment check on cardboard.

That same year Chrysler would make an operating profit of $975 million—the best ever in the company's history.

To stabilize Chrysler Iacocca downsized the corporation. He sold off profitable units such as the tank division. A union representative was appointed to the board of directors. Then in the early 1980s Chrysler introduced the K-Cars, along with the mini-van that would become best sellers.

K-Cars were introduced in the Plymouth Horizon and Dodge Omni models and then expanded. The mid-sized sedans featured a solid beam rear axle and independent front suspensions with McPherson Struts. They came in front or all-wheel drive with a base model starting price at $5,880.00. It was the perfect car for a country working its way out of the recession and American's embraced it.

The K-Car was the brainchild of Hal Sperlich a former Ford engineer and product planner who had been fired by Henry Ford II in 1977.

Hal Sperlich, born in 1931, was raised in Detroit and Saginaw, Michigan. In 1951 he graduated from the University of Michigan with a degree in Industrial/Mechanical Engineering. Prior to joining Ford, he spent three years in the U.S. Navy (Seabees).

Sperlich had been crucial in the design of both the Mustang and Fiesta while at Ford. According to Iacocca, Henry Ford II didn't care for Sperlich because he was brash and didn't show deference to the king. At planning meetings

Sperlich would sit next to Iacocca and occasionally whisper something in his ear which would agitate Henry a lot. At one point, Henry told Iacocca that he didn't want Sperlich sitting next him anymore.

But the key factor that got Sperlich into Henry Ford II's doghouse was that he saw the future and advocated building smaller cars. Iacocca and Sperlich had wanted to build a version of the K-Car at Ford, but Henry wouldn't approve it.

When Iacocca was reunited with Sperlich at Chrysler he described the experience as "like finding a tall, cool beer in the middle of the desert."[11] It was however a lot more for Iacocca. It could be argued that with the development of the Mustang, K-car and mini-van, it was Hal Sperlich that made Lee Iacocca famous.

By turning Chrysler around Lee Iacocca became a corporate rock star. In 1984 he wrote his autobiography *Lee Iacocca—An Autobiography*. The book was a best seller and Iacocca was booked on every TV talk show on the air in America and Canada.

Although military historians claim that it was General George Patton who first said it, Lee Iacocca is now popularly credited with adding the phrase "lead,

General George S. Patton reviews troops with Soviet Marshall Aleksandr Vasilevski in Torgau, Gerany, 1945.

follow or get out of the way" as part of the American dialogue. For over a decade in the late 1980s and into the early 1990s Iacocca's corporate culture edict was bellowed by just about everyone in a position of authority in America; small and large business managers, athletics coaches, teachers, politicians even the everyday man-on-the-street. The phrase became America's corporate rallying-cry of the late 1980s and early 1990s.

On September 27, 1987 Henry Ford II died of pneumonia at the Henry Ford Hospital in Detroit a facility that his grandfather had founded. He was 70-years old.

Lee Iacocca retired from Chrysler in 1992, but despite his success with the company he was far from happy. In 1995 Iacocca sued Chrysler claiming the company blocked him from exercising $42 million in share options. The case was settled with Iacocca receiving $21 million.

On May 15, 1983, Lee's wife Mary died in Royal Oak, Michigan following a stroke. For years she had suffered from heart disease and diabetes. She was just 57-years old. Through-out their marriage Mary had been Iacocca's source of inspiration, his strength and his confidant. Even after Iacocca had been fired, Mary attended the Ford annual meeting. Why not she reasoned, after the Ford family we're the largest stockholders.

She had also encouraged Lee to go to Chrysler. Iacocca would later state that if he had one regret it was that Mary never lived long enough to see the success of the K-Cars.

In 2014 Lee Iacocca then 92-years old was living in Bel Air, California with a rescue dog he had adopted. He named the pooch Sparky after the first dog he had grown-up with back in Allentown. Still leading a full life, he kept active with family and friends and various philanthropic activities through his Iacocca Foundation. The automobile industry had been very good to Lee Iacocca; his network had grown to $100 million.

15.
Japanese Imports, Mini-Vans, and SUVs

Beginning in the late 1970s into the 1990s the flood of fuel-efficient Japanese imports continued to gain popularity with American car buyers at a rapid pace. The flood gates for Japanese imports had been opened in the American market as a result of the 1973 fuel crises that followed the Arab-Israeli war. In 1974 sales at General Motors dropped by a million and half vehicles and sales at Ford dropped by a half-million.

When the Japanese auto makers first started to export cars to the US, the CEOs of The Big Three met the challenge with arrogance and indifference. Roger Smith CEO of GM mocked the Japanese industry; "What did the Japanese invent in cars"? Smith mocked. "The only thing I can think of is that that little coin holder."[1] Henry Ford II refused to take the Japanese manufacturers serious. In 1978 Ford predicted that American manufacturers would drive Japanese imports "back into the sea."[2]

Nissan had been one of the first Japanese automakers to begin exports to the US in 1958 with the Datsun Bluebird. Soon the Datsun pick-up followed and by 1967 the company had sold 100,000 cars in the US.

When the great surge of Japanese imports was about to begin toward the end of the 1960s only two major companies Toyota and Honda were seriously competing with the American manufacturers. Within a decade just about every automaker in Japan; Suzuki, Nissan, Mazda, Mitsubishi, Subaru and others would have their cars lined-up at the docks ready for shipment to America.

For over a decade American car manufacturers had been in a muscle car mindset, but it wouldn't be long before they would have to swallow their two-door, high-performance engine pride and form alliances with Japanese manufacturers. The first was Chrysler which began marketing Mitsubishi products under the Dodge name. GM agreed to a partnership with Toyota and formed New United Motor Manufacturing building the Chevrolet Nova. Ford bought a 25% share of Mazda.

The Japanese just didn't penetrate the American market—they did likewise in the European market. As a result, British Leyland formed a partnership with Honda and later in the 1980s Toyota formed a partnership with Volkswagen to build a small pick-up truck in Germany and the trend would continue into the 21st century.

As a result, a new economy was emerging—globalization. To Wall Street globalization meant quick profiteering. To business, globalizations meant more markets to sell their products in. In addition, it offered the opportunity to save money through standardization and sharing products world-wide. To consumers it was a double-edged sword; while globalization meant more options in the marketplace, it was clouded by the possibility of jobs being exported and lower wages. Suddenly, an economy emerged where anything could be made and sold elsewhere. Of all the industries affected by globalization the auto industry personified the term more than any other.

It just wasn't the oil crises or the movement toward the global economy that started to pull the American car manufacturers under; Detroit itself did a lot to exacerbate the problem with the declining quality in the cars it was putting on the market.

Beginning in the late 1960s American car buyers began to advance the theory "never buy a car made on a Monday" implying that at the beginning of the work week a condition existed on the assembly lines in Detroit were workers still recovering from the effects of weekend binge drinking were prone to making mistakes.

The assembly line was even ridiculed in a huge country music hit that crossed over to the pop charts in 1976 when Johnny Cash and the Tennessee Three recorded "One Piece At A Time." The lyrics tell the story of a man who leaves his Kentucky home in 1949 and heads to Detroit to work on the Cadillac assembly line. The man covets the cars he is assembling and while they are out of reach for him financially, he devises a plan to get one by stealing auto parts one piece at a time to build an eclectic Caddy.

"One Piece At A Time" reached number one on the Country Music charts in both the US and Canada and the recording did a lot to reinforce negative feelings about the quality of American cars with consumers.

For a while in the 1980s some industrial engineers and psychologists were toying with the idea that Henry Ford's assembly line model had outlived its usefulness in producing automobiles. Some researchers began to take notice of a manufacturing model being used in Sweden and wondered if it might work in Detroit to solve problems with quality, efficiency and costs associated with producing automobiles.

In 1969 in Sweden the Saab-Scania plant located at Sodertalje outside of Stockholm which manufactures automobile and heavy truck engines began experimenting with having groups of 20 people of various skills manufacture an entire truck engine rather than using the traditional assembly line. If the experiment was successful Saab planned to incorporate it in a new factory that was being planned to be built at Malmo.

Group assembly was tested at the plant between 1969 and 1972 showing some remarkable results; unplanned stoppages dropped from 6% to 2% of total time. Also extra work and adjustment needed to correct omissions and errors in the finished product dropped by one-third. Furthermore personnel turn-over on the chassis line dropped from 70% annually to 20% or less.

But there were problems with the group model; the most compelling was that an insufficient system of materials transporting that was needed to accompany the group assembly task environment that did not exist in the traditional linear assembly line. Saab came-up with a solution by locating the assembly groups transversely to the conveyor line and began using the model in 1972.

Volvo took notice of the group engine assembly model at Saab and expanded the model to have teams build an entire car at a new factory the company opened in 1988 at Uddevalla located in southwest Sweden. It was a bold attempt by Volvo chairman, Oehr R. Gyllenhammar to show the industry that a small team of highly skilled workers could build an entire car with support of advanced materials handling that could compete with the assembly line.

Meanwhile Volvo continued to run its traditional assembly line at its plant at Kalmar in southwest Sweden which provided researchers with a parallel system to evaluate the efficiency of the group model.

After Volvo lost money for the first time in a decade in 1990 the company reviewed the progress of the group or team building concept at Uddevalla and discovered that it took 50 hours to build a car using that model whereas it only took 37 hours to build a car on the traditional assembly line at its Kalmar plant. Furthermore, it was noted that at the Volvo plant in Ghent, Belgium with workers using a traditional assembly line it took only 25 hours to build a car.

While both the Saab and Volvo group/team assembly models were bold attempts at humanistic manufacturing they were slow and quality standards did not seem to be improved. Consequently in 1991 Saab closed its new assembly plant at Malmo that had been using the team assembly concept. In 1994 the Kalmar plant was also closed, and Saab ceased manufacturing cars.

In 1989 General Motors had bought a 50% stake in Saab for $600 million with a condition that after 10 years it could acquire the remaining 50% for $125 million. The acquisition appeared to have a potential win-win potential. GM now had a foothold in the European luxury car market that was becoming very popular with a rising sub-culture of buyers in the US known as yuppies (young urban professionals), while Saab could use its affiliation with GM to advance as a global dealer and benefit from GM's huge supply chain to lower costs.

In 2000 GM exercised its option and bought the remaining 50% of Saab turning it into a wholly owned subsidiary. However, the Saab acquisition was never a profitable venture. When GM filed for bankruptcy during the Great Recession in 2010 it jettisoned Saab.

Volvo would also abandon the team assembly concept.

Several factors brought about the scuttling of the group/team model. First, at Saab, GM was not committed to it. Second, too many employees at Saab and Volvo did not realize the demands inherent in the job redesign. And finally, the training period to provide the workers in the new group/team model with the necessary skills to build an entire car turned-out to be much longer than had been anticipated.

It was simply inconceivable that Detroit auto manufacturers would have ever attempted to implement a system that did not support a mechanically driven paced conveyor system, i.e. the assembly line. There was no interest in providing for paralleled, relatively autonomous, self-paced groups building complete engines or cars. As innovative as it seemed, it was just too slow for Detroit and for Japan too.

The Toyota Motor Company began as the Toyoda Loom Works in 1926 and manufactured automatic textile looms. In 1933 a subsidiary of Toyoda was created by Kiichiro Toyoda the son of the company's founder Sakichi Toyoda to begin manufacturing cars. Four years later the company name was changed to Toyota.

During World War Two Toyota manufactured trucks for the Japanese army. Following the war transition to peacetime truck manufacturing was problematic and the company was facing bankruptcy. Toyota was saved when during the Korean War the US Army placed an order for 5000 military vehicles.

The company then began building automobiles and in 1957 exported its first car to America, the Toyota Crown. In 1963 Toyota established a manufacturing plant in Melbourne, Australia and slowly began its climb to becoming a global auto manufacturing powerhouse with reliable, four-door compact cars such as the Carina and Celica as well the second generation Corolla and fourth generation Corona that would become popular in the US during the early 1970s in the wake of the oil crisis.

By 1980 Toyota was completely confident that they could compete head-to-head in the US with General Motors, Ford and Chrysler in the mid-sized car market and began manufacturing the Camry which was much larger and powerful than the Corona. The Camry was reliable, well-equipped, had very good re-sale value and became an overnight success. By 1997 the Toyota Camry was the best-selling car in the US.

Honda had been the trailblazer for the Japanese to begin manufacturing cars in America. The company had been founded by Soichiro Honda. Born in 1906 in a rural area southwest of Tokyo, Honda did not see his first car, a Ford Model T, until he was 8-years old. Fascinated by auto mechanics he left school early to become a self-taught engineer. During World War Two he managed a company that made piston rings for Japanese military vehicles.

In 1948, Honda now 42-years old, drawing on the production experience he had gained during the war started his own company Honda Giken Kogyo to build motorcycles. At first the company only produced motorbikes with small motors. By the 1950s as Japan's post-war recovery expanded rapidly, Honda became the largest motorcycle manufacturer in Japan and in 1954 went public on the Tokyo stock exchange.

For a while growth seemed to affect the quality of the Honda motorcycles being produced and sales plummeted. Then in 1955 Soichiro Honda came up with an idea to showcase his motorcycles. He announced a corporate goal to win the Tourist Trophy at the races held at England's Isle of Man. It was the most prestigious motorcycle race in the world and just like Henry Ford a half-century before, Soichiro believed that showcasing your products in competitive racing was a very good way to get them noticed. In 1961 Honda accomplished his goal when he swept the top five positions in the Isle of Man races.

In 1959 Honda began selling motorcycles in the US with a small bike called the Super Club 50. It was hardly a competitor for the big bikes of the day but a clever advertising campaign followed that took aim at the sub-culture of motorcycles in America by taking care to point-out that the Honda was not a California Hell's Angels or New Jersey Amboy Dukes motorcycle gang prototype. The key advertising line that defined the Honda as mainstream was "You meet the nicest people on a Honda."[3]

Within a couple of years The Beach Boys would extoll the virtues of the Honda when they wrote the hit song "Little Honda." While the song was first recorded in 1964 by the Hondells later The Beach Boys recorded their own version in the album *All Summer Long*.

Honda was a late entry into the Japanese auto manufacturing business and didn't make its first car until 1962 the S360. The company began to consider the American market because as hard as it tried in Japan, Honda perpetually lagged in sales behind Toyota and Nissan. So, the company decided to explore building a factory in the US.

The man sent by Honda to explore the possibility of a manufacturing plant in the US was Shige Yoshida who had grown-up in Japan during World War Two, joined the company in the early 1960s and had played a key role in expanding Honda's sales operations in the US.

Finding the best place to assemble Hondas in America was a daunting task considering the vast expanse of the country and difference in state laws and local customs. Yoshida quickly ruled out such locations as California, Las Vegas, Kentucky and Tennessee as not having a potential workforce with talents suitable for accomplishing the task of building Honda's product line.

But when he came to rural central Ohio, Yoshida found an environment he believed was conducive to Honda's corporate culture and goals. In Ohio there was cheap land available; good roads and a large potential labor pool existed made-up mostly of men and women from farm families who had been raised by their parents with a strong work ethic.

Yoshida decided on Marysville, Ohio a small town about 30 miles northwest of Columbus. When he returned to Japan, out of respect he sought-out the approval of Soichiro Honda the company's founder who had retired four years earlier. When Yoshida approached Honda and asked if he approved of the site he had selected in America, the company's founder abruptly snapped at him—why was he asking him? Honda told Yoshida that he knew nothing about America, that the decision was his.

While it was a risky venture for Honda the board approved Yoshida's plan on October 1, 1977. Soon after back in Ohio Governor James A. Rhodes held a press conference and announced that Honda was coming to the state to build a motorcycle factory.

In September 1979 Honda opened its manufacturing plant in Marysville, Ohio. At first Honda only produced motorcycles at the facility.

When Honda opened its Marysville facility it had planned to hire 100 workers to build motorcycles. In fact, the first team of workers at Marysville only numbered 64. Then in 1982 the company built a new the facility right next door for cars and began producing the mid-sized Accord which became very popular. During the period of 1990 to 1993 the Honda Accord was the most popular car in the US replacing the Ford Taurus as the top selling model.

By 2002 the Marysville plant was employing 14,000 workers. That same year Honda opened a second plant near Birmingham, Alabama. At that point in time Honda had become the largest importer of cars in the US and had total earnings for 2002 larger than The Big Three (GM, Ford and Chrysler) combined.

With its success in the US at Marysville, Honda took the next step and in 1985 became the first Japanese automaker to open a manufacturing plant in Europe located outside of Swindon a town in southwest England between Bristol and Reading.

It didn't take long for other Japanese car manufactures to take notice of Honda's successful operations in Ohio. Toyota formed a joint venture with GM in Freemont California and then in 1984 began constructing a new plant in Georgetown, Kentucky.

On March 31, 1985 Nissan became the third Japanese auto manufacturer to open a plant in the US when its plant in Smyrna, Tennessee opened. A huge celebration took place in Smyrna the day the Nissan plant was dedicated with high school bands and dignitaries on hand. Although Nissan had planned to build only trucks at Smyrna soon after the plant opened, they began producing cars too.

The Big Three called foul ball! They contended that the Japanese automakers were not opening plants in cities like Detroit or Cleveland with a typical urban labor pool, but in rural areas where they hired healthy farm boys to build their cars that used very little healthcare benefits and had virtually no loyalty to organized labor thereby keeping production costs down.

In fact, the UAW had decided to launch a union representation drive at Marysville, but backed off when it became cognizant of the fact that it would be defeated. It turned-out that the Marysville Honda plant became the first US auto manufacturing plant since the early 1930s to be non-union.

The primary-market for sales of Japanese cars in the US was mainly young buyers in their twenties and thirties—baby boomers. Veterans of World War Two and those who had been of military age during the war tended to waive the bloody shirt still harboring resentment toward Japan over the attack on Pearl Harbor and the war. Also, Hollywood productions such as the Academy Award winner *The Bridge on the River Kwai* and *King Rat* that depicted harsh treatment of Allied POWs did much to reinforce the negative feelings of many. At first the World War Two generation was very slow to enter Toyota and Honda showrooms instead remaining loyal to Ford and GM.

In the 1950s and 1960s Detroit had the largest middle-class population of any city in America. But by the 1970s Detroit faced the possibility of becoming the world's largest ghost town. A lot of auto workers had lost their jobs because of the rise in popularity of Japanese cars and some were very angry. In June of 1982 a tragic and senseless incident took place in Detroit that personified the pent-up emotions growing in some of them.

June 19, 1982 was a hot early summer night in Detroit and it would be that night when a hideous case of blind street justice would occur when two bigoted white men alleging that they (Asians) all look alike, would take the life of a decent man who happened to be in the wrong place at the wrong time.

A 27-year old Chinese American by the name of Vincent Chin had gone to a strip club on Woodward Avenue in Detroit to enjoy his bachelor party with friends. Also, at the club were a group of autoworkers who after consuming a few beers began taunting Chin and his friends. It wasn't long before two white men approached the Chin party and blamed them for the success of the Japanese auto industry in America. One of the men yelled at Chin, "It's because of you (little mother fuckers) we're out of work."[4]

As the situation began to escalate Vincent Chin began to fear for his personal safety. So, Chin with his party left the club and went to a nearby fast food restaurant. However, two of the men followed them into the restaurant, Ronald Ebens, a laid-off Chrysler plant supervisor, and his stepson Michael Nitz. The two proceeded to drag Chin outside and bludgeoned him with a baseball bat until his head cracked open. Four days later on June 23, 1982, Vincent Chin died at Henry Ford Hospital.

Neither, Ebens or Nitz would ever serve jail time for the murder of Chin. While the two never denied their acts, they insisted that the incident had simply been a barroom brawl that ended badly for one of the participants. In a plea bargaining agreement with prosecutors the two pleaded guilty to manslaughter (a reduced charge from second-degree murder) and were sentenced to three years of probation and fined $3,000.

In 1983 federal prosecutors brought civil rights charges against Ebens and Nitz and once again the two dodged a legal bullet when both denied that they had used any racial epithets in the attack. Ronald Ebens was ultimately convicted of violating Vincent Chin's civil rights and sentenced to 25 years in prison, but the conviction was overturned on appeal.

Eventually a wrongful death judgment was brought against Ronald Ebens, but in late 2015 the estate of Vincent Chin was still seeking payment. By that time Ronald Ebens was 76-years old and living in Nevada and still owed the Chin estate more than $8 million.

In November 2015 an attorney for Ebens filed a motion to remove the lien the Chin family had placed on his home. According to Eben's attorney his home was protected by Nevada's Homestead Act and the lien was placed on it with malice...to annoy and harass him to the point where he is unable sell or refinance his home. The motion was even so brazen as to ask for attorney's fees.

The Chin murder had been committed in a volatile economic environment. The early 1980s were a time of high double-digit unemployment and inflation not just in Detroit but across the nation. The unemployment levels were much like those which would be seen during the Great Recession during the first few years of the Obama administration. The Japanese entry into the American auto manufacturing market had a devastating effect on the status quo and for a while imported cars became a symbol of all that was wrong with the economy. It was this environment that Honda and Toyota were building their American import empires in.

Employment was down in the auto industry from the 1970s and the UAW refused to settle for lower wages for greater job security.

In 1981 President Ronald Reagan told Japanese automakers to limit their exports to about one-fifth of the American market or face tougher restrictions imposed on them by Congress. Reagan's edict immediately drew fire from critics who believed that using restrictions to limit imports only helped to promote inefficient American auto producers and their unions to continue their lethargic practices.

It is estimated that the Reagan quotas saved 44,000 jobs, but the costs that resulted in higher auto prices soared to about $90,000 a year per job.

The Japanese Ministry of International Trades and Industry decided how to divide the Reagan quotas among the country's cartel of auto makers made up of Toyota, Honda, Nissan, Mitsubishi, Suzuki and Isuzu

The Japanese cartel complied with Reagan's request and soon they began to embrace the quotas. They were good for business. No longer did the Japanese automakers have to compete against each other for the American market. As a result, the Japanese cartel began to raise prices on their exports resulting in windfall profits of about $2 billion a year.

Also, in a larger sense the quotas had the effect of holding down the Japanese trade surplus with the US, and reduced the pressure to open Japan to more American products.

By 1984 the Reagan quotas on Japanese imports had been lifted. It was back to business as usual and economists in the US began speculating that competition from within would benefit consumers with dealing with the Japanese cartel.

It wouldn't be long before South Korea began to export cars to the US. In 1986 Hyundai arrived in America and the following year sold 264,000 cars. For several years following its peak year in 1987 sales fell off for Hyundai and in 1997 just 107,371 vehicles were sold in the US. Then Hyundai bought into its Korean competitor Kia and sales began to grow by leaps and bounds.

Kia had entered the US market in 1992 and each subsequent year its sales totals slowly increased. By 2014 Hyundai owned a 33.88 % stake in Kia and the two had formed the Hyundai-Kia Motor Group. Engines for both Hyundai and Kia are manufactured by GEMA (Global Engine Manufacturing Alliance) which also builds motors for Mitsubishi. In 2015 sales of both vehicles in the US were solid with Hyundai selling 761,710 vehicles and Kia selling 625,818 for a total of 1,287,328.

There was even a certain stupidity that started to permeate the export car market as some importers believed that anything sent to America would automatically find a market. One of the worst examples was the Eastern European attempt to export the Yugo to the US in 1985.

It has generally been accepted that during the cold war the Soviet Union and some of its satellite nations produced some very sophisticated military hardware such as tanks, machine guns, nuclear bombs and ICBMs. However, when it came to consumer products technology everything, they manufactured in the Soviet block was a piece of crap. Nothing could have personified that notion more than the Yugo.

Designed in Italy under the name Fiat 144, the Yugo was manufactured in Yugoslavia. The car was cheap in price $4,400 and cheap in design. Inside the Yugo was fitted with a dashboard and center console made from a single mold. All most everything was cheap plastic and there was an enormous bolt that held the seat belt in place. Under the hood one found that the underpowered 55 hp, 1.1liter, carbureted 4-cylinder engine shared space with the spare tire.

Although the car was a constant butt of jokes the Yugo survived on the US market until 1992. By that time people who only had $4,400 to spend on a car had come to the conclusion they could get better value with a used car than a new Yugo.

American car manufacturers had acted blindly to the rise of Japanese compact and mid-sized models, but further damage to the industry was to come in the late 1980s and early 1990s when they left the back door of the industry wide-open for the Japanese to enter the luxury car market.

In 1988 Nissan introduced the Infiniti. Initially sales were low because of a poor advertising campaign that left buyers with the impression that the Infiniti was nothing more than a spruced-up Nissan Maxima J30 full-size car.

But then Toyota introduced the Lexus and the company took great care to distinguish it from the Camry and the car found a market quickly. American car buyers liked the fact that the Lexus cost less than the German BMW and Mercedes. Ford and GM where shocked when they learned that buyers were trading-in Lincolns and Cadillacs on the Lexus.

The introduction of the Infiniti and the Lexus would cause all the talk that the Japanese cars were just utilitarian to cease—it was serious business for Detroit and Germany too.

Both the Americans and Germans began to fight back with redesigned luxury cars and by the early 1990s Ford with the second generation Lincoln Town Car had developed a substantial market share with sales exceeding 100,000 a year, but for the moment the Japanese had pulled-off another coup.

At Chrysler on November 3, 1983 two former Ford employees, Lee Iacocca and Hal Sperlich, both fired by Henry Ford II, would introduce a new era to American automobile manufacturing when their first minivan rolled off the assembly line. Over-night the vehicle would define a new generation of baby boomer American families while neither of its creators Iacocca and Sperlich even remotely had any notion of the massive cultural change the vehicle would bring about.

A minivan is a small van that drives like a car. It is typically fitted with seats in the back designed to enhance passenger safety and comfort. The minivan is designed for family use, with room for five or more passengers.

Hal Sperlich had been toying with the idea of a minivan for years going back to his days with Ford. His vision was to build a truck like vehicle on a car chassis with front wheel drive –something easy to drive with high utility. While promoting such creativity got him fired at Ford by Henry Ford II, at Chrysler he got the backing from Lee Iacocca he needed to proceed.

In 1984 Chrysler introduced the mini-van in the Dodge Caravan and Plymouth Voyager models; both would quickly replace the station wagon as a large passenger car of choice for families and set-off a new trend in automobile buying that would have lasting cultural connotations.

The four-cylinder engine Caravan and Voyager sold for between $9,000 and $14,000 and were particularly popular with families. You could easily get three or four kids in the back and the high seating provided both short people and women with a clear view of the road, something inherently lacking in sedans that gave both a sense of safety.

The Chevrolet Corvair Greenbrier manufactured from 1960 to 1965 is acknowledged to be the first minivan. Ford had attempted to get into the minivan line in the early 1970s with a cut-down version of its full-size commercial delivery van the Econoline, but the vehicle fell victim to the energy crisis and was scrapped.

As minivans increased in popularity in the 1980s a new term entered into the American lexicon, "soccer moms." However, by the 1990s the term soccer moms would be used more in a political sense than in a marketing sense. While mini-vans had been used by suburban moms across America to shuttle kids to after-school sports, weekend sports and do grocery shopping as well as for family vacations since first coming off the assembly line, the use of the term soccer moms didn't really came into popularity until the 1996 presidential race between Democrat incumbent President Bill Clinton and Republican challenger Senator Bob Dole.

Bob Dole wanted the suburban mom's votes, regardless if they were democrat leaning or republican leaning and to expedite the matter, he conveniently compressed them into a single class of voters he called soccer moms.

In reality the term soccer moms was a bit of a misnomer and perhaps the term soccer dads would have been more appropriate. At the time of the Clinton-Dole presidential campaign youth soccer was being played in Montclair, New

Jersey, a town about 15 miles west of New York City with a population of about 38,000, by about 1,800 kids. To keep the Montclair soccer program running required about 280 volunteers, but only 10% of them were women. That same ratio (10 to 1) of men to women running the program would have easily been found in other suburban youth soccer programs through-out the country at that time and probably still exists today.

Of course, it was all political nonsense, youth soccer had no more influence on the outcome of the 1996 presidential race than Little League baseball or Pop Warner football had. There were 23 candidates in the 1996 presidential race with a total of 96,277,634 votes cast and the top four finishers were in order, Bill Clinton who took most of the soccer moms votes and won the election with 49% of the total vote, followed by Bob Dole with 40%, Ross Perot 8% and Ralph Nader with 0.71%.

In 1990 Chrysler decided to take the next step and introduced a luxury mini-van the Town & Country. Suddenly, the Chrysler mini-van came in a stretched version with a powerful V-6 engine, leather seating and sliding side doors that opened by pushing a button.

The new luxury mini-van replaced the Chrysler Town & Country 4-door station wagon that had been in production since 1940 (1940-1941, 1945-1989). When the Town & Country luxury mini-van model was discontinued at the end of 2016 it had sold over 12 million.

Chrysler's minivan had caught Ford, GM and the Japanese snoozing in their design departments. Coming to grips with their lapses in foresight they all responded with one form or another of dysfunctional designed minivans.

Ford rushed the Aerostar into production and GM quickly had the Chevy Astro on the market. While the Astro outsold the Aerostar, neither was well accepted by buyers who came to see the vehicles as hastily designed downsized versions of the companies' full-sized, rear-wheel drive vans. They both drove like trucks and were often difficult to park.

Although it was designed with some luxurious amenities such as second row captain's seats and rear stereo controls with head jacks, the Ford Aerostar was hardly any automotive star. According to a report published by The Center for Automobile Safety, in 1990, 30,000 Aerostars were recalled by The Traffic Safety Administration for poor brake performance. Also, problems were reported in the 1989 to 1991 Aerostar models with the automatic transmission. But the most frequent complaint reported with the model was peeling paint in the 1985 to 1992 models.

A few years later GM would attempt to recoup its losses in the minivan market by introducing the front-wheel drive Chevy Lumina which also found a limited market.

The Japanese didn't have any better luck than their American competitors. In 1990 Toyota launched the Previa which was designed with the engine under the front seat. The design allowed for more people and cargo which was considered the most desirable feature of the minivan. But Previa's mid-engine design caused the chassis to be elevated making it difficult for short people and women to get into the vehicle. ·

The Previa also proved to be too small and too under-powered to compete with the larger and cheaper Chrysler mini-vans and was off the American market after just one year.

But Toyota would return to the minivan market in 1998 with the Sienna featuring a powerful V-6 194 hp engine with seating for seven people. The Sienna became a big seller and remains on the market in 2020 available in seven models.

The mini-van craze even created some strange bedfellows in the automotive manufacturing world. In 1992 Ford and Nissan teamed up at the Ford truck plant in Avon Lake, Ohio to manufacture the Mercury Villager and the Nissan Quest minivans.

The minivan had clearly been a corporate slam-dunk for Chrysler. Both Hal Sperlich and Lee Iacocca were amazed at how their design, engineering and marketing of the vehicles had somehow outfoxed their larger competitors. Perhaps even more amazing was the fact these two men, both raised during the depression era, had the vision to foresee a product that would have mass appeal to the baby boomers whose generation would form the largest market ever for the consumption of automobiles.

In 1988 Hal Sperlich retired from Chrysler to be followed by Lee Iacocca in 1992. Both would be inducted in the Automotive Hall of Fame (Sperlich 2009), (Iacocca 1994). Sperlich remained loyal to his creation and continued to drive a minivan well into his seventies.

The Chrysler minivan remains the company's best-selling vehicle of all-time. While all the other manufacturers attempted to duplicate it, they continually fell short. The minivan will always be synonymous with Chrysler and the minivan concept synonymous with the engineering genius of Hal Sperlich.

By the early 1990s the SUV era had descended upon the auto manufacturing industry. A SUV or 4X4 is a vehicle with similarities to a station wagon. It is equipped with four-wheel drive built on a truck chassis. The body is spacious, and it is designed for off-road travel. Since SUVs are classified as trucks, they are exempt from EPA emissions standards.

As the popularity of SUVs grew and evolved into the 1990s and beyond, manufacturers took note of the fact that very few SUVs were being used for off-road driving on mountainous paths or in deserts, and more often than not were being driven as a family vehicle to suburban schools, supermarkets and shopping malls. So, some of them were designed to look like SUVs in regard to the interior and under the hood, but were built with lower ground clearance and suspension making them generally confined to use on paved roads with limited or very little ability to go off-road.

SUVs have been around for quite a while in one form or another beginning with the Chevrolet Suburban in 1935. But all SUVs today are descendants of either the Willys-Jeep or the Land Rover. Jeep introduced the Jeepster Commando in 1948 and it remained in production until 1950 then reintroduced it on the market between 1967 and 1973.

During World War Two the Japanese Army had captured an American Jeep in the Philippines and following the war in 1951 an adaptation of the vehicle was used to produce the Toyota Land Cruiser that by 1980 would become one of the first luxury, compact, off-road vehicles produced.

While there were other early SUVs such as the 1970 Range Rover and the gas guzzling International Travelace produced between 1953 and 1975 the first modern SUV is more often than not acknowledged as the 1963 Kaiser Jeep Wagoneer.

But the SUV that brought the concept into the minds of mainstream American car buyers was the Jeep Cherokee developed by AMC and Renault and introduced in 1984. The Cherokee was helped into becoming a trend-setter by a skillful request made by AMC to the EPA for a waiver for the vehicle on the Clean Air Act which saved the company countless millions of dollars.

Following Chrysler's acquisition of AMC in 1987 the Jeep Cherokee manufactured in both Toledo, Ohio and China was heavily promoted and quickly found a lucrative market. While the Cherokee caught both Ford and GM by surprise, both who had been adapting light trucks into two-door SUVs such as the Ford Bronco and Chevrolet Blazer/Jimmy, by 1990 every major car manufacturer, foreign and domestic was producing 4-door SUVs.

The market fallout created by the SUV craze in the US with the success of Jeep and the rush by Ford and GM to catch-up may have been responsible in part for those manufacturers losing additional ground on both the luxury car and full-size car markets as Mercedes-Benz, Toyota, Nissan and Volkswagen took direct aim at the US car buyer. By 1988 the manufacturing facility that Toyota had begun constructing in Georgetown, Kentucky in 1984 was operational and that year produced 900,000 Camrys.

Jeep had always been out in front in popularity in the SUV class. In 1998 for $38 billion Daimler-Benz acquired control of Chrysler and the Jeep brand. But the Germans mismanaged Jeep and millions of dollars of losses followed.

Drivers began to notice more road noise in Jeeps built by Daimler. Daimler even cut the cost of manufacturing the interior of the Compass and Patriot models by 40% causing them to appear cheap.

For a while the production on SUVs was cut back by all automakers. But by the mid-1990s the SUV had found a new market becoming the vehicle of choice for women. Women had been growing as a consumer market and many who were tired of the stereotype "soccer mom" would now purchase hundreds of thousands of SUVs.

While women were unlikely to buy an SUV to tow a boat or camper, they liked the taller ride height. As on the minivan, they said that they felt safer. SUVs could be driven through snowbanks and in addition, women liked the space provided in SUVs and the three-row seating. Of course, there was a safety downside as all drivers of SUVs, women or men, short or tall, were less likely to see objects and distractions low on the ground.

By 1985 one-half of all college graduates in the US were women. Women were occupying more positions in the workforce. According to the US Census Bureau in 1967 14.8 million women had been in the labor force, by 1980 that number had risen to 30 million and by 2002 there were 41 million women working in full-time jobs. In just thirty years the number of women in management positons had risen from 16% in 1970 to 38% by 2000. What this meant was that purchasing power of women had risen dramatically and they were now calling the shots when they walked into a car dealership.

Gone were silly days such as in 1955 when Dodge designed the La Femme for a female market. It was a pink car that came with a matching purse, lipstick and umbrella.

By 2011 women were buying 41% of the luxury vehicles on the market, most notably luxury SUVs. Writing for bloomberg.com in May 2016, Melissa Mittleman stated, single women dominate the small SUV sales. From 2010 to

First Jeep Cherokee. (Wikimedia Commons)

2015 mainstream small SUV sales to women rose 34%, compared to 22% for men. Today an SUV could be marketed as a woman's car that men like too.

During the SUV craze a lot of models have come and gone. Between 1990 and 2017 a total of forty-three SUVs became extinct. Some of the models that had a short existence include the Accura SLX 1996-2000, Accura 2DX 2009-2012, Chrysler Aspen 2007-2009, GMC Envoy XW 2004-2005, Honda Passport 1994-2002, Isuzu Amigo 1990-1994, 1995-2000, Mazda Navajo 1991-1994, Mitsubishi Endeavor 2002-2011, Suzuki XLT 2007-2009, Pontiac Torrent 2006-2011, Lincoln Aviator 2003-2005 and Kia Borrago 2009-2010.

But other SUV models such as the Jeep Cherokee, Jeep Wrangler, Jeep Patriot, Toyota RAV4, GMC Acadia, Chevrolet Equinox, Buick Enclave and Dodge Journey continue to have strong sales and going forward the demand for these models show no signs of slowing down.

16.
Hard Times and Hope for The Big Three

When the Great Recession arrived in 2008 the automotive industry was hit hard again. General Motors and Chrysler would go through bankruptcy and stay afloat by accepting bailouts from US Government funds provided by the Obama administration.

But Detroit automakers had been in deep trouble long before the financial meltdown caused by the bottom falling out in the sub-prime mortgage market fiasco, the resurgence in oil prices and the Wall Street panic that followed.

Steve Rattner served as Lead Advisor to the Presidential Task Force on the Auto Industry in 2009; he states in his book *Overhaul—An Insider's Account Of The Obama Administration's Emergency Rescue Of The Automobile Industry*, when gas prices surged to over $2 a gallon in 2004 and suddenly it took $60 to fill the tank of an SUV, car buyers wanted to quickly return to fuel-efficient sedans but dealers had nothing to offer them. "The Big Three had never controlled expenses, especially labor costs, enough to be able to make money on such cars. In 2006 Ford lost $12.6 billion on $160 billion in sales."[1]

Hurricane Katrina didn't help matters either. The gargantuan storm that was a direct hit on New Orleans in late August 2005 caused $90 billion in damage and crippled oil production in the Gulf of Mexico sending gas prices to a national average high of $3.59 a gallon and causing gas shortages.

The devastation of Katrina also left 571,000 flooded or damaged cars in its wake—many which found their way onto the used car market and were still being sold for nearly a decade after the storm.

In September 2005 GM. reported a sales drop of 24% compared with the same month the previous year. Ford sales declined 20%. Somehow Daimler Chrysler bucked the trend with a 4% gain in sales. It was almost predictable that the major Japanese automakers would report strong U.S. sales in September 2005 with most posting increases of 10 to 12%, as car buyers began snapping up Toyota, Honda and Nissan passenger cars and smaller trucks.

Both GM and Ford seemed to be completely out of touch with reality, they attempted to reassure themselves that the downturn in sales in September was not caused by Katrina, but rather the slump was predictable following their record sales during the summer that had resulted from their marketing gimmick where they had offered cars to buyers at factory employee's discounts. But the fact was that car buyers believed that the aftermath of Katrina signaled a turning point for the long-term effects of high gas prices. Of course, that was bad news for The Big Three, market changes seemed always to leave Detroit behind because they were too blind to see it.

Then came the summer of 2008 and gas prices went through the roof topping $4 a gallon in many states. Car-dealers through-out the country suffered double-digit decreases in sales. At the same time housing prices were tanking and as the coming recession intensified credit began to dry-up. Consequently, potential car buyers could not get loans and dealers couldn't finance their inventories. It was a perfect economic storm as sales hit bottom cash was being syphoned from automakers financial accounts at a lightning speed rate.

By 2007 Daimler gave up on Chrysler and sold its 80% stake in the company to Cerberus, a private equity firm based in New York but things only got worse and billions of additional dollars where lost.

During the summer of 2008 Chrysler approached General Motors asking CEO Rick Wagoner and the board if they would consider a merger. At that time GM was attempting to work-out its own financial problems with a plan to reduce production of gas guzzlers, cuts jobs, cut orders with suppliers, while cutting inventory and working capital. GM was even working on a plan to restructure retirees' healthcare benefits into a new fund.

GM gave the matter serious consideration coming to the conclusion that by absorbing Chrysler into its company might prove to be an opportunity to attract new investment, even if demand continued to fall. But when the panic in housing market hit Wall Street in September it killed any chance of the merger happening.

Now as the recession pulled the economy in like quicksand the possibility of both GM and Chrysler filing for bankruptcy became a scary situation. Ford, GM and Chrysler employed hundreds of thousands of workers. In addition, The Big Three supported several million more workers in related industries such as auto parts manufacturing and sales. Also if either or both of the automakers filed for bankruptcy the US Government would be on the hook for picking-up some of the tab as the government pension guarantee corporation would have to pay some of the benefits for hundreds of thousands of retirees.

Recently the US Government had given the auto industry $25 billion in subsidized loans to retool their plants to build fuel-efficient cars. Now suggestions were being made by auto workers that the companies could use another $25 billion in low-cost loans to pay into the retiree health care plan.

In Washington politicians and bureaucrats alike started to worry. What would happen if the largest industry in the country went bust—would there be riots in the streets?

The U.S. Government was going to have to act and it would ultimately require a $50 billion bailout from the taxpayers to get GM back on its feet.

In the first two quarters of 2008 General Motors had lost $6.3 billion and the automaker was nearly out of cash and on the verge of collapse. Also, another huge loss was eminent for the third quarter. GM president Rick Wagoner decided to seek relief from the Bush administration. On October 12, 2008, Wagoner along with two GM board members called on Hank Paulson, Treasury Secretary in President Bush's cabinet.

On October 3, Congress at the urging of President Bush had created TARP (Troubled Asset Relief Program) which set-aside $700 billion for the Treasury Department to use in an effort to prevent a total financial and economic collapse. At the moment $350 billion of that money was at Paulson's disposal without review. Paulson was aware that GM might come calling soon and he was concerned because TARP funds were intended for use by banks not automakers. What would happen if he diverted some of the money to Detroit, would other cash strapped businesses be knocking on his door the very next day?

As the meeting began Rick Wagoner didn't pull any punches, he got right to the point and told Hank Paulson and his staff that without government assistance GM was facing bankruptcy. If that happened it would lead to the company's liquidation and a domino effect would occur when GM locked its factory gates and it would cause the collapse of suppliers and dealers all over the country and have a devastating effect on millions of lives.

Then Wagoner heightened the anxiety levels of Paulson and his staff when he announced that GM's collapse could come as early as November 3, the day before the company would announce its third quarter results, the day before a multi-billion dollar payment was due to suppliers and day before the 2008 presidential election between Senators Barrack Obama and John McCain.

To prevent the collapse of General Motors Wagoner asked Paulson for a loan of $10 billion in TARP money, to be paid back with interest and also giving the Treasury Department a 19.9% ownership in the company.

The proposal was a huge gamble for the government. When Treasury officials asked why Wagoner was so confident that $10 billion would bail out the company, he stated that they were expecting big things from the new Chevy Malibu and cited the company's recent gains in J.D. Powers quality studies.

Paulson kept the meeting short and reminded Wagoner that TARP was intended to attempt to stabilize the financial system, not bail out failing industries. Perhaps GM would have to go to Congress.

When Wagoner and his associates had departed, Hank Paulson turned to his staff and said, "This is complete Bullshit."[2]

Only weeks before Hank Paulson had let Lehman Brothers go down the tubes; then he turned around and became instrumental in approving an $85 billion TARP bailout for A.I.G. setting the government and taxpayers up to take a large risky equity stake in the company. After getting bailed out by the government A.I.G. would promptly change the name of its commercial property casualty operations to Chartis, Inc.

At that time Paulson had reasoned that A.I.G. like the banks was too big to fail. In 2007 A.I.G. had lost $10 billion and in the first six months of 2008 the company had lost $14.7 billion by selling credit default swaps. In short, the company promised to insure other's serious defaults including risky sub-prime mortgages. But Hank Paulson's reasoning was that with the company's assets topping $1 trillion, they were too global and too interconnected to fail.

Within a week of the GM meeting with Paulson, Chrysler announced that it too was facing a possible bankruptcy

Ford had avoided being caught between a rock and a hard place by borrowing money earlier in the year before the banking industry began to collapse. The only concern expressed by Ford president Alan Mulally to the government was that he wanted some sort of assurance that bailout money for General Motors and Chrysler would not put his company at a competitive disadvantage.

The New York Times offered an opinion on the automakers plight that was tantamount to setting-up a short-term industrial welfare program. In a piece published the same day that Rick Wagoner had met with Hank Paulson *The Times* advocated a bailout for The Big Three because it might benefit the economy in the short term to keep them from going bankrupt and in so prevent the recession from widening. It was stated in part in the article, "If Detroit's car companies do not manage to survive in the long term, it may still be worthwhile to keep them from going bankrupt next year. The economy and job market will have their hands full dealing with the fallout from the near collapse of the financial system. Major job losses in the auto sector would not only cause enormous economic and social distress around the country but would be extremely costly to the government."[3]

As sorry as Detroit was perceived to be, as incompetent as some of the automaker's top executives may have been and in fact, they were building cars that consumers didn't want to buy, it was not all the automakers' fault.

In large part the banks had caused the problem and some of their actions resembled fraud. In 2007 Citigroup paid out $107 billion in dividends, the third highest dividend total in America. This took place despite the fact that Citigroup had lost $9.8 billion in the fourth quarter of that year.

Looking back on those dark days Matt Tibbi writing in the *Rolling Stone* in 2013 stated that the Federal rescue of Wall Street had created a Ponzi-like confidence scheme. "The whole financial sector, in fact, had taken on Ponzi-like characteristics, as many banks were hugely dependent on a continual influx of new money from things like sales of sub-prime mortgages to cover-up massive future liabilities."[4]

Now with TARP money flowing into their vaults the banks where off the hook for their egregious behavior.

Election Day 2008 arrived amid a storm of voter outrage over the bailouts handed-to A.I.G., Bank of America, Citigroup, Goldman –Sachs, Wells Fargo and others. Unemployed workers and those that suddenly found themselves with under-water mortgages were starting to ask, "where's my bailout?"

Barrack Obama defeated John McCain for the presidency and GM continued to hang-on by a thread. The company withheld its dismal third quarter financial report until the day after the election which revealed that the company was losing approximately $3 billion a month.

Following the election Rick Wagoner went to Washington to meet with Democrat Congressional leaders and plead GM's case for government assistance.

Wagoner asked in particular that the government ease restrictions on the use of the $25 billion in loans that had been set-aside to re-tool factories for the development and production of more fuel-efficient cars.

Hank Paulson was now becoming concerned that half of the $700 billion TARP money authorized by Congress, $350 billion, was going to run out before the end of the year and there might not be any funds left for the automobile industry. In fact, a few days before Thanksgiving Citigroup which had already received $25 billion in TARP funds requested a second bailout of $20 billion. With a new administration coming into the White House the auto companies might have to wait for Barrack Obama and the new heavily Democrat Congress to release the money and that raised the question of whether or not they could hold-out.

When Congress reconvened on November 18 Senator Christopher Dodd of Connecticut and chairman of the Banking Committee held a meeting to explore the General Motors bailout request. The presidents of the Big Three were all in attendance, Rick Wagoner, GM, Alan Mulally, Ford and Robert Nardelli, Chrysler, as well as the president of the UAW Ron Gettlefinger, and they all testified.

The problems of the Big Three were no secret and Wagoner summarized them in a couple of sentences telling the committee that the dilemma the auto manufacturers were facing had been caused by the global financial crisis that made it hard to get credit and thereby reduced sales. It had nothing to do with any management competence, employee productivity issues or the cars they were producing.

Nothing really came out of the committee hearing that day, other than it laid the auto industry's troubles square on the steps of the Capitol Building. The Big Three hadn't even submitted a plan to the committee on how they would divide-up the $25 billion if it was authorized to be diverted from developing fuel-efficient cars.

The current Congressional session ended just before Thanksgiving and Senate majority leader Harry Reid and Speaker of the House Nancy Pelosi announced to The Big Three presidents that in December Congress would reconvene for a lame duck session devoted entirely to addressing the auto industry problems. However, the promised lame duck session came with a caveat—each company would be responsible for submitting a restructuring plan prior to the session.

By this time Hank Paulson had reached the conclusion that a bailout for the automakers using the second half of the TARP funds could not wait any longer. So, he advised out-going President George W. Bush of the circumstances.

The Detroit bailout was not particularly popular with Republicans and some notable members of the party openly opposed it including Newt Gingrich, Mitt Romney and Rick Santorum. It just wasn't Republicans who were opposed to rescuing the automakers. Supposedly the "liberal Brookings Institution put out a report saying they should be allowed to go bust, with their factories and machinery being sold to the highest bidder."[5]

If President Bush was going be successful in obtaining bailout money for the automakers, he was going to need support of Democrats who might be inclined to wait until the new Democrat President Barrack Obama was sworn-in on January 20, 2009.

Another danger in advocating the use of TARP funds for the rescue was that the banks had quickly adjusted to the comfort zone provided by TARP and diverting some of the funds to the automakers might cause a secondary panic in the stock market.

The House Democrats and President Bush decided to attempt a solution to the automakers dilemma outside of TARP by putting together a proposed bill that would provide $14 billion in loans to be drawn upon from the $25 billion (Advanced Technology Vehicles Manufacturing Loan Program) that had been allocated for re-tooling plants to produce more fuel-efficient cars. The program also called for a so-called car-Czar to over-see the loans and extended the deadline for the automakers to put together turn-around plans until March 31, 2009.

Speaker Pelosi was confident that she could get enough Republican support in the House to pass the measure and that happened with 32 Republicans, most from districts affected by auto manufacturing industries, joining 205 Democrats in voting yes.

The Senate was another matter, the recession had hurt the Republican Senators politically and they were in a mood to punish the automakers and the UAW.

Many Republicans felt President Bush had demanded too little from the automakers in return Many Republican Senators felt that giving money to General Motors and Chrysler without restructuring liabilities and expenses didn't make financial sense. They also felt that the proposal didn't call for large enough wage cuts on the UAW.

On December 11 when Republican Senator Bob Corker asked the UAW to accept wage cuts that would put them in-line with Japanese automakers operating in the US by the end of 2009 it killed the bill.

Chrysler was the most desperate of The Big Three. CEO Robert Nardelli called Hank Paulson and asked him to have the Treasury Department force General Motors to buy Chrysler. When that effort failed a few days later Steve Feinberg the CEO of Cerberus called the Treasury Department and offered to sell Chrysler to the US Government for $1.

The troubles of General Motors and Chrysler caused considerable confusion and disappointment among various legislators due to the fact that at the time they were attempting to find a way for the automakers to continue operations, Honda had just opened a new assembly plant in Greensburg, Indiana.

It was now up to President Bush to handle the matter. On December 19 President Bush unilaterally agreed to loan General Motors and Chrysler $17.4 billion in TARP money of which $13.4 billion was to be made available immediately.

President Bush, Hank Paulson and his staff members at the Treasury Department had to twist the law a little to make the TARP funds available, but a bridge had been built which gave the automakers and the incoming Obama administration time to come up with a more lasting solution.

Surprisingly, the Canadian government announced that it would add $2.8 billion to the US bailout total. Prime Minister Stephen Harper stated that the Canada wanted to be part of the solution and the amount they pledged was commensurate with production that took place in that country.

In February 2012 former President George W. Bush would state while addressing a meeting of the National Automobile Dealers Association in Las Vegas that he used the TARP money to help the country avoid a 21% unemployment rate. "I didn't want history to look back and say, "Bush could have done something but chose not to do it."[6]

As a candidate and as president-elect Barrack Obama had supported the widely unpopular bailout of the Wall Street banks so it was inconceivable that after taking office, he could ignore the financial troubles of the largest industry in the country. After being sworn-in as president on January 20, 2009 President Obama put together an auto task force and they began to distribute additional billions of dollars in emergency funding.

While *The New York Times* had referred to The Big Three as The Sorry Three, there remained a lot of optimism in the general public for the American automotive industry even though the Great Recession was crippling the American economy and gasoline prices were hovering just under $4.00 a gallon.

Everyone knew that Ford still built the best trucks in the world. Trucks have higher profit margins than cars and investors looking for bargains knew that Ford's stock was under-valued. Furthermore Chrysler, although in deep trouble financially, was still building the number one minivan albeit they were assembled in Windsor, Ontario, and their Dodge Ram trucks were popular too. The problem with GM was that it had become an industrial dinosaur; it was just too big, had to many unprofitable subsidiaries and needed to be downsized.

In the second quarter of 2009 Ford would suffer the worst quarterly loss in its history—$8.7 billion. General Motors had even a bigger quarterly loss of $15.5 billion. While Ford would attempt to restructure its product line, GM cut production by 300,000 vehicles.

Chrysler was forced to file for bankruptcy on March 30, 2009. The company's creditors were highly concerned. Less than two years ago JP Morgan, Citibank, Bear Stearns, Goldman Sachs, and Morgan Stanley had lent Cerebus $10 billion to assist with its purchase of Chrysler and Chrysler Financial. Now there was high anxiety on Wall Street about the automaker going belly-up.

To compound matters in March 2008 JP Morgan had acquired Bear Stearns when it collapsed thereby taking in an additional chunk of the Chrysler debt making its total exposure $2.7 billion.

President Barack Obama wanted to save Chrysler and under a deal brokered by his task force and the US Treasury Department, control of Chrysler was transferred to the Italian automaker Fiat. Both the Canadian government and the Treasury Department would have equity stakes in the deal. Initially Fiat only purchased 20% of Chrysler but following Chrysler's bankruptcy Fiat led by its dynamic CEO Sergio Marchionne took over total control of the company.

Of course to some it was absolutely ironic and absurd that Willys-Jeep, the vehicle brand which had helped to defeat both Germany and Italy in World War Two had been transferred from American ownership to two of its former enemies in an attempt to save it. Although the taxpayers would eventually lose $1.3 billion on the Chrysler bailout, under Fiat within only a few years the Jeep would once again be a very popular brand and Chrysler would start to rise from the ashes.

Now the time had come for General Motors to face its uncertain future. The plan to save GM had actually started to be formulated right before Thanksgiving. On Sunday morning, November 23, 2008 Jay Alix an expert on corporate bankruptcy called on Rick Wagoner at his home and laid out a provocative and innovative plan to the GM CEO for the company to file bankruptcy.

What Alix proposed to Wagoner that morning was that prior to filing bankruptcy GM should split into two separate companies: "NewCo," a new company with a clean balance sheet, taking on GM's best brands and operations: and "OldCo," the leftover GM with most of the liabilities."[7] All of the operational restructuring to make "NewCo" profitable would occur before the bankruptcy filing. That would permit GM to go through the bankruptcy in days rather than a protracted period of months or even years with creditors fighting over what remained in the company as the revenue line began to crash. At that time world-wide GM had 500,000 supplier contracts.

To seek funding from the government GM would use Bankruptcy Code Section 363, which permits a company to sell assets under a court-approved sale. The bankruptcy codes allowed for the company to segregate and spin out its valuable assets—with the Federal government providing operational funds. It also permitted GM to postpone filing a plan of reorganization and disclosure statement which would take months and no doubt occur during a flurry of litigation while the company's market share and enterprise value slowly withered away.

Jay Alix knew his plan was unprecedented and controversial, but nonetheless it was legal. Rick Wagoner saw the plan as a creative way for GM to restructure.

There were many critics of the Section 363 plan, primarily in respect to the asset sale which was termed as a "Sham" sale. Under a regular bankruptcy plan process, all the affected creditors of the company are given the right to vote on the proposed plan. But in a 363-asset sale there is no such requirement. Critics of GM bankruptcy plan charged that company was using it to avert paying legitimate claims to its creditors.

Rick Wagoner would never see the GM bankruptcy occur or head-up the new company. In late March 2009, President Obama at the request of his auto task force would ask Wagoner to step-down as CEO due to a failure of leadership. He would be replaced by Fritz Henderson who would take-over as acting CEO on March 20 and hold the position for 247 days. The pain inflicted on Wagoner in his forced departure by the task force would be eased when he was granted a golden parachute in $7.1 million in severance pay.

Rick Wagoner didn't really have much of a chance of surviving the bankruptcy at General Motors, the deck was stacked against him on the Obama auto task force which included a lot of arrogant Wall Street types who were smitten by the fact that he had come to Washington in his private corporate jet to testify at the Senate hearing in late 2008, then proceeded to blame everything that happened to his company on Wall Street. The auto task force members held the belief that Wagoner should have laid himself prostrate before the committee and taken personal responsibility for the company's circumstances.

It was a double standard; because the new Treasury Secretary Tim Geithner or any member of the auto task force would have never demanded the same from any of the CEOs of Bank of America, Chase, A.I.G., JP Morgan or other Wall Street banking institutions that had caused the recession.

In an attempt to demean all three of the auto company CEO's and the UAW's appearance before the Senate committee, an auto task force member later proclaimed with brash self-assurance, that they came to Capitol Hill in private jets and begged for a bailout.

The fact is that The Big Three CEO's were sensitive to the criticism of their arriving in Washington by private jets and made sure that any subsequent trips to the nation's capital were made in one of their respective company's most eco-friendly cars.

But the worst example of the auto task force's self-edification on their work was when they would attempt to historically credit themselves and Matt Feldman, the bankruptcy attorney they had hired as being the ones that had developed GM's bankruptcy plan that had in fact been suggested by Jay Alix and advanced by Rick Wagoner and the GM board of directors before President Obama pushed him out the door.

Nonetheless it should be pointed-out that a similar plan had been used in the Chrysler bankruptcy and Matt Feldman had been the auto task force lead bankruptcy attorney where a judge had approved a new company to be created and ran by Fiat. However, the GM bankruptcy had far greater global consequences than the Chrysler case.

On May 29 with its bankruptcy about to become a reality General Motors common stock fell on the New York Stock Exchange to 75 cents a share, the lowest it had been since the Great Depression.

On June 1, 2009 General Motors filed for bankruptcy in New York listing $82 billion in assets and $173 billion in liabilities. It was the largest industrial bankruptcy in history.

Furthermore, with GM joining Wall Street investment firm Lehman Brothers and savings and loan Washington Mutual it meant that three of the largest bankruptcies in history had happened within the past nine months.

At that time the government had poured $19.4 billion into GM to keep it running. Now it would add $30 billion to that total to fund operations during the company's reorganization.

Those brands designated by General Motors for the old company and to be discontinued included Pontiac, Saturn, Hummer and Saab. In addition, GM planned to cut ties with 2000 of its 6000 dealerships in the US. The unemployment fall-out was that the move had a potential to cut thousands of jobs. Also at least twelve factories would be closed possibly resulting in the loss of 20,000 jobs. Two of those assembly lines targeted for closure were located in Pontiac, Michigan which made full-size pick-up trucks and at Wilmington, Ohio where roadsters for Pontiac and Saturn were manufactured. In addition, three parts warehouses were targeted for closure.

The new General Motors would consist of four brands: Chevrolet, Cadillac, GMC and Buick, as well as several of the companies more successful overseas operations.

At the time it filed for bankruptcy GM had approximately $54 billion in debt. The new company was expected to have $17 billion in debt. However, the lower debt was due in part to the sale of shares in Ally Financial and Delphi.

It was proposed that the taxpayers have a 60% stake in the new company with the unions, creditors and federal provincial government of Canada owning the rest. So, for a time the Treasury Department would own more than 500 million shares of GM. The move prompted many people to refer to General Motors as Governmental Motors.

With the bankruptcy filed the New York Stock Exchange announced that it would no longer list General Motors shares. The company had traded publicly on the exchange since 1925.

President Obama praised the action stating, "GM and its stakeholders have produced a viable plan that will give this iconic American company a chance to rise again. But GM can't put this plan into effect on its own. Executing this plan will require a substantial amount of money that only a government can provide."[8]

It did take a lot of government money to put GM back on its feet and in the end the taxpayers lost $16.6 billion on the deal.

In 2000 General Motors had twenty-six plants in the USA, Canada and Mexico that turned-out 5,631,771 cars and trucks that year. By 2011 GM had reduced the number of it plants to seventeen and built 2,565,616 cars and trucks.

Both Ford and Chrysler also downsized. Ford cut its production from 4,669,253 vehicles in 2000 to 2,619.797 in 2011. Chrysler went form 2,972,355 cars and trucks built in 2000 to 1,993,455 in 2011.

On November 25, 2010 General Motors returned to trading on the New York Stock Exchange. The IPO for common stock was set at $33.00 a share. The stock closed that day better than expected at $34.19. While the government needed the stock to reach $50 a share to have any hopes of breaking even, 358 million shares of common stock had been traded reducing the government's ownership by 61%.

GM's recovery was slow; in 2009 the company lost $4 billion before finally showing positive earnings of $6.2 billion in 2010 and $9.2 billion in 2011. But once again by 2014 GM was sliding toward red ink again as the company's earnings had slipped to just $0.1 billion.

President Obama stated in his 2014 end of the year press conference that, "effectively today, our rescue of the auto industry is officially over. We've now repaid taxpayers every dime and more of what my administration committed."[9]

Well, it really depends on how you do the math. According to Conn Carroll writing for *townhall.com* in 2015 it's true that taxpayers did get back "every dime" of that cash if you look only at the new money the Obama administration spent bailing out General Motors, Chrysler, and Ally Financial.

"But that completely ignores the $17.4 billion President Bush promised General Motors and Chrysler in December 2008. If you take the entire Troubled Asset Relief Program (TARP) bailout into account, taxpayers spent a total of $79.7 billion on the auto bailout, received only $63.1 billion back, for a total loss of $16.6 billion."[10]

In the years immediately following GM's $50 billion bailout the company displayed a rather disingenuous attitude toward the American taxpayers that had saved it. Relying on the Federal Reserve's cheap-money policies GM began to outsource its operations. During the first four years following the bailout the new GM invested $11 billion in China to create new production facilities and 6,000 new jobs in the country. In same period GM invested only $8.5 billion in the US while cutting 76,000 jobs.

GM would rationalize the China move by stating that creating manufacturing facilities in the country would give it an alternative to developing small cars in Europe. GM would use the new China facilities to build a new low-cost vehicle lineup for Asia and Latin America with its Chinese partner Shanghai Automotive Industry Corp.

By 2014 Fiat Chrysler had risen to become the 7th largest automaker in the world behind Ford, General Motors, Toyota, Volkswagen, Renault-Nissan and Hyundai-Kia. This was hardly a small feat considering how bad things had been for the company in 2007.

On Columbus Day, October 12, 2014 shares of Fiat Chrysler began selling on the New York Stock Exchange under the symbol FACU for the first time since 2007. Chrysler opened at $9 a share that day and moved as high as $9.55 before trading closed. With lower gas prices once again at the pump Jeep sales and sales of Chrysler Ram Trucks were surging.

Ford alleged that it had avoided a government bailout, an assertion that resonated with car buyers and permitted the company to gain a significant market share position while General Motors and Chrysler were going through bankruptcy proceedings. Regardless of the fact that Ford did not accept any TARP money, both GM and Chrysler were of the opinion that Ford had gotten a free pass.

In September 2006 Alan Mulally succeeded Henry Ford's great-grandson William Clay "Bill" Ford as CEO of The Ford Motor Company. Mulally a native of Kansas was educated at the University of Kansas where he earned a BS and MS in aeronautical engineering. Later in 1982 he earned a master's in management at M.I.T. as an Alfred P. Sloan fellow. He came to Ford from the Boeing Company where he had served as executive vice president and president and CEO of Boeings commercial airplanes.

Mulally was on the job for about 90 days when he went to New York on November 29, 2006 and addressed 400 of the nation's biggest bankers at the Marriott Marques. In his address that day Mulally told the bankers he was going to take Ford in a different direction. He stated that if necessary, he would close factories, lay-off workers and cut costs in order to develop new technology to accomplish his goals. If necessary, he would mortgage the company. But to do all that he told the bankers it would require $23.6 billion in loans.

At one point in his address Mulally amused the bankers by lampooning the auto industry as he displayed a large chart that made an analogy between them and the NCAA basketball tournament. On the chart it boldly proclaimed, The Final Four—Toyota, Honda, Volkswagen and Ford. The room exploded with laughter.

The bankers liked what Mulally said and signed-on. So, with nearly $24 billion in low interest loans Ford got the money it would need to continue operations during the early months of the on-set of the Great Recession in late 2008 and early 2009.

However, it is not entirely true that Ford did not accept government money during that period. In late 2008 the Federal Reserve had created the TALF program (Term Asset-Backed Securities Loan Facility) after mortgage defaults started rising. The function of TALF was to lend money to investors so they could buy securities to fund student loans, cars and other consumer loans. Ford Credit offered new bonds backed by the company to obtain loans for car buyers and dealerships.

The leadership of Alan Mulally had resulted with Ford having moderate prosperity during the Great Recession. In June 2014 Mulally retired from Ford and was succeeded as CEO by Mark Fields.

While General Motors and Chrysler were struggling Ford had been out in front of its American competitors in developing new technology. Today there is about 400 pounds of plastic on a typical car. Since 2000 Ford had been researching the use of sustainable materials and was starting to outfit its cars with byproducts from castor oil, cellulose, coconut fiber, kenaf fiber, rice hulls, soy foam, wheat straw and wood. By 2017 Ford was even partnering with tequila distiller Jose Cuervo to use agave a byproduct in the booze to make items such as storage bins, a wiring harness or even a go cup.

Also, Ford had been granted $5.9 billion in low cost loans from the Obama Administration to assist the company in developing more fuel-efficient cars.

It was President Obama's goal to have a million electric cars on the road by 2015. The money from the administration to attempt to accomplish that goal was channeled through Ford, Nissan and Tesla.

By January 2017 there were 540,000 electric cars sold. The top five models with sales figures were the following: Tesla Model S (23,714), Chevy Volt (21,048), Ford Fusion (14,839), Tesla Model X14 (14,450), Nissan Leaf (12,107).

By 2018 world-wide there were seven auto manufacturers producing electric cars, Tesla, BMW, Nissan, Chevrolet, Ford, Volkswagen and Kia.

For some reason, Fiat-Chrysler has been reluctant to enter the electric car market. But that could change with the company's new leadership. In July 2018 CEO Sergio Marchionne died from complications following surgery in a Swiss hospital. It had been Marchionne that had led Fiat-Chrysler's remarkable comeback. In the second quarter of 2017 the company had reported net income of 1.2 billion euros on revenue of 27.9 billion euros.

Mike Manley who had been leading Fiat-Chrysler's two most popular divisions Jeep and RAM was chosen to follow Marchionne as CEO and it's possible he may take the company into the electric market.

Some automotive analysts believe that there will be 10 million electric cars on the road by 2020. For the moment and foreseeable future Tesla is the leader in developing electric cars.

Tesla began operations after it bought the defunct GM/Toyota (New United Motors Manufacturing Inc.) plant in Fremont, California. GM/Toyota had been producing cars at the plant since 1984 until the partnership ended in 2009. In 2010 Tesla remodeled the facility and the first Model S rolled off the assembly line in June 2012. Today the facility is both one of the largest in the world consisting of 5.3 million square feet and one of the most advanced in auto manufacturing technology.

In 2016 Tesla produced 84,000 electric vehicles at its non-union Fremont plant. The production goal for 2017 was to produce 500,000 cars. However serious safety concerns were raised by Tesla assembly line workers at the plant. The results of a test commissioned by Tesla workers released in late spring 2017 found "that the electric vehicle maker's factory in the last two years had about one-third more worker accidents and twice the rate of serious injuries as other auto manufacturers."[11] The study conducted by a non-profit worker advocacy group also stated that recorded safety incidents at the Freemont plant were 31% higher than the average auto assembly plant.

As Tesla began gearing up to soon begin producing the Model 3 broad sweeping changes in the long hours and demand on workers to produce cars in the plant needed to be put in place. Tesla management rationalized its poor employee safety record by asserting that they are learning how to become a car company.

The CEO of Tesla is 48-year old Elon Musk a man that would appear so foreign to Henry Ford, Walter Chrysler and Alfred P. Sloan that they would have believed he was from outer-space.

Born on June 26, 1971 in Pretoria, South Africa today Elon Musk holds tri-citizenships in South Africa, Canada and the United States. He came to the U. S. from Canada as a transfer student to the University of Pennsylvania where he graduated from the Wharton School of Business in 1997.

He made his first millions as one of the co-founders of PayPal an early entry into online banking. Today Elon Musk is not only CEO of Tesla but also CEO of SpaceX and ranked on the *Forbes* list of richest Americans at #24 being worth $19.5 billion USD.

In early 2018 as production was sagging on the Model 3 by April the Tesla stock fell significantly on NASDAQ to $244.59 a share. To shore-up the production schedule Musk came to the conclusion that he had to take matters into his own hands. So, he began working in the plant 17 hours a day, 7 days a week. At times he even slept on the factory floor. While things improved, Musk due to his exaggerated work ethic began to exhibit some goofy behavior that bothered the board.

In September Tesla was featured on the popular Joe Rogan Pod Cast taking a puff of marijuana. For a follow-up he began rambling on Twitter and was also known to be taking the sleep aid Ambien. Questions were raised if Musk had violated the Tesla substance abuse policy for its workers. Some questioned if his use of Ambien had been the cause of his rambling on Twitter.

But the biggest shock to the board and the stock market was to come when in late September Elon Musk announced that he wanted to take Tesla private. Musk was of the opinion that the company would be more effective as a privately held company, rather than private. He was also concerned about growing outside influence. Quietly Saudi Arabia had built a $2 billion stake in the company by accumulating Tesla shares on the open market.

Despite all the controversy Tesla and Elon Musk survived and by mid-October 2018 the stock had rebounded to $269.73 share.

Still a lot of skeptics on the outside looking at Tesla were convinced that the company really wasn't building cars, but rather batteries. That opinion was aided by the fact that Tesla has been very slow in producing the version of the Model 3 sedan that was supposed to sell for $35,000 that Elon Musk had promised for 2018.

Instead the company started taking orders in 2018 for the mid-range battery Model 3 that operates for 260 miles before requiring charging that sells for $45,000. In addition, Tesla was making an all-out effort to manufacturer and sell its high-performance cars with a long-range battery of 310 miles between charges that sold for $80,000.

Elon Musk advanced the production priority of the higher priced version of the Model 3 by expressing his belief that Tesla needs to reach higher levels of production and reduce its costs before selling lower end cars that could cause the company to lose money and collapse.

On December 10, 2013 Mary Barra was named CEO of General Motors succeeding Dan Akerson thereby becoming the first female CEO of a major global automaker.

Mary Barra had fallen in love with cars at a very young age, in particular with a red Chevy Camaro. A graduate of Kettering University (BA, electrical engineering), Stanford University Business School (MBA) and the GM Institute, Barra had been working at GM for 34 years when appointed CEO. Barra's father had been employed as a die maker at GM and together the two have spent nearly eight decades working at GM.

Prior to her appointment Mary Barra had been working as the company's executive vice president of Global Product Development, Purchasing & Supply Chain. She had also served as GM vice president Global Human Resources and vice president Global Manufacturing & Engineering Plant Manager at the Detroit Hamtramck assembly plant.

There was no honeymoon period for Mary Barra as she got her baptism under fire when two months after being appointed CEO on February 6, 2014 GM recalled 600,000 of its small cars due to faulty ignition switches. The switches could shut off the engine during driving that would prevent the airbags from inflating.

By early June 2015 the recall had affected 2.2 million vehicles in the US and would be blamed for 21 deaths and 500 injuries, resulting in a $400 million victim compensation fund to be distributed by the company.

General Motors had known about the problem since 2001, but due to a corporate culture of silence, buck passing and obfuscation existing in the company, no one had taken steps to correct the problem, all which was laid out in a 325 page report written by former US Attorney Anton Valukas following an internal investigation and several Congressional testimonies by Barra.

While fifteen GM employees were fired who allegedly had been involved in the switch crisis, Mary Barra and her top team were spared on the basis they had not been aware of the problem.

Mary Barra said the day she read the Valukas Report was one of the saddest days of her career. "The most frightening part to me was that (the report) said everything that everyone's criticized us about over the years. It was like a punch."[12]

While Mary Barra has had a tough road to hoe during her tenure as CEO of General Motors she has done a remarkable job of steadily moving the company further out from its near collapse and back into a strong market position.

In 2015 GM posted a record profit of $9.5 billion. To show support for Mary Barra and GM, financial tycoon Warren Buffett bought a Cadillac.

Under Mary Barra's leadership the decision to end operations in Russia was made, the company got through the ignition switch crisis and went on to introduce various new models such as the 2015 Cadillac ATS Coupe, the brand's first compact luxury model, and also improved such popular models as the Corvette Stingray featuring a 460 hp engine with a fully electric top that can be lowered remotely with the key fob. In addition, GM began selling two new midsize pickup trucks that had been approved by Barra when she was head of product development: the Chevy Colorado and the GMC Canyon both capable of getting 27.6 mpg on the highway, Both trucks have 200 hp four cylinder engines.

Going forward the company wanted a greater ability to return cash to shareholders in a continuing bid to raise its stock price. Since the bankruptcy GM had been considering selling Opel and in 2017 Mary Barra did just that. On March 6, 2017 GM sold Opel Vauxhall to the PSA Group of France for $2.3 billion. GM determined that due to Europe's changing geo-political and regulatory climate demands it would require more investment at a time when the company should be putting a greater focus on North America, China and emerging technologies such as autonomous vehicles (self-driving cars).

Mary Barra is a technological visionary who believes that the automotive industry will experience more change in the next five years that it has in the last fifty. She had hoped to put a self-driving car on the market by 2016, but at this point there is no industry timeline for such vehicles. While the technology is definitely available consumers ranging in age groups from Baby Boomers to Gen Xers are hesitant about giving up the steering wheel. Nonetheless some dream of the day when you can get in your car and take a nap, tune-out or tune-in, or shop on your laptop computer while your car whisks you to your destination.

The largest complication in getting self-driving (autonomous) cars on the road is safety. It is estimated by the Rand Corporation in Santa Monica, California that it would take 5 billion miles of testing to demonstrate that the failure rate of autonomous cars is statistically lower than those with human drivers.

Nidhi Karla and Susan M. Paddock of the Rand Corporation ran the math on this premise and the results were staggering. "With a fleet of 100 autonomous vehicles test-driven 24 hours a day, 365 days a year at an average speed of 25 miles per hour, this would take about 225 years... (which) is an impossible proposition if the aim is to demonstrate their performance prior to releasing them on the roads."[13]

The other major hurdle that must be crossed before artificial intelligence rules the road in autonomous vehicles is human nature. Gill Pratt, CEO of the Toyota Research Institute speaking at the Consumer Electronics Show at Las Vegas in early 2017 stated, "Human nature, not surprisingly, remains one of our biggest concerns. There are indications that many drivers may either under-trust or over-trust a system."[14] Self-driving cars simply raise the question of while you know who is driving the car, who is doing the thinking?

In 2016 led by high-profit trucks, crossovers and pick-up trucks General Motors achieved US vehicle sales of $12 billion. It was good news for investors as returns were $6.12 a share. For hourly workers that meant a record bonus check of $12,000. Global revenue for GM topped $166 billion in 2016 with high sales of full-size trucks and SUVs, mainly in North America.

In 2015 there were 17.5 million cars and light trucks sold in America representing $570 billion in sales. While there were still approximately fifteen Japanese automobile assembly plants in the US turning out 12 models, the most popular cars and trucks manufactured in order were by GM, Toyota and Ford.

Still as a result of auto production surging in lower wage countries such as Mexico and a strong dollar that hindered exports, in August of 2015 Japanese imports hit a new all-time high in the first half of the year. For that period the overall US trade deficit rose 7.1%—when adjusted for seasonal fluctuations—to $43.8 billion in June 2015. Autos which include not only vehicles, but parts and engines, accounted for more than one-third of the trade deficit. In the first half of 2015 auto exports were down by $3 billion to $74.8 billion as opposed to auto imports which had increased $10.8 billion to $171.5 billion.

The Japanese market is almost unattainable for US auto manufacturers. In Japan about 300,000 foreign cars are sold each year, but only about 15,000 of those are American cars. By comparison the Germans fare much better with yearly average sales figures of 46,000 BMWs, 65,000, Mercedes and 55,000 Volkswagens. Overall, there are 289 European models for sale in Japan and only 24 American models.

The American Automotive Policy Council (AAPC) a lobbying group for Ford and General Motors has urged Japanese Prime Minister Shirizo Abe to open up Japan's auto market in a meaningful way for American cars and trucks. While Japan hasn't had import tariffs on automobiles since 1978 it doesn't preclude the fact that Japanese currency manipulation with constant devaluations of the yen make sales of US cars and trucks in Japan very difficult.

Canada continues to play a significant role in automobile manufacturing as well. Plants in Ontario build 2.4 million cars annually of which 80% are exported to the US. Among the 21 models of American cars being manufactured in the Canadian province are the Chrysler 300, Cadillac XTS, Dodge Challenger, Ford Edge, Chevrolet Impala (some are built in Detroit too) and Lincoln MKT.

In September 2016 Ford CEO Mark Fields, seeking to appeal to investors, announced that over the next two to three years the company was going to shift all of its small car production to Mexico. The announcement immediately drew strong criticism from presidential candidate Donald Trump who was advancing his "America First" theme in his campaign. If elected Trump threatened to impose tariffs on cars imported from NAFTA assembly plants and of course that meant Canada as well Mexico.

After candidate Trump attacked Ford the company put its plans to build a new $1.6 billion plant in Mexico on hold. But Ford was not alone in its plans to shift manufacturing to Mexico. Earlier in the year Fiat Chrysler which was considering expanding its manufacturing facility in Mexico announced that it was planning to end production of all cars in the US by the end of 2016 as it ceased production of the Dodge Dart in Belvidere, Illinois and the Chrysler 200 in Sterling, Heights Michigan. Furthermore, General Motors had recently completed a $5 billion expansion in Mexico.

Previously foreign car manufactures Honda, Hyundai, Nissan, Toyota and Volkswagen all had announced they either had plans to expand manufacturing facilities or build new ones in Mexico.

The auto manufacturing jobs had been going south of the border rapidly since the financial meltdown of 2008. In the period between 2008 and 2016 Mexico saw a 40% increase in auto manufacturing jobs while during the same period the US saw only a 15% increase. In 2015 over 2 million vehicles had been imported into the US from Mexico.

Of course, there was unprecedented hypocrisy in Trump's criticism of Ford. Donald J. Trump the businessman had made tens of millions of dollars over the years selling shirts and ties with his name on them that had been manufactured in China. It seemed to beg the question of why Ford should be singled-out for political chastisement for wanting to build some cars in Mexico for sale in the US when Donald Trump manufactured shirts and ties in China for sale in the US.

Furthermore, Trump had never criticized the computer barons such as Bill Gates—Microsoft and the late Steve Jobs—Apple, whose companies for decades have assembled their software and computer products in China and other foreign countries.

Also, during his presidential campaign Donald Trump avoided any mention of the fact that the greedy Silicon Valley leaders of Google and Facebook invest a pittance of their company's wealth in the US. The fact is that "Google with a market capitalization five times larger than GM's employs only one-fourth as many US workers."[15]

In January 2017 the American auto industry coming off a record sales year with 17.5 million vehicles sold and record profits recorded entered the Trump era with uncertainty and caution.

In the 2016 presidential election Donald Trump ultimately won 12 of the 14 states where car manufacturing plants are located. He won a lot of union votes with his campaign promise to bring manufacturing jobs back to the US.

Four days after taking office on January 23, 2017, President Trump by executive order cancelled the US participation in the Trans-Pacific Partnership.

Critics of the Trans-Pacific Partnership stated that it would allow Japan unrestricted movement in the Asian market in Malaysia, Viet Nam, Singapore and Brunei as well as Central and South American countries such as Mexico, Chile and Peru. Proponents of the treaty advanced the belief that it would bolster America's influence in the Asian Pacific region where China's influence continues to grow.

The next day, President Donald Trump met in Washington with the CEOs of the Big Three; Mary Barra—General Motors, Mark Fields—Ford and Sergio Marchionne—Fiat Chrysler, and sticking to his America First pledge, urged them to build new plants in the US and promised to change environmental regulations to encourage the creation of jobs.

Following the meeting the CEOs were congenial in their remarks as all three expressed what seemed like an artificial excitement about creating a renaissance in American car manufacturing by participating with the government. But it was clear to all observers that in reality what all three of the CEOs wanted more than anything else was to get out of the White House and leave town as quickly as possible.

The Big Three only account for 60% of the automobile manufacturing in the US. Foreign automakers such as Toyota and Honda who account for the other 40% were not invited by President Trump to participate in the meeting. So it is pure speculation as to how much more production capacity The Big Three could effectively add at this time in the US with no real data concerning consumer demand for the near future. As 2017 began to unfold with low gas prices at the pump, all the automakers really knew was that right now consumers seemed to prefer pick-ups, higher-riding SUVs and cross-over vehicles for their personal use.

The Trump agenda for The Big Three meeting left a lot of important questions still open for discussion and gave the meeting an appearance of being more ceremonial than substantive.

No one can really predict what impact the future policies of the Trump administration will have on fuel economy issues. Currently the US automakers continue to lobby the EPA to ease their 54.5 mpg CAFÉ (Corporate Average Fuel Economy) standard by 2025.

Then there are finance issues existing from the previous century that still in effect in the early twenty-first century that seem a bit shady and discriminatory in auto lending practices; inflated interest rates, questionable debt collection practices and high subprime loans, all will need to be addressed. The subprime loan practice is particularly troubling to auto industry analysts who pointed-out that in 2017 there were about the same number of subprime loans being issued to buy cars as before the financial meltdown in 2008.

Also the time table for further development of electric cars and self-driving (autonomous) cars is still sketchy at most.

Where President Trump is heading with the import-export deficit issue is very vague. Speaking at the European Union meeting in Brussels in late May 2017 Trump advanced his America First agenda telling EU leaders, "The Germans are bad, very bad. Look at the millions of cars they're selling in the US. Terrible. We will stop this."[16]

Previously Trump had told a German newspaper he wanted a 35% import tax on BMWs assembled in Mexico as an incentive to move manufacturing to the US. What Trump failed to acknowledge or possibly not know was that in 2017 and 2018 more BMWs were manufactured in South Carolina than any other factory in the world.

Trump seems to have a habit of not doing his homework or repeating what the last person told him. As German Chancellor Angela Merkle pointed out to Trump during a meeting in March 2017, trade agreements with Germany can't be done alone, since Germany is a member of EU.

By mid-2018 the entire auto industry was filled with uncertainty as it sought-out strategies to deal with what seemed like an impending trade war being forced on the industry by President Trump who was advocating tariffs on imported cars and car parts. While Trump is an expert in estimating pricing for building materials he seems to be naïve on the complexities of the supply chain inherent in manufacturing automobiles. No longer is building autos about V8 engines and chrome, today it is an extremely complex process that requires advanced research into computers and sophisticated electric systems. Costs of auto parts can run into the billions.

Everyone in Detroit was in agreement that if the American auto industry is to continue its economic recovery, what the industry needs least is global hyperbole from the nation's president, but rather one who is knowledgeable and capable of negotiating a competent long-term plan of action void of apathy.

But massive change has already begun in the American auto industry. Industry analysts predict that by 2022 nearly 75% of consumer sales in the United States will be SUVs, trucks and cross-overs. So manufactures are developing long-term plans to build and sell high-margin vehicles as a means of survival.

Ford has conceded that Americans now prefer SUVs, trucks and crossovers. In early 2018 Ford decided to forget about seeking-out new customers and began to direct its advertising to retaining those customers that already buy their brand. Going forward Ford has decided to reduce its passenger car line it manufacturers to two models in North America, the Mustang and Focus Active crossover.

It appears that GM is headed in the same direction. While the iconic Corvette will remain in production, the fact that GM has introduced the Cadillac XT4 is proof that the company is attempting to catch-up in the luxury cross-over market.

Today as the auto industry continues to recover remnants of the old industry take on new forms. While the ruins of the massive former Packard plant have become a tourist attraction, in Pontiac, Michigan on the site of the former GM Pontiac Division's 87 acre factory a facility called M1 is rising out of the ashes that includes a mixed-use road course with private garages for classic auto collectors and events. The facility includes a 1.5-mile racetrack and skidpad. Further development plans include shops and restaurants.

Also high nostalgia for the golden days of the Motor City takes center stage one time each summer on the third Saturday of August when approximately 40,000 hot rods, custom cars and classic muscle cars descend upon the city for Detroit's Woodward Dream Cruise. The event which is billed as the world's largest classic car show draws about 1.5 million visitors who come to celebrate and watch for 12 hours every move of the mass of American automotive ingenuity and motor muscle cruise the 16-mile stretch of Woodward Avenue

2018 Ford Escape 4-Door SUV. (Author's private collection)

that runs from Ferndale to Pontiac. The family-friendly event has become a must for car enthusiasts of all generations. From 9 AM to 9 PM chopped tops and lowriders with wild paint jobs along every conceivable classic car; a 1932 Ford Roadster Street Rod, 1969 Shelby Mustang GT-500-KR, 1968 Chevrolet Camaro 228, 1970 Plymouth Road Runner or a 1964 Pontiac GTO Tri-Power will cruise down Woodward Avenue to the delight of the spectators. The saying at the event is; wait long enough and you'll see one of everything,

Regardless of the uncertainty that exists there is one rising hot spot on the map for automobile manufacturing in America—the southeast. Between 2000 and 2015 the percentage of autoworkers located in the southeast rose from 20.8% to 29%. There is currently a total of 70,000 auto related jobs through-out Georgia alone; suppliers make-up the bulk of the operations. Atlanta is fast becoming the hub of southeast auto industry activity.

In 2013 GM opened a new technology center in Atlanta that brought a 1000 white collar jobs to the area. This was followed in 2015 by Mercedes-Benz making Atlanta the company's North American Headquarters, thanks in part to tax incentives of $40 to $50 million a year to move the operation from

Montvale, New Jersey to a new facility in Georgia. Also in 2016 Porsche moved its headquarters to Atlanta creating an additional 1000 jobs and building a 27 acre state of the art facility complete with a 1.6 mile driver performance track.

There are four auto assembly plants within a short distance of Atlanta; VW has a plant in Chattanooga, Tennessee, Kia Motors has a plant in West Point, Georgia, BMW builds cars in Spartanburg, South Carolina and Mercedes-Benz has an assembly plant in Vance, Alabama.

Meanwhile the old guard is still very much in evidence in the manufacturing process. The UAW still has a strong presence in the industry with 148,200 members in 2019 (Ford 55,000, GM 46,000, Fiat-Chrysler 47,200).

The UAW workers had made significant economic concessions to GM during the recession by taking cuts in hourly pay and healthcare benefits. By late 2019 with the stock market up 25% and GM again making huge profits the workers believed that it was time for them to share in the prosperity that they helped attain for the company. They were quick to point-out that in 2018 GM CEO Mary Barra's total compensation package was valued at $21.87 million a year. Barra's pay was 281 times that of the median company employee.

Labor negotiations broke-down and a 40-day strike against GM began on September 16, 2019. It was the longest walkout against an automaker since the 67-day strike in 1970. The work stoppage also caused production to come to a halt in GM's assembly plants in Mexico and Canada due to the lack of parts. When it was all over the UAW agreed to a 4-year deal for workers and GM had lost over $2 billion in lost vehicle production.

While the automobile in America has had both a complex and interesting history how the next chapter in this saga will read is anyone's guess. At this point in time it's all a waiting game and the future of Detroit and whether or not it will remain the capital of automotive culture hangs in the balance.

Source Notes

ONE—BEGINNINGS
1. Drive Electric For Ten Years, *The Indianapolis Sunday Star,* July 27, 1913.

TWO—HENRY FORD AND THE MODEL T
1. Associated Press Sports Staff, Supervising Editor: Will Grimsley, Photo Editor: Thomas V. diLustro, (Auto Racing by Bloys Britt), *A Century of Sports,* (The Plimpton Press, 1971, P212).
2. Watts, Steven, *The People's Tycoon—Henry Ford and the American Century,* (Alfred A. Knopf, New York, 2005, P179).
3. *Ibid,* P242.
4. A Longworth-Ford Story—Congressman Tells Why He Declined to Do a Political Errand, *The New York Times* November 27, 1922, P13.
5. Ford to operate the Ford Motor Company…, http://en.wikipedea.org./wki /dodge_v._ford_motor_co.

THREE—"CRAZY CARL" FISHER AND THE INDIANAPOLIS 500
1. Judy Keene, The "500"s Four Members, *Indianapolis Magazine, May 1978.*
2. Jane Watts, *Fabulous Hoosier,* http://www.firstsuperspeedway.com/books/fabulous-hossier, P1.
3. The Fabulous Hoosier and Friends, *500 Souvenir Book*, Carl Hungness Publishing, Speedway, Indiana, 1983 P4.
4. Drivers Will Get Final Instructions, *The Indianapolis Star,* May 27, 1911.
5. Dick Farrington, Auto Racing At Night Tried At The Fairgrounds, *The Indianapolis Star,* April 20, 1915. P8.
6. Jeff Gluck, Would Brickyard be better under the lights?, *USA Today,* July 26, 2013, www.usatoday.com/
7. Associated Press Sports Staff, Supervising Editor: Will Grimsley, Photo Editor: Thomas V. diLustro, (Auto Racing by Bloys Britt), *A Century of Sports,* (The Plimpton Press, 1971, P219).
8. The Fabulous Hoosier and Friends, P5.
9. *Fabulous Hoosier,* P228.

FOUR—WALTER P. CHRYSLER'S RISE TO POWER
1. S. J. Woolf, A Motor Car Magnates's Rise To Power, *The New York Times,* August 19, 1928, P69.
2. Ibid.

3. Curcio, Vincent, *Chrysler, The Life and Times of an Automotive Genius*, (Oxford Press, New York, New York, 2000, P419).

4. 1934 Chrysler/DeSoto Airflow—The 50 Worst Cars of All Time—*Time*, http://content .time.com/time/specials/2007/article/0.28804.1658545_1657686_1657675,00...

5. Dammann, George H., 70 years of Chrysler, (Crestline Publishing, Glen Ellyn, Illinois, 1974, P192)

FIVE—ALFRED P. SLOAN AND GENERAL MOTORS

1. Taken for a Ride—How General Motors (GM) Conspired to Destroy Rail Trolley Systems, http://culturechange.org/issue10/taken-for-a-ride.htm

SIX—HENRY FORD PRESIDENTIAL AMBITIONS AND BIGOTRY

1. Collier, Peter and Horowitz, David, *The Fords—An American Epic*, (Summit Books, New York, London, Toronto, Sydney, Tokyo P105).

2. Jewish Degradation of American Baseball, http:///www.jrooksonline.com/Intl _Jew_version/ij46.htm

3. Ibid.

4. Ford Denying Hate, Lays War To Jews, *The New York Times*, October 29, 1922, P5.

5. Ibid.

6. Reply To Henry Ford, letter to the editor, F.P. Merritt, *The New York Times*, November 17, 1920, P12.

7. "Ford Five-Day Week Approved By Labor," *The New York Times*, March 26, 1922, P17.

8. New Era Here, Henry Ford Says, *The New York Times*, August 21, 1922, P26.

9. Ford Expects Auto To End War Forever, *The New York Times*, January 18, 1923, P8.

10. Politicians Cool To The Ford Boom, *The New York Times*, May 29, 1923, P2.

11. Ford Is Charged With Backing Klan, *The New York Times*, May 29, 1923, P2.

12. Ford Leads Harding In Collier's Poll, *The New York Times*, June 6, 1923, P24.

13. Ford Might Run If a Crisis Came, *The New York Times*, August 1, 1923, P3.

14. Ford Urges Army Keep Country Dry, *The New York Times*, June 10, 1923, P1.

15. Couzens Ridicules Ford's Candidacy, *The New York Times*, October 31, 1923, P2

16. Ford For Coolidge; President Sends Him Thanks For Support, *The New York Times*, December 20, 1923, P1.

17. "Statement By Henry Ford," June 30, 1927, www.bjpa.org/publications/ downloadPublications.cfm?PublicationID=17906

18. Black, Edwin, The Transfer Agreement, Chapter 3, The Nizer Project, www.feature group.com

SEVEN—THE 1930S AND THE RISE OF ORGANIZED LABOR

1. Letter from Clyde Barrow to henry ford Praising the Ford V-8 Car, https://.thehenry ford.org.collections-and-research/digital-collections/artifact/281082/

2. Ford Might Run If A Crisis Came, *The New York Times*, August 1, 1923, P3.

3. Distributors of Cards Routed, *Cincinnati Enquirer,* May 27, 1937, P1.
4. *Cincinnati Enquirer,* May 26, 1937, P2
5. Farber, David, *Sloan Rules—Alfred P. Sloan and the Triumph of General Motors,* (The University of Chicago Press, Chicago—London, 2002, P209).
6. Alfred P. Sloan Jr. Dead at 90; G.M. Leader and Philanthropist, By *The New York Times,* http://www.nytimes.com/learning/general/onthisday/bday/0523.html
7. Ibid
8. Anti-Trust Enforcement Through Consent Decrees, A Document from the CQ Researcher archives, http://library.cqpress.com/cqresearcher/document.php?id =cqresrre1938121900.
9. Marvin Miller, *A Whole Different Ball Game—The Inside Story of Baseball's New Deal,* (Fireside—Simon & Shuster, New York, 1992, P32.)

EIGHT—WORLD WAR TWO AND THE AUTO INDUSTRY

1. General Motors & the Third Reich/Jewish Virtual Library, http://www.jewish virtuallibrary.org/jsource/Holocaust/gm.html
2. Ford Werke, A.G., Financial Compensation for Nazi slave laborers, http://www. religioustolerance.org/fin_nazi.htm
3. Iwanowa v Ford Co., 67supp2d424,
4. www.legal.com/decision/199949167FSupp2d424_1453
5. National Affairs, *Time,* December 3, 1945, Vol. XLVI No. 23, P19.
6. Ibid, P20.

NINE—THE VOLKSWAGEN BEETLE COMES TO AMERICA

1. Torchinsky, Jason, The Real Story Behind The Nazis and Volkswagen, http://jalop-ink.com//the-real-story-behind-the-nazis-and-volkswagen-1733943186
2. Melvin Lasky, The Volkswagen: A Success Story, *The New York Times,* October 2, 1955, pg. SM15.
3. Lesser Known Facts of WWII 1944, 1945, http://members.iinet.net. au/~gduncan/1944.html
4. Patton, Phil, *Bug—The Strange Mutations of the World's Most Famous Automobile,* (Simon & Schuster, New York, 2002, P74.)
5. The Volkswagen: A Success Story, *The New York Times,* October 2, 1955, pg. SM15.
6. Parissien, Steven, *The Life Of The Automobile,* (Thomas Dunne Books, New York, 2013, P179)
7. Volkswagen Gives Up Plans to Produce Here for the American Market, *The New York Times,* January 25, 1956, P41.
8. Iacocca, Lee with William Novak, *Iacocca—An Autobiography,* (Bantam Books, New York, New York, 1984, P62)
9. Edward Hudson, Nader Scoredon Volkswagen, *The New York Times,* March 12, 1972, http://www.nytimes.com/1972/03/12/archive/nader-scored-on-volkswagen.html ?_r+0

10. Boston, William, Class-Action Suit Filed Against Volkswagen in U.S. Court—WSF, February 24, 2016, http://www.wsj.com/articles/class-action-suit-filed-against-volkswage-in-u-s-court-14563...

11. Mark Rechtin, What the Trump presidency may mean for the future of the auto industry, *Motortrend.com*, February 2017, P20

TEN—THE 1950S, FINS, ROCK N' ROLL, SUBURBS & INTERSTATES

1. Halberstam, David, *The Fifties*, (Fawcett Columbine, New York, 1993, P126)

2. Marti Benedetti, Hard-charging Charles Wilson ran GM—and then the Pentagon, *Automotive News*, September 14, 2008, http://www.autonews.com/article/20080914/OEM02/309149916/hard-charging-charles-wi...

3. *The Fifties*, (P135)

4. Ibid, P141

5. Crystal Gayean, U.S. History Scene, Levittown, The Imperfect Rise of American Suburbs, www.ushistoryscene.com/article/levittown

6. Text of President's Message Outlining His Roads Program, *The New York Times*, February 23, 1955, P17.

7. Cincinnati Museum Center, Kenyon-Barr: Lost City: Queensgate, West End, from an article by Alyssa Konnermann published in the University of Cincinnati, School of Planning Newsletter, November 1, 2017.

8. Mark Armour, Jim Brosnan/Society for American Baseball Research, http://sabr.org/bioproj/person.bl5e9d74

ELEVEN—RALPH NADER'S CRUSADE—UNSAFE AT ANY SPEED

1. Nader, Ralph, *Unsafe at Any Speed—The designed-in dangers of the American automobile*, (Grossman Publishers, New York, 1972, P223).

2. Car Safety Crusader—Ralph Nader, *The New York Times*, March 23, 1966, P32.

3. *Unsafe at Any Speed—The designed-in dangers of the American automobile*, (1xii).

4. Walter Rugaber, Critc of Auto Industry's Safety Standards Says He Was Trailed and Harassed; Charges Called Absurd, *The New York Times*, March 6, 1966, P94.

5. Ibid.

6. Ibid.

7. Walter Rugaber, G.M. Acknowledges Investigating Critic, *The New York Times*, March 10, 1966, P66.

8. Ribicoff Summons G.M. on Its Inquiry of Critic, *The New York Times*, March 11, 1966, P18.

9. Walter Rugaber, G.M. Apologizes for Harassment of Critic, *The New York Times*, March 23, 1966, P1.

10. Ibid.

11. Iacocca, Lee with William Novak, *Iacocca—An Autobiography*, (Bantam Books, New York, New York, 1984, P161)

12. Walter Rugaber, Henry Ford Sees Economic Hazard In Curb On Autos, *The New York Times,* April 16, 1966, P1.
13. Congress Acts on Traffic and Auto Safety, an article from CQ Almanac 1966, CQ Almanac Online Edition, https://library.congress.com/cqalmanac/document. php?id=cqal66-1301349

TWELVE—AMC ATTEMPTS TO RUN WITH THE BIG DOGS
1. Chapin's gusto kept AMC going, http://www.autonews.com/article/20010813 /SEO/108130760/chapins-gusto-kept-amc-going
2. AMC V8 engine—Wikipedia, https://en.wikipedia.org/wiki/AMC_V8_engine

THIRTEEN—JOHN Z. DELOREAN, A MAVERICK ENTRAPPED
1. Joseph B. Treaster, Superstar and Maverick, DeLorean Never Fit Mold, *The New York Times,* October 20, 1982, PD26.
2. DeLorean, John Z. with Ted Schwarz, *DeLorean,* (Zondervan Publishing House, Grand Rapids, Michigan, 1985, P126.)
3. *DeLorean* (P199).
4. Joseph Volz, John DeLorean, automobile engineer and executive, is arrested for drug dealing in 1982, *New York Daily News,* October 21, 1982, http://www.nydailynews .com/news/crime/john-delorean-arrested-drug-dealing-1982-article...

FOURTEEN—LEE IACOCCA, VISIONARY ENGINEER OR OPPORTUNIST
1. Lee Iacocca looks back at the 1964 sensation that was Ford Mustang, *Automotive News,* April 12, 2014, http://www.autonews.com/article/20140412/OEM02/304149996/ lee-iococca-looks-back-att...
2. Ibid.
3. Nader, Ralph, *Unsafe at Any Speed—The designed-in dangers of the American automobile,* (Grossman Publishers, New York, 1972, 217).
4. Case: The Ford Pinto / Business Ethics, https://philosophia.uncg.edu/phi361-metivier /module-2-why-does-business-need-ethics/cas...
5. The Ford Pinto Case, https://users.wfu.edu/palmitor/law&valuation/papers/1999 /leggett-pinto-html
6. Ford Pinto https://en.wikipedia.org/wiki/ford_pinto#state_of_indiana_vs._ford _motor_company
7. Iacocca, Lee with William Novak, *Iacocca—An Autobiography,* (Bantam Books, New York, New York, 1984, P162)
8. Ibid, (P118)
9. Henry Ford 2nd Is Dead at 79; Led Auto Maker's Recovery, September 30, 1987, http://www.nytimes.com/1987/09/30obituaries/henry-ford-2d-is-dead-at-70-led -auto-mak...
10. Goldwater, Barry M., with Jack Casserly, *Goldwater,* (Doubleday, New York, 1988, P18).

11. Iacocca—An Autobiography, (P170)

FIFTEEN—JAPANESE IMPORTS, MINI-VANS AND SUVS

1. Parissien, Steven, *The Life of The Automobile,* (Thomas Dunne Books, New York, 2013, P319).
2. Henry Ford 2nd Is Dead at 79; Led Auto Maker's Recovery, September 30, 1987, http://www.nytimes.com/1987/09/30obituaries/henry-ford-2d-is-dead-at-70-led -auto-mak
3. Ingrassia, Paul, *Engines of Change—A History Of The American Dream In Fifteen Cars,* (Simon & Schuster, New York, P196)
4. Frank H. Wu, Why Vincent Chin Matters, *The New York Times,* June 22, 2012, http://www.nytimes.com/2012/06/23/opinion/why-vincent-chin-matters.html

SIXTEEN —HARD TIMES AND HOPE FOR THE BIG THREE

1. Rattner, Steve, *Overhaul—An Insider's Account Of The Obama Administration's Emergency Rescue Of The Automobile Industry,* (Houghton Mifflin Harcourt, Boston, New York, 2010, P17)
2. Ibid, (P24)
3. More Money for Detroit, *The New York Times,* October 31, 2008, PA30
4. Matt Taibbi, Secrets and Lies of the Bailout, *The Rolling Stone,* January 4, 2013, www.rollingstone.com/politics/news/secrets-and-lies-of-the-bailout-20130104
5. John Cassidy, An Inconvenient Truth: It Was George W. Bush Who Bailed out the Automakers, *The New Yorker,* March 16, 2012, http://www.newyorker.com/news /john-cassidy/an-inconvenient-truth-it-was-george-w-bus...
6. Ibid.
7. Dan Bigman, How General Motors Was Really Saved: The Untold True Story Of The Most Important Bankruptcy in U.S. History, *Forbes,* November 13, 2013, www .forbes.com/.../how-general-motors-was-reallu-saved-the-untold-true-story-of-th...
8. Chris Isidore, General Motors Bankruptcy: End of an era—Jun. 2, 2009, http:// money.cnn.com/2009/06/01mews/companies/gm_bankruptcy/
9. Conn Carroll, It's Official: Tax Payers Lost $16.6 Billion On The Auto Bailout, townhall.com, February 4, 2015, http://townhall.com/...its-official-the-auto-bailout -cost-taxpayers-1666-billion-n-195...
10. Ibid.
11. Louis Hansen, Tesla workers: Factory less safe than other automakers, The Mercury News, May 24, 2017, http://www.mercurynews.com/2017/05/24/tesla-worker -report-factory-less-safe-than-other...
12. Rana Foroohar, Mary Barra's Bumpy Ride, *Time,* October 6, 2014, P34.
13. Jim Gorzelany, Detours on the road to self-driving cars, *The News Transcript,* August 3, 2016, P54.
14. Mike Floyd, Editor's Letter, The Future Is Now-ish, *Automobilemag.com,* Volume 32, No. 1, April 2017, P10.

15. Robert W. Patterson, "What's Good for America…," National Review, July 1, 2013, http://www.nationalreview.com/node/352429/print
16. Peter Mueller, President Trump calls Germans 'very bad' and promises to stop care imports' report, *USA Today*, May 25, 2017, http://www.usatoday.com/story/news/politics/onpolitics/2017/05/25/president-trump-calls-germans-very...

Bibliography

BOOKS

Ambrose, Stephen E., *Eisenhower—Soldier and President—The Renowned One-Volume Life*, New York: Touchstone, 1990.

Angelo, Frank, *Yesterday's Detroit*, Seemann's Historic Cities Series No. 9, Miami, FL: E. A. Seemann Publishing, Inc., 1974.

Associated Press Sports Staff, Supervising Editor: Will Grimsley, Photo Editor: Thomas V. diLustro, (Auto Racing by Bloys Britt, *A Century of Sports*, The Plimpton Press, 1971.

Carter, Jimmy, *A Full Life—Reflections at Ninety*, New York: Simon & Schuster, New York, 2015.

Collier, Peter and Horowitz, David, *The Fords—An American Epic*, New York: Summit Books, New York, London, Toronto, Sydney, Tokyo, 1987.

Cook, William A., *August "Garry" Herrmann—A Baseball Bibliography*, Jefferson, NC: McFarland & Co. Inc., Publishers, 2008.

Cook, William A., *Bibb Falk—The Man Who Replaced Shoeless Joe*, Jefferson, NC: McFarland & Co., Inc., Publishers, 2015.

Cook, William A., *Diamond Madness—Classic Episodes of Rowdyism, Racism and Violence in Major League Baseball*, Mechanicsburg, PA: Sunbury Press, 2013.

Curcio, Vincent, *Chrysler—The Life and Times of an Automotive Genius*, New York, New York: Oxford University Press, 2000.

Dammann, George H., 70 years of Chrysler, Glen Ellyn, Illinois: Crestline Publishing, 1974.

DeLorean, John Z. with Ted Schwarz, *DeLorean*, Grand Rapids, Michigan: Zondervan Publishing House, 1985.

Edited by Philip L. Cottrell, *Events—A Chronicle of The Twentieth Century*, New York, New York: Oxford University Press, 1992.

Editors: Carl Hungness, Jack Fox, Justyn Blackwell, *500 Souvenir Book*, Carl Hungness Publishing, 1983.

Farber, David, *Sloan Rules—Alfred P. Sloan and the Triumph of General Motors*, Chicago—London: The University of Chicago Press, 2002.

Ford, Henry in collaboration with Crowther, Samuel, *My Life and Work*, (Garden City Publishing Co. Inc., New York 1922)

Halberstam, David, *The Fifties*, New York: Fawcett Columbine, 1993.

Hayes, Walter, *Henry—A Life of Henry Ford II*, New York: Grove Weidenfeld, 1990.

Iacocca, Lee with William Novak, *Iacocca—An Autobiography*, New York, New York: Bantam Books, New York, New York, 1984.

Ingrassia, Paul, *Engines of Change—A History of The American Dream in Fifteen Cars*, New York: Simon & Schuster, 2012.

Katz, Daniel, Kahn, Robert L., *The Social Psychology of Organizations 2ed*, New York: John Wiley & Sons, 1978.

Nader, Ralph, *Unsafe at Any Speed—The designed-in dangers of the American automobile*, New York: Grossman Publishers, 1972.

Patton, Phil, *bug—The Strange Mutations of the World's Most Famous Automobile*, New York: Simon & Schuster, 2002.

Parissien, Steven, *The Life of The Automobile*, New York: Thomas Dunne Books, 2013.

Rattner, Steven, *Overhaul—An Insider's Account of The Obama Administration's Emergency Rescue of The Auto Industry*, Boston-New York: Houghton-Mifflin-Harcourt, 2010.

Ritchie, Barbara, *The Riot Report—A shortened version of the Report of the National Advisory Commission Civil Disorders*, New York: The Viking Press, 1969.

Russell, Francis, *The Shadow of Blooming Grove—Warren G. Harding in His Times*, (McGraw-Hill Book Company, New York—Toronto, 1968)

The Stars and Superstars of Rock, London: Octopus Books Limited, 1974.

Ward, Geoffery C., with Burns, Ric and Burns, Ken, *The Civil War—An Illustrated History*, Alfred A. Knopp, Inc., 1990.

Watts, Steven, *The People's Tycoon—Henry Ford and the American Century*, New York: Alfred A. Knopf, New York, 2005.

LIBRARIES

The Indiana State Library
Monmouth County Library (NJ)
The Cincinnati and Hamilton County Public Library
The New Brunswick Public Library (NJ)
The New York Public Library

MAGAZINES, PAMPHLETS, PROGRAMS, ETC.

Editor & Publisher, William R. Donaldson, Indianapolis Motor Speedway, Associate Editor Kurt Hunt, *Official Program, Seventy Fourth Indianapolis 500, May 27, 1990*

Editor & Publisher, William R. Donaldson, Indianapolis Motor Speedway, Associate Editor Kurt Hunt, *Official Program, Seventy Fifth Indianapolis 500, May 26, 1991* Published by Indy 500 Publications—IMS Corporation

500 Souvenir Book, Carl Hungness Publishing, Speedway, Indiana, 1983.

Indianapolis Magazine, (May 1978)

McCuen, General Manager, General Motors Research Laboratories Division, *1900 To 19XX—A Report On Automobile Engine Progress*, General Motors, Detroit, Michigan

Rechtin, Mark, We Say…What the Trump presidency may mean for the future of the auto industry, *Motortrend*, (February 2017)

Riser, Lee, Travel Tour Director, Mount Rushmore National Memorial, *Trailways Magazine, Victory*, Volume VIII, No. 4 (*July- August 1942*)

Sciolla, Angelina, All Roads Lead Through America—Celebrating 50 Years of the Interstate Highway System, *AAA World*, Vol. 7, No.6 (July/August 2006)

Slater, Cliff, General Motors and the Demise of Streetcars, *Transportation Quarterly*, Vol. 51, No 3 Summer 1997 (45-66), 1997 Eno Transportation Foundation, Inc., Lansdowne, Virginia

Snelt, Bradfod, *The Streetcar Conspiracy—How General Motors Deliberately Destroyed Public Transit*, http://www.lovearth/net/gmdeliberatelydestroyed.htm

Time, Vol. XLVI No. 23, December 3, 1945

Time, Vol. 184, No. 13, October 6, 2014

NEWSPAPERS

The Cincinnati Enquirer
The Cincinnati Post
The Daily Home News (New Brunswick, NJ)
The Indianapolis Star
New Brunswick Times (New Brunswick, NJ)
The New York Times

WEBSITES

http://en.wikipedia.org/wiki/rocket_88
http://www.allpar.com/history/military/red-ball-express.html
http://www.automotivehalloffame.org/inductee/hal-sperlich/789/
http://www.automotivenews.com/article/20030616/SUB/306160748/ford-motor -battles-befreinds
http://www.automotivenews.com/article/20030616/SUB/306160758/iacocca-shot -ddown-the-cardi...
http://ww.autonews.com/article/20030616/SUB/306160708/landmark-patent-case -broke-seldens-lock-on-auto-industry
http://culturechange.org/issue10/taken-for-a-ride.htm
http://www.fhwa.dot.gov/interstate/brainiacs/eisenhowerinterstate.htm
http://gangsterreport.com/henry-fords-relationship-with-the-mafia-godfather-of-auto- indust...
https://history.gmheritagecenter.com/wiki/index.php/Wilson,_Charles_E
http://jalopink.com//the-real-story-behind-the-nazis-and-volkswagen-1733943186
https://library.cqpress.com/cqalmanac/document.pho?id=cqal66-1301349
http://linclonhighway.jameslin.name/historypart2.html
http://mediaford.com/.../01/chronology-of-the-life--of-henry-ford.pdf
http://members.iinet.net.au/~gduncan/1944.html
http://www.natinalreview.com/node/352429/print
https://philosophia.uncg.edu/phi361-metivier/module-2-why-does-business -need-ethics/cas...
http://ultimateclassicrock.com/beatles-drive-my-car/

http://www.ebony.com/entertainment-culture/thedifference-between-rap-hip-hop
http://www.firstsuperspeedway.com/books/fabulous-hoosier
http:///www.jrooksonline.com/Intl_Jew_version/ij46.htm
http://www.nps.gov/nr/travel/detroit/d38.htm
http://www.nydailynews.com/news/crime/john-delorean-arested-drug-dealing
    -1982-article...
http://www.nytimes.com/learning/general/onthisday/bday/0523.html
http://www.nytimes.com/1991/07/07business/edges-fray-on-volvo-s-brave-new
    -humanisti....
http://www.pbs.org/wgbh/amex/miami/peopleevents/pande02.html
hht://revolutionaryworkersgroup.org/files/pampitels/riverrouge-strike.pdf
http://unofficialamericangraffiti.weebly.com/the-1956-t-bird/http

About the Author

William A. Cook is an internationally recognized author of seventeen books on sports, true crime and automotive history. He has appeared in documentary productions on ESPN2 and the MLB Network and will appear in a forthcoming documentary on the Lindbergh baby kidnapping produced by Blizzard Road Productions of Perth, Australia. His work has been recognized for literary and artistic achievement by the Hamilton County Committee of the Ohioana Library Association and the Public Library of Cincinnati and Hamilton County. In addition, his Jim Thorpe biography received a favorable review in the American Indian Culture and Research Journal published by UCLA. A graduate of the University of Cincinnati and the University of Illinois at Chicago, he is a former health-care administrator and township councilman in North Brunswick, New Jersey. He currently lives in Manalapan, New Jersey.

www.ingramcontent.com/pod-product-compliance
Lightning Source LLC
Chambersburg PA
CBHW021353090426
42742CB00009B/835